"*Dream Gear* is just that — an excellent gear guide with all the toys a filmmaker could need and some you may not even know exist. It's a must-have for every production pro's library."

— DAVID INSLEY | Award-winning Director of Photography whose credits include the feature films *Crybaby* and *Hairspray*, the television series *Homicide: Life on the Streets*, and more than 1,000 commercials

"If just for the sheer speed of accessing over 200 of the top film and video gear manufacturers quickly and efficiently, get this book. *Dream Gear* is a fantastic research tool that let's you get connected and stay current with the best tools out there."

— JOE LEWIS | President of General Lift, a provider of motion control gear for major motion pictures, including T*he Lord of the Rings Trilogy, Matrix Reloaded,* and *X-Men 2*

"This cutting-edge book is for gearheads and professionals alike. It contains all of the information you need to achieve your creative goals."

— DAVID URGO | Independent Video Graphics Designer for Black Entertainment Television and The Jim Lehrer News Hour

"This versatile book speaks to many audiences. It's for any production professional looking to get a handle on a broad spectrum of technologies available today."

— ELINA FUHRMAN | Producer, CNN International

D1520601

MICHAEL WIESE PRODUCTIONS
www.mwp.com

We are delighted that you have found, and are enjoying, our books.

Since 1981, we've been all about providing filmmakers with the very best information on the craft of filmmaking: from screenwriting to funding, from directing to camera, acting, editing, distribution, and new media.

It is our goal to inspire and empower a generation (or two) of filmmakers and video-makers like yourself. But we want to go beyond providing you with just the basics. We want to shake you and inspire you to reach for your dreams and go beyond what's been done before. Most films that come out each year waste our time and enslave our imaginations. We want to give you the confidence to create from your authentic center, to bring something from your own experience that will truly inspire others and bring humanity to its full potential — avoiding those urges to manufacture derivative work in order to be accepted.

Movies, television, the Internet, and new media all have incredible power to transform. As you prepare your next project, know that it is in your hands to choose to create something magnificent and enduring for generations to come.

This is not an impossible goal, because you've got a little help. Our authors are some of the most creative mentors in the business, willing to share their hard-earned insights with you. Their books will point you in the right direction but, ultimately, it's up to you to seek that authentic something on which to spend your precious time.

We applaud your efforts and are here to support you. Let us hear from you.

Sincerely,

Michael Wiese
Filmmaker, Publisher

DREAM
GEAR

COOL & INNOVATIVE **TOOLS** FOR **FILM, VIDEO, & TV** PROFESSIONALS

CATHERINE **LORENZE**

Published by Michael Wiese Productions
11288 Ventura Blvd, Suite 621
Studio City, CA 91604
Tel. (818) 379-8799
Fax (818) 986-3408
mw@mwp.com
www.mwp.com

Cover Design: agdesign.com
Layout: Gina Mansfield
Editor: Bob Somerville

Printed by Sheridan Books, Ann Arbor, Michigan
Manufactured in the United States of America

Library of Congress Cataloging-in-Publication Data

Lorenze, Catherine, 1966-
  Dream gear : cool and innovative tools for film, video, and TV
professionals / by Catherine Lorenze.
       p. cm.
   ISBN 0-941188-88-4
  1. Cinematography--Equipment and supplies. I. Title.
TR885 .L67 2004
778.5'028'4--dc22

                                                    2003025147

TABLE OF **CONTENTS**

FOREWORD

As filmmakers we are all tool users. All our visions, and our many efforts to realize those visions, ultimately come down to the moment when we set the stop and roll the camera. This interplay between our imagination and our tools is the essence of what we do. Through the barrel of the lens, our vision ends up on the film or tape. Success rides on our preparation and preconception of what that desired vision is going to look like.

Like a carpenter who lives by the code of "Measure twice, cut once," we select gear to realize our vision. If we select wisely, our tasks are easier, our results usually better. *Dream Gear* is a book by Catherine Lorenze that promises to keep all of us abreast of what is tried-and-true and also introduce us to equipment that may make our jobs easier, our images fresher. This book will also act as a reference for producers and other non-camera department people. For them, *Dream Gear* will explain the gear's purpose and, at times, why we are asking for it.

Whether it is a simple tip such as using saran wrap and a drier to quickly add water resistance to your meter or deciding you want to put the camera on a 20-foot boom arm with a three-axis remote head while panning at 30 knots over the water; we all are eager for inside info about how to get something done. What used to be trade secrets is now public information. *Dream Gear* is a welcome sign of the times, and as you'll see in this book, the times are good for gear.

Back when I was in college on a football scholarship, I was also lucky enough to be in a training program at a local television station during the summers. A clip wiped out my football career, but since I was at the University of Colorado, I took my athletic skills into the mountains and cliffs of Boulder. I knew I wanted to capture the excitement of climbing on film, but there were no handy instruction booklets about how to get motion picture cameras off the ground. I learned by trial and error. At that time, my good friend Greg Lowe — whose products you'll see in this book — had a backpack company, and his efforts allowed us to haul delicate gear safely up vertical cliffs. Those early prototype packs were the forerunner of the company's Lowepro and Lowe Alpine systems. By the early 1990s, and lots of adventure films later, we hauled a 35mm camera and "air station" 2,500 feet up the sheer wall of Yosemite Valley's El Capitan for 2nd unit work on the *Star Trek V* movie. And a couple of years later, master rigger Earl Wiggin's electrical winches and jibs were making the job a lot easier on the cliffs we were shooting on in America and Europe.

That initial desire to take on challenging projects has led me down a career path of sports shooting, adventure documentaries, action commercials, and feature stunt sequences. Recently, I worked with a DP named Scott Duncan who brought 57 cases of gear for a History Channel project we were working on in Alaska. That's a lot of gear for one guy, but Scott Duncan isn't your typical guy. Scott has an uncanny knack of being able to juggle multiple tasks at once. He'll be shooting an interview with an 800-foot magazine on his Aaton XTR Prod while outside his A-Minima time-lapse camera is ticking away. In between loads, he may be shooting stills with an SLR or Medium-format still camera. His results are spectacular, as a visit to his Web site *Scottduncanfilms.com* will attest. I always make it a point to look through Scott's cases to see what new tools he has up his sleeve. Scott is always looking for that new lens, or light, or mini-DV, or still hard drive he can use — any piece of gear that will help in his push to discover new perspectives and new looks for his work. Like lots of us, Scott is a gear freak.

The goal for all of us is to grow, to find new inspiration and new depth in our story-telling. To do that, we force ourselves out of safe, tried-and-true initial impulses to try new compositions and challenge ourselves to see and reveal our subjects in new ways. Let's face it: If we don't, someone else will.

All of us in the film business pride ourselves on finding new applications for equipment. We scour all the articles to keep abreast of who is doing what and how. In a clear sign that the film/video business is no longer the good old boys club, a book like *Dream Gear* appears. I invite you to thumb through the pages of this book and see if you can discover new ways to help capture your vision, and while you're at it keep Catherine up to date at *DREAMGEAR@cox.net* on any new gear that will help in the next edition.

Bob Carmichael
Director/Cameraman
Denali Productions
www.bobcarmichael.com

Bob Carmichael is an Emmy award-winning Director/Cameraman based in Malibu, California. He has extensive experience directing and shooting in commercials, documentaries, and 2nd units on features. Carmichael has specialties in aerial, automotive, marine, mountaineering, sports, and stunt sequences. A partial list of clients includes: the Ford Motor Co., Merrill Lynch, Bayer Aspirin, Sprite, Molson Beer, Cadillac, Adidas, Kawasaki, EA Sports, National Geographic Explorer, Six Flags, and the U.S. Marine Corps. In 1980, his film Fall Line*, a look into the sport of extreme skiing, was nominated for an Academy Award.*

INTRODUCTION

Welcome to *Dream Gear*, the book where you supply the imagination and *Dream Gear* provides the wish list for the coolest and most innovative filmmaking technologies available today. From cameras and cranes to lenses and lighting, I invite you to become captivated and engrossed with the endless possibilities presented in *Dream Gear*.

Dream Gear is a book born from an interest in mechanics, a passion for fine engineering, and an appreciation of both. For where would our industry be without the talented engineers whose skills continue to make the incredible products that help make film-making easier, more interesting, and no doubt more creative?

What filmmaker won't acknowledge that there is something truly awesome about sitting high atop a movie crane, zipping around the skies in a helicopter with a camera mount, or creating astounding effects in an edit suite? It's an adrenaline rush, sure. But it's more than that. It's an acknowledgment that what we as filmmakers, producers, editors, gaffers, sound designers, and visual artists are creating is all possible due to the capabilities of the gear itself. Filmmaking is an art, and so is the engineering that went into making the gear that makes our industry possible.

Dream Gear is an engaging photo book that showcases top new film, video, and audio production technologies as well as those that have become true staples of our industry. I hope you will use this dynamic book to ignite your creativity and as a reference tool for professional inspiration. Take it to production meetings for planning purposes. Use it to discuss options with your DP, soundman, grip, or gaffer. Or just keep it around for entertainment during those long edit sessions.

Each featured piece of production gear has its own purpose, with a functionality and versatility to speak to many audiences — from Hollywood cinematographers and commercial producers to news and Webcast engineers. Immerse yourself in the world of Sony, Arriflex, and Fostex, and visualize yourself working with gear like Thomson's Viper FilmStream Camera or one of Shotmaker's Camera Cars.

I have designed *Dream Gear* as an opportunity for manufacturers to demonstrate their skills and for you, the reader, to check out the highlights. And to keep you truly current with the latest developments, *Dream Gear* provides Internet and complete address information for contacting every vendor mentioned within these pages.

It took an intensive, ten-month effort to research, compile, and organize the hundreds of products, manufacturers, and distributors seen within these pages. Undoubtedly, there are undiscovered products and companies out there who should be included in *Dream Gear*. If you are aware of some and want to share your own experiences, comments, and suggestions about the gear with others, I invite all self-described gearheads and interested manufacturers to e-mail me at *DREAMGEAR@cox.net*.

In order to easily access information, *Dream Gear* is arranged alphabetically by product category, and in some cases by product application. Preference was not given to any particular piece of gear or to any particular manufacturer or distributor. All companies that were contacted were invited to submit their product descriptions, product images, and testimonial quotes. Of the thousands of products out there, the products represented in *Dream Gear* were chosen because of their acknowledged benefits, their popularity in the market, the willingness of manufacturers to provide product photos and descriptions in time for publication, and in some cases because the products simply appeared cool and useful.

I think you will find that whether you are a seasoned professional or a gearhead whose fantasy is to create productions using really cool tools, this book is definitely for you. So read on and dream on with *Dream Gear* — a showcase book designed to ignite and unleash all of your creative possibilities.

Enjoy!

Catherine Lorenze

Catherine Lorenze is a veteran commercial producer whose credits include the Miami Heat Basketball Team, the American Cancer Society, Blue Cross Blue Shield, and three U.S. presidential candidates. For nearly 10 years, she served as Director of Production and Senior Producer for The Murphy Pintak Gautier Hudome Agency, a subsidiary of InterPublic Group (IPG), overseeing multi-million-dollar media budgets and high-profile clients. She is also a former radio network news producer and editor. Following a three-year sabbatical in Paris, she now resides with her husband and children in suburban Washington, DC.

(Contact Information: DREAMGEAR@cox.net)

ACKNOWLEDGMENTS

This project would not have happened were it not for the professional support I have received from two important people. The first is my former employer, Director/Producer Mike Murphy. Mike is the ultimate gearhead, and his push for perfection on every shoot demanded nothing less of my skills as a producer. My knowledge base about film/video/audio gear, how to use it, how to find it, and how to discuss it with my crew, is solely due to him. Thanks for taking a fellow Detroiter under your wing for so many years, Mike!

Secondly, a big thanks to my publisher, accomplished Director/Producer Michael Wiese. It was through discussions with Michael that the idea of *Dream Gear* was born. Thanks for giving me the opportunity to run with the ball, Michael!

Special thanks to the following people whose support and suggestions made *Dream Gear* possible, including: Director/Cameraman Bobby Carmichael of Denali Productions; Suzanne Paul, freelance producer for Animal Planet's *Emergency Vet*; Chris Fleszar, executive producer for Channel 13, Grand Rapids; Kathleen Redmond, former producer for *America's Most Wanted*; Robin Massin, executive producer for AFI Filmworks in Miami; Jennifer Martin-Donahue, former producer of CNN's *Burden of Proof*; Bill Murray, former National Public Radio producer; Addie Moray, freelance producer; Creative Director Jerry Cappa of CC Design Group; Giovanni Galvez, Craig Maniglia, and the rest of the gang at MVI Post in Falls Church, VA; Central Michigan University Broadcast & Cinematic Arts Chairperson Peter B. Orlik and friend Irene Nagaraj, both of whom shared their extensive experience and advice about book publishing. Thanks as well to my husband and children, who put up with the hundreds of packages, videotapes, and product CDs that cluttered our home while I compiled this book. And lastly, much gratitude to Gina Mansfield, who laid out all of the graphics and images for *Dream Gear*, and to my editor Bob Somerville, who has the eyes of a hawk!

Lastly, additional thanks and photo credits are due to the following manufacturers who provided their time, expertise, and product images to *Dream Gear*: Aaton, Abel Cine Tech, AccuScene Corporation, Adobe, ADS Technologies, AKG, Alan Gordon Enterprises, Amphibico, AMS Neve, Angenieux, Apogee Electronics Corporation, Apple, Arri Inc., Astro Systems, Inc., Audio-Technica, Audix, Aurora Video Systems, Avid, The Badham Company, Band Pro Film/Video, Inc., Barber Tech Video Products, BeachTek, B. E. Meyers & Co. Inc., Bogen Photo Corp., Boom Audio and Video, Boris FX, CamMate, Canada Camera Car, Canon, Canopus, Cartoni, Century Optics, Chapman/Leonard, Chimera, Chyron, Cinekinetic, Cinetransformer, Cool-Lux, Coptervision, Core Digital, Crystal Partners, Datavideo, Davis & Sanford, Digidesign, Digital Anarchy, Discreet, Doggicam Systems, DPA Microphones, The Easy Budget Company, Edirol, Electrophysics, E-N-G Mobile Systems, Entertainment

Partners, Euphonix, Ewa-Marine, EZ FX, Filmair International, FLIR Systems, Flying-Cam, Focus Enhancements, Fostex America, Frezzi, Fujinon, Gillard Industries, Inc., Glidecam, GPI, Ground Support Equipment, Herman Miller, HHB, Hitachi, Hollywood General Machining, Inc., Hollywood Lite, HydroFlex, Ikegami, IMP Electronics, Innovision Optics, J. L. Fisher, JVC, Kata, Kinetic Impulse, Kino-Flo, Leitch, Losmandy, Lowel Lighting, Lowepro, LTM Lighting, Manfrotto, Marketec, Microdolly Hollywood, Mirror Image, Mole-Richardson, Nagra, NCS Products, 1 Beyond, Optex, PAG, Panasonic, Panavision, Panther, Photoflex, Photo-Sonics, Pinnacle Systems, Portabrace, PowerProduction Software, Preston Cinema, Professional Sound Corp., ProMax, Quantel, Russ Bassett, Sachtler, Satellight, Shotmaker, Shure, Silicon Graphics, 16x9 Inc., Solid State Logic, Sonic Foundry, Sony Corp. of America, Sound Devices, Spintec, SpyderCam, StageTools, Ste-Man, Inc., StuffBak, Tascam, Telemetrics, Telescript, Television Equipment Associates, Thomson/Grass Valley, Tiffen/Steadicam, Trew Audio, Tyler Camera Systems, VariZoom, Videotek, Vinten, Wescam, Wide Screen Software, Winsted, Wohler Technologies, Y-Vamp, Zaxcom, Inc., Zeiss, and ZGC.

Special photo credits for Apple products are as follows: Screen shots reprinted by permission from Apple Computer, Inc.

Special photo credits for Coptervision products are as follows: NASA/CALTECH/JPL, "Goldstone Antenna with Coptervision Helicopter" photo taken by Carlos Hoyos, HIS Circle Productions, "Nissan X-terra" Whistler, British Columbia, Canada, photo taken by Daniel Hernandez, Clap Productions "Prince Alwaleed Ben Palal" Saudi Arabia photo taken by Andres Navia, ABC "Dreamkeepers" Calgary, Canada, photo taken by Art Santamaria, Rollvision on Crane photo taken by Carlos Hoyos.

AUDIO
ACCESSORIES

"Now that pro-audio has finally arrived in OS X, the Apogee Mini-Me is the perfect piece of gear to complete a portable, laptop-driven studio. It has worked perfectly and hassle-free in various applications since the moment I first plugged it in. And nobody comes close to the quality of the mic-pre's and converters in a little package like this. It's really in a class of its own!"

— Mike Knobloch,
   Vice President, Fox Music,
   20th Century Fox
   Quote from Apogee Web site — Reviews & Testimonials
   2002 Blue Ribbon Award from EQ magazine

MINI-DAC PORTABLE 192 KHZ D/A CONVERTER

MINI-ME PORTABLE CONVERTER/PREAMP | By Apogee Digital

Mini-DAC: This professional-quality 192kHz D/A converter is the ultimate portable and compact solution for studio playback, reference monitoring, USB connectivity to your DAW, and premium home audio systems. If you are doing digital, you need connectivity options. Through Mini-DAC's ability to interface directly with your computer and virtually any DAW via USB, you get maximum flexibility for a myriad of input formats.

Mini-Me: By popular demand, Apogee has returned to home territory with the release of a new, portable, two-channel A/D converter with built-in mic/instrument preamps, featuring a special low-power, wide-range, supply-voltage design for maximum flexibility. The Apogee Mini-Me is a completely new design — from its 24/96 sampling capability to its direct computer interfacing via USB — so you can use almost any software you choose.

Apogee Electronics Corporation
3145 Donald Douglas Loop South
Santa Monica, CA 90405-3210
(310) 915-1000
www.apogeedigital.com

DXA-4C AUDIO ADAPTER | By BeachTek Inc.

This audio adapter, made exclusively for the Canon XL1 or XL1s, fully exploits the powerful audio capabilities of this camcorder, increases flexibility, and simplifies setup and operation. The DXA-4C can be used with the Canon MA-100 adapter for four discrete, balanced, XLR inputs at the same time! Other features include: two balanced XLR inputs for stereo recording, auxiliary mini-jack from wireless mics, dual MIC/LINE level switches for versatility, dual, drift-free trim controls for reliable operation, and mono/stereo switch for single input recording. The DXA-4C is super quiet: It generates no hiss.

BeachTek Inc.
53 Bellefair Ave.
Toronto, Ontario
Canada M4L 3T7
(416) 690-9457
www.beachtek.com

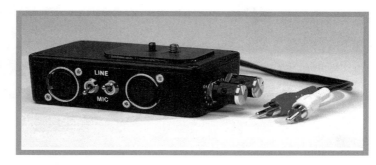

KIT COOL MICROPHONE BOOM POLE SUPPORT SYSTEM | By Boom Audio & Video

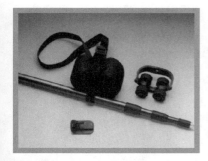

This unique support system offers total freedom, moving forward and back, and rotating around its own axis for precise microphone positioning. Kit Cool enables single-handed and full operation of the boom pole while on the move. The other hand is free to operate the mixer, or to hold the support when using a long pole. This ingenious device allows a fishpole to be supported by one hand, even overhead. The three-section, telescopic support pole is adjustable from 550 to 1,100mm with an innovative and effective 1/4 turn clutch. Simply adjust to the correct height, then twist the vertical markers into alignment to lock. Weight: 450 grams.

Boom Audio & Video
18, avenue Jules Tricault
35170 Bruz, France
+33 (0)299-05-35-83
www.boom-audio.com

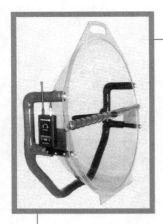

BIG EARS PARABOLIC REFLECTOR | By Crystal Partners, Inc.

Constructed from a patented plastic material made of a kevlar, buterate, and acrylic combination that was specially developed after years of testing and research, the result is a material that allows remarkable audio clarity over a wide frequency range. Big Ears Parabolic Reflector's modified parabolic design was calculated in conjunction with a major university to ensure that the contours would provide the most ideal reflective pattern, resulting in a "sweet spot" that can be fine-tuned to optimize its use in varying situations. Big Ears accepts wireless Sennheiser, Beyer Lavs, Audio Technica, CO90s, and most other standard mics.

Crystal Partners, Inc.
321 Village Drive
Carol Stream, IL 60188
(800) 244-3277
www.parabs.com

HUSH HEELS | Distributed by Professional Sound Corporation

Hush Heels save valuable production time on film and television sets. Designed by Hollywood sound mixer Hank Garfield, Hush Heels easily and quickly quiet on- and off-camera shoes.

Do you shoot in public buildings with hard floor surfaces such as marble? Does the Steadicam™ operator or boom man have to walk on these same hard, noisy surfaces? Do you need to provide some form of damping when an actor sets down a plate or other noisy prop? Hush Heels can help. Hush Heels are a set of very high quality foam pads that are precut to various shapes that can be easily and quickly applied to shoes and other props.

INDUCTIVE EARPIECE | By Professional Sound Corporation

Professional Sound Corporation has met the high demands for discreet cueing with the development of the Inductive Earpiece. This inductive cueing system is quite simple to use. Audio is transmitted from a source via an inductive loop. The talent can wear a small, flexible neck loop that couples audio via a low-level magnetic field into a hearing aid-style earpiece. Alternately, a perimeter or "room loop" may be used to encircle an entire room or stage, allowing many people to receive the same cue. The Inductive Earpiece is made of a flesh-color ABS plastic to provide better on-camera concealment. Its small size allows it to be worn by adults and children alike.

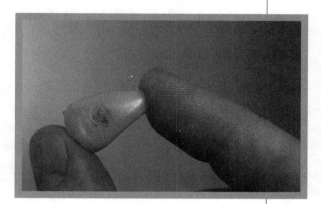

PHONE TAP | By Professional Sound Corporation

This device can be connected to virtually any standard telephone line via the supplied cables and adapters. The PSC Phone Tap, once connected, will emulate a standard telephone. When that telephone line is called, a red "ring" LED will flash. The operator of the PSC Phone Tap then flips the switch to "on" and the line will be seized just as a normal phone would do. The red "ring" LED will stop flashing and the green "seize" LED will light, indicating that the line has been seized. Audio received over the phone line is then available on the output XLR for recording purposes. Two sides of a conversation can also be recorded if a standard telephone is connected in parallel with the PSC Phone Tap. A dual phone jack is provided to allow this configuration. This device adheres to part 15 of the FCC regulations. Licensing is the responsibility of the owner/user.

Professional Sound Corporation
28085 Smyth Drive
Valencia, CA 91355
(661) 295-9395
www.professionalsound.com

THE MICROEAR EAR PROMPTER | By
Television Equipment Associates

Just insert microEar into your ear canal and you will receive information or prompting at distances of up to a mile (depending on transmitter and radio conditions). A VHF user-specified crystal-controlled receiver available in the range of 138 to 240MHz will receive signals up to several kilometers. Features include an automatic squelch circuit, a high-sensitivity superheterodyne circuit that provides maximum receiver sensitivity, a self-adapting filter to reduce background noise, battery life of 15 to 30 hours, and a volume control.

Television Equipment Associates
P.O. Box 404
Brewster, NY 10509
(310) 457-7401
www.swatheadsets.com

DREAM GEAR | LORENZE | 6

APA APK007 ADAPT-A-PAK KIT | By
Trew Audio, Inc.

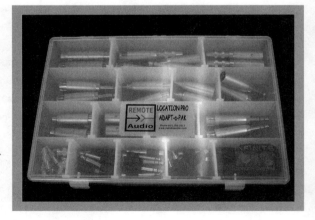

The Remote Audio Adapt-a-Pak Kit features 25 different types of common audio adapters needed in the field and includes a total of 53 pieces.

REM VM VOLT-METER

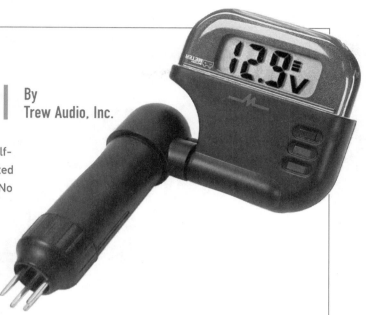

| By Trew Audio, Inc.

The Remote Audio Volt-Meter is a self-powered voltage meter with illuminated display that measures 9 to 24 volts. No batteries required.

Trew Audio, Inc.
240 Great Circle Road, Suite 339
Nashville, TN 37228
(800) 241-8994
www.trewaudio.com

PANORAMADTV PENPAL-SDI

| By Wohler Technologies

2003 TV Technology Award Winner

Introducing the world's smallest serial digital video test-pattern generator. PENPAL-sdi generates 26 video test patterns and four stereo audio signals. Each 10-bit video test pattern is encoded according to Rec.ITU-R BT.601 and transmitted serially according to Rec.ITU-R BT.656. AES digital audio signals are embedded according to SMPTE 272. Operating in 625- or 525-line standards, PENPAL-sdi is the perfect tool for every broadcast engineer. Powered by a three-volt lithium battery or an optional AC adapter, and weighing in at less than six ounces, PENPAL-sdi is a device you can take anywhere, confident that you can generate serial digital test patterns and audio tones at the touch of a button whenever you want them.

Wohler Technologies
713 Grandview Drive
South San Francisco, CA 94080
(888) 5-WOHLER
www.wohler.com

If you have used this gear and want to share your own experiences, comments, and suggestions in our next edition, send an e-mail to Catherine Lorenze at *DREAMGEAR@cox.net*. We are particularly interested in innovative ways you have used the gear that will help inspire other film, video, and TV professionals.

AUDIO
EDITING MIXING CONSOLES AND SOFTWARE

2

AMS Neve:	Libra Post
	Logic MMC
Digidesign:	Mbox – Micro Studio Music Production System
	Pro Tools HD
	Digi 002 – FireWire-based Pro Tools LE Music Production System
Euphonix:	System 5 Digital Mixing Systems
Sony:	DMX-R100 Digital Audio Mixing Console

LIBRA
POST | By AMS Neve

Libra Post is a world-class post-production system engineered for the time-critical requirements of television, DVD, and budget-conscious feature film mixing. Libra Post harnesses the power of the award-winning DFC. Applications include documentaries, dramas, sitcoms, movies, trailers, and commercials.

"The console lets me quickly move through the layers and access the things I need on the surface. A second pot allows me to access any layer I want for volume and level control, so I can hold onto two pots, so to speak, without going down to another layer. And the sonic and dynamic qualities of the console are exceptional. The MMC has a rich, warm sound rather than that sterile sound you often get with digital boards."

— Dave West, Owner of Emmy Award-Winning West Productions

Quote obtained from AMS Neve's Web site/Case Study

LOGIC MMC | By AMS Neve

The stunning new Logic MMC is the spiritual successor to the famous AMS Neve Logic 2 console and features power from the award-winning DFC console alongside multitrack music excellence. The combination of 24-bit/96kHz operation and a brand-new suite of state-of-the-art I/O restarts the technology clock. The Logic MMC is here to power the next decade of business success.

AMS Neve
Billington Road
Burnley, Lancashire
England BB11 5UB
+44 (0)1 282-457-011
www.ams-neve.com

MBOX – POWERFUL MICRO STUDIO MUSIC PRODUCTION SYSTEM | By
Digidesign (a division of Avid)

Mbox is a full-featured, USB-powered studio-in-a-box that works with your Windows XP or Macintosh computer to give you a compact, portable, professional-quality audio production system. Comprised of a small, upright I/O unit and the latest Pro Tools LE software and featuring two Focusrite mic preamps, Mbox works in conjunction with your computer to provide the firepower necessary for quality results. Complementing Mbox's analog and digital I/O, Pro Tools LE software offers 24 tracks of record and playback, 128 MIDI tracks, real-time plug-in support, and a host of additional features. From beginning to end, Mbox places you in an ideal position to realize any project.

Digidesign, Inc.
2001 Junipero Serra Blvd.
Daly City, CA 94014-3886
(800) 333-2137
www.digidesign.com

PRO TOOLS HD | By
Digidesign (a division of Avid)

The most comprehensive system of its kind, Pro Tools HD offers audio professionals superb quality and efficiency through one intuitive, integrated production environment. This High-Definition system embodies the latest Digidesign innovations, incorporating cutting-edge technology to deliver unprecedented sonic fidelity and price/performance. Featuring dramatic DSP power, sweeping sample rate support, brand-new high-resolution audio interfaces and peripheral options, abundant track count and I/O capacity, extensive routing flexibility, and much more, Pro Tools HD gives you control over your audio world like never before.

DIGI 002 – FIREWIRE-BASED PRO TOOLS LE MUSIC PRODUCTION SYSTEM | By Digidesign (a division of Avid)

Working with your computer through a single FireWire connection, Digi 002 pairs Pro Tools LE software with an integrated control surface to provide you with an ideal, finger-friendly music production environment. Record, edit, process, mix and master your projects with hands-on efficiency, then tuck Digi 002 under your arm, take it to a gig, and use it as an 8x4x2 digital mixer complete with EQ, dynamics, delay, and reverb with snapshots.

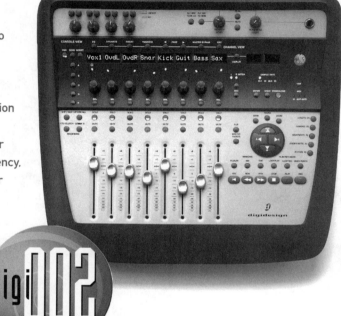

Digidesign, Inc.
2001 Junipero Serra Blvd.
Daly City, CA 94014-3886
(800) 333-2137
www.digidesign.com

SYSTEM 5 DIGITAL MIXING SYSTEMS | By Euphonix, Inc.

"David (Lynch) and I love the total control of all the parameters of the mix. With such control, we can fully concentrate on molding the sound we are looking for without worrying about any hardware limitations. Our Euphonix always sounds solid and clear."

— John Neff, Chief Engineer at David Lynch's studio — Asymmetrical Productions

Quote obtained from Euphonix's PR Department

"The Lord of the Rings soundtrack was a very important element of the film. To create the fantasy world, there had to be sometimes hundreds of layers. The Euphonix System 5 excels at managing all these elements and keeps the sound pristine. When we decided we needed to expand the facility and get more consoles, System 5 was the logical choice."

— John Neill, Sound Department Manager of The Film Unit studios

Quote obtained from Euphonix's PR Department

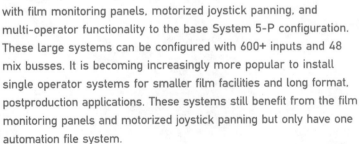

The all-digital System 5 can be configured for TV audio post (System 5-P) or for feature film dubbing applications (System 5-F). The System 5-F adds up to four operator positions with film monitoring panels, motorized joystick panning, and multi-operator functionality to the base System 5-P configuration. These large systems can be configured with 600+ inputs and 48 mix busses. It is becoming increasingly more popular to install single operator systems for smaller film facilities and long format, postproduction applications. These systems still benefit from the film monitoring panels and motorized joystick panning but only have one automation file system.

Euphonix, Inc.
220 Portage Avenue
Palo Alto, CA 94306
(650) 855-0400
www.euphonix.com

DMX-R100 DIGITAL AUDIO MIXING CONSOLE (UNCONFIGURED) | By Sony Electronics

Sony's DMX-R100 is a high-quality, 48-channel digital audio mixer designed for professional recording and audio postproduction applications. The mixing console can interface with a variety of professional digital audio recorders with the installation of optional I/O cards. Incorporating an ergonomic user interface, professional automation, full 5.1 surround sound capability, and machine control, the DMX-R100 can efficiently fulfill most production requirements.

AUDIO
MIXERS
3

Edirol:	M-100FX 10-Channel Audio Mixer with Effects
Professional Sound Corp.:	AlphaMix Mixer
	M3 Audio Mixer
	M6 Portable Audio Mixer
	Mjr Mixer
Shure:	FP42 4-Channel Stereo Microphone Mixer
	FP410 Automatic 4-Channel Mixer with IntelliMix
	M367 Six Input Portable Mixer
Sony:	DMX-P01 Portable Digital Mixer
Sound Devices:	MixPre Compact Field Mixer
	302 Compact Production Mixer
Zaxcom:	Cameo II Location Recording Console

M-100FX 10-CHANNEL AUDIO MIXER WITH EFFECTS

| By Edirol Corporation

The M-100FX is a 10-channel audio mixer with a number of useful voice and sound processing effects. The M-100FX is primarily designed to target the video editing market with such features as direct USB connection to computer, voice effects suited for voice-overs, and a variety of input types, including XLR/TRS, 1/4", and RCA inputs. The many inputs allow the video editor to record from almost any source straight into the computer without the added noise common with most internal sound cards. The M-100FX also has phantom power for use with high-end condenser microphones more suited to narration. Although the M-100FX is clearly targeting the video market, the particular toolset will fit almost any small computer-based audio studio.

Edirol Corporation
425 Sequoia Drive, Suite 114
Bellingham, WA 98226
(360) 594-4273
www.edirol.com

ALPHAMIX MIXER | Distributed by Professional Sound Corporation

The new PSC AlphaMix contains all of the features required by today's demanding ENG (electronic news gathering) recordist. Do you regularly do two camera shoots, work with demanding producers, or have complicated IFB feeds? Then the new PSC AlphaMix is for you. This all-new design contains four inputs each with switchable line or microphone level inputs, 12T or 48PH microphone power, low noise preamplifiers with continuously variable gain trims, active 12dB/Octave low-cut filters, balanced line level outputs per input channel, pre-fader-listens and simple three LED meters per input channel. The AlphaMix is also equipped with a boom pole-mounted remote control that can be used to control the gain of the first input channel, thus allowing the operator to boom with both hands.

M3 AUDIO MIXER | Distributed by Professional Sound Corporation

The new Professional Sound Corporation M3 Audio Mixer offers the features required for today's ENG mixer. It combines rugged construction, high-quality components, and ease-of-use ergonomics in a compact package. The M3 Mixer's input panel includes: three XLR transformer-balanced inputs each with switchable "T" Dynamic or 48PH microphone powering as well as three-way input pads D, C, L (Dynamic 0dB Pad, Condenser -15dB Pad, Line Level -50dB Pad). The M3 Mixer's outputs panel is also loaded with connections. While other mixers offer the ability to monitor from two cameras at once, only the M3 gives you two 10-pin connectors.

Professional Sound
Corporation
28085 Smyth Drive
Valencia, CA 91355
(661) 295-9395
www.professionalsound.com

M6 PORTABLE AUDIO MIXER | By Professional Sound Corporation

The new PSC M6 Portable Audio Mixer is designed to fulfill the needs of the field recordist. It offers many of the features found in our flagship M8 Mixer, but with reduced complexity and cost. This new PSC M6 Mixer is designed for extreme field operating conditions and thus utilizes rotary pot faders because of their immunity to dirty and dusty conditions. In addition, it offers provisions for direct mounting of your favorite RDAT or DVD recorder. This allows for a simple and convenient means of recording in the field whether you are working on a sound stage, in an insert car, or at some other remote location.

MJR AUDIO MIXER | By Professional Sound Corporation
(WITH OR WITHOUT CAMERA MOUNT)

The Professional Sound Corporation Mjr Audio Mixer is perfect for use with today's small digital video cameras, standard Betacams™, RDAT, and MiniDisc™ recorders. The PSC Mjr Mixer offers the features found on many full-size mixers yet is built in a small and concise format. The Mjr Mixer is housed in a rugged aircraft aluminum case barely 4.75" by 6" in size and weighing less than 1.5 pounds. In addition, the entire mixer may be mounted to the bottom of any small video camera via the supplied 1/4-20 thumb screw. The mixer also contains a 1/4-20 threaded attachment point so that the mixer/camera combination can be mounted to any standard tripod.

Professional Sound
Corporation
28085 Smyth Drive
Valencia, CA 91355
(661) 295-9395
www.professionalsound.com

FP42 4-CHANNEL STEREO MICROPHONE MIXER | By Shure Incorporated

With full stereo capability, the FP42 is perfect for mixdown in video editing suites. It includes four XLR transformer-balanced mic/line inputs and two outputs (one for each stereo channel). Pull-pot cueing on all inputs provides channel previewing. Other features include low-cut

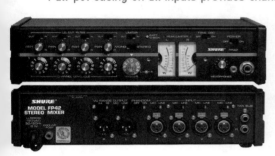

filters, mono/stereo switch, mix bus linking, headphone amplifier, tone oscillator, switchable limiter, phantom power and dual VU meters. The FP42 is rack-mountable with A16R and runs on three standard 9-volt alkaline batteries or 120/240 Vac power.

FP410 AUTOMATIC 4-CHANNEL MIXER WITH INTELLIMIX | By Shure Incorporated

The FP410 uses Shure IntelliMix® to dramatically improve audio quality by providing greater gain-before-feedback, reducing the pickup of ambient noise and reverberation, and virtually eliminating comb filtering effects. IntelliMix combines three key features: Noise-adaptive threshold activates a microphone for speech but not for constant room noise; maxbus limits the number of activated microphones to one per talker; LAST microphone lock-on keeps the most recently activated microphone open until a newly activated microphone takes its place. Primary applications include video production, broadcast, conference recording, and field production.

Shure Incorporated
5800 West Touhy Avenue
Niles, IL 60714-4608
(800) 25-SHURE
www.shure.com

M367 SIX INPUT
PORTABLE MIXER | By
Shure Incorporated

The Shure Model M367 is a six-input, portable microphone mixer/remote amplifier specifically designed for professional applications in electronic news gathering (ENG), electronic field production (EFP) and general audio mixing. Exceptional low-noise design makes the M367 ideal for use with digital transmission links and digital video/audio recording media, including ISDN and DAT. Compact and rugged, the M367 is built to withstand the most demanding field production conditions. In addition, its excellent performance, versatility, and features make it an ideal choice for studio, remote, or sound reinforcement use, and as an add-on mixer for expanding existing facilities.

Shure Incorporated
5800 West Touhy Avenue
Niles, IL 60714-4608
(800) 25-SHURE
www.shure.com

DMX-P01 PORTABLE
DIGITAL MIXER | By
Sony Electronics

The DMX-P01 digital mixer is a lightweight and portable field mixing unit developed for electronic news gathering (ENG) and electronic field production (EFP) recording. The unit has 32-bit, full digital sound processing, and its unique Scene Memory Recall feature enables users to instantly recall up to 10 different user-defined parameter settings, providing the DMX-P01 portable digital mixer with the ability to store and recall settings including limiter and compressor. This allows users to recall favorite settings instantly, which is very useful when switching between different recording environments.

Sony Electronics
One Sony Drive
Park Ridge, NJ 07656
(800) 686-7669
www.sony.com/professional

302 COMPACT PRODUCTION MIXER | By Sound Devices

Developed specifically for audio-for-picture applications, the 302 mixer is the perfect tool for production companies and camera operators wanting to take control of their audio. The 302 is stunning for its size, flexibility, control, and performance; it is the most compact and cost-effective battery-powered professional audio mixer in its class. With important features to accommodate nearly any over-the-shoulder production, the 302 interfaces with wireless transmitters and receivers, camera audio inputs of all kinds, and external audio recorders.

MIXPRE COMPACT FIELD MIXER | By Sound Devices

The MixPre from Sound Devices is a studio-quality two-channel portable stereo microphone mixer. Its impressive audio performance and comprehensive features, including pan switches, built-in slate microphone, 1kHz tone oscillator, and head- phone monitoring, make it ideal for the front end of any studio or field production system. Radio, television, and film production engineers value the compact size and ability to withstand extremes in the field. The MixPre combines rugged mechanical and electrical construction, compact size, and high-quality components. The MixPre gives no-compromise performance for any application.

Sound Devices
P.O. Box 576
300 Wengel Drive
Reedsburg, WI 53959
(608) 524-0625
www.sounddevices.com

CAMEO II LOCATION RECORDING
CONSOLE | By
Zaxcom, Inc.

Cameo II Digital Recording Console is the second generation of the Cameo LRC, and is designed primarily for use on location to record feature films, television programs, and high-end audio venues. This new console offers upgraded mic preamps as well as multi-frame output audio delay for use in High-Definition motion picture and television production. Cameo is designed to be a high-performance, easy-to-use mixer. It provides a high-end professional touch that lower-cost music industry mixers are not able to do. While the system is optimized to function with Deva and Zaxcom wireless, it has been designed to ensure perfect compatibility with existing Nagra, DAT, and third-party wireless equipment.

Zaxcom, Inc.
230 West Parkway, Unit 9
Pompton Plains, NJ 07444
(973) 835-5000
www.zaxcom.com

AUDIO
RECORDERS

CANTAR-X AUDIO DISK RECORDER | By
Aaton and distributed by Abel Cine Tech NY/LA

Every detail of Cantar has been honed to perfection to make the task of a location recordist as easy as possible while providing the utmost flexibility. All five mic inputs are equipped with the high-quality isolation transformers used in the best stand-alone mixers. Since these transformers handle up to +10dBu signals, they can also be used as balanced line inputs. Another important point is the high sensitivity (-25 +8dB) of the four line inputs, which allows direct RF mic connection and makes Cantar a nine-mic input machine! A Bluetooth-connected PDA controls the "18 inputs to 8 track" routing, recalls the user's routings and settings, and allows the script supervisor to enter scene and take IDs from up to 15 meters (45 feet), and a built-in CDR driver burns the mixdown of the day in less than six minutes. The external CDR burner is powered through FireWire, with no delay at wrap-up.

Aaton S.A.
bp 3002
38816 Grenoble
cdx1 France
+33 (0)4 76-42-95-50
www.aaton.com

Abel Cine Tech
66 Willow Avenue, Suite 201
Staten Island, NY 10305
(888) 223-1599
www.abelcine.com

R-1 MULTI-TRACK DIGITAL AUDIO RECORDER | By
Euphonix, Inc.

The R-1 is a high-quality digital audio recorder with up to 96 tracks and has 24-bit 96kHz capability. It is supplied with an easy-to-operate remote. It can also be supplied with TransferStation, which allows for back-up and archiving of disks and offline editing with Steinberg's Nuendo.

Euphonix, Inc.
220 Portage Avenue
Palo Alto, CA 94306
(650) 855-0400
www.euphonix.com

DV40 DVD MASTER RECORDER | By Fostex

The Fostex DV40 Master Recorder is designed to record and play back audio data directly onto a DVD-RAM disk. The unit offers high-reliability recording by employing a Verify/Write mode, which examines all recording data, all the time, while in the record mode. And to ensure the widest range of compatibility throughout the industry, and maximizing the DVD-RAM technology, the DV40 can record up to four channels of simultaneous audio in a vast number of permutations. The DV40 is used by Academy Award-winning sound mixer Chris Munro.

PD-6 DVD-RAM TIMECODE FIELD RECORDER | By Fostex

The PD-6 Portable Location Recorder offers spectacular 24-bit/96kHz audio quality, six independent audio tracks, and time code-locked DVD-RAM recording to an easy-to-use 8cm removable media. The PD-6 also features a full-function, feature-rich six-channel mixer, "easy access" monitoring, and all the connectivity one would expect, and need, from a thoroughly professional unit. It is already proving itself in motion pictures, TV productions, and outside broadcast. The removable 8cm DVD-RAM cartridges provide two 1.46GB sides, offering, for example, 108 minutes per disk of four-track recording at 48kHz/16-bit. And the disks fit right into conventional DVD drives.

Fostex America
a Division of Foster Electric, U.S.A., Inc.
15431 Blackburn Avenue
Norwalk, CA 90650
(562) 921-1112
www.fostex.com
www.fostexdvd.net

PORTADISC MDP500 PROFESSIONAL PORTABLE MINIDISC RECORDER | By HHB Communications

HHB's Portadisc is a rugged, fully featured MiniDisc (MD) portable and has become standard issue in TV, film, and broadcast audio acquisition. Developed in consultation with leading sound recordists, the Portadisc optimizes the many advantages of the MD format — sound quality, random access, editing, etc. — in a robust, portable package loaded with features essential for life on location. Of particular interest to radio journalists is the provision of a USB interface for the real-time transfer of files to laptop editing systems, enabling the production of finished news pieces in the field.

PORTADRIVE PDR2000 8-TRACK LOCATION SOUND RECORDER | By HHB Communications

The Portadrive combines eight-track recording on a removable hard drive, simultaneous recording of mono or two-channel rushes to an external DVD-RAM/DVD-R/DVD-RW drive, 24-bit/96kHz performance, sophisticated onboard mixing, comprehensive time code facilities, and flexible, session-based file transfer with Mac and PC work stations — all in a rugged, portable device. And with input from leading sound recordists, the Portadrive is packed with essential features placing everything just where it's needed to deliver reliable recordings and pristine audio on even the most demanding location.

HHB Communications USA, Inc.
743 Cochran Street, Buildings E & F
Simi Valley, CA 93065-1976
(805) 579-6490
www.hhbusa.com

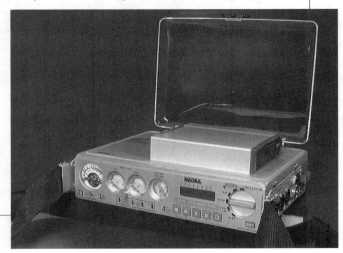

NAGRA ARES-P PORTABLE HANDHELD RECORDER/PLAYER | By Nagra

The concept behind the ARES-P and the RCX220 is to put a modern, solid-state recorder/player firmly in the reporter's hand, for rapid access and easy use in the heat of things. It is powered by five AA cells and provides four hours of uninterrupted recording. External power is also available. A single 12-pin connector on the top of the unit serves as the microphone and stereo line inputs. Nagra-built electret capsules can be screwed directly onto this connector for an ultra-compact, all-in-one unit. For those who prefer a traditional microphone, the cable is connected instead of the capsule, allowing the machine to be hung on a belt or put in a pocket.

NAGRA V 24-BIT LINEAR LOCATION RECORDER | By Nagra

For over 50 years Nagra recorders have established a well-deserved respect from audio professionals all over the world. The tradition continues with the new Nagra V, a two-track, direct-to-disk location recorder using a removable sealed hard drive that records 24- or 16-bit linear PCM data at selectable 44.1 or 48kHz (88.2 and 96kHz optional) with audio stored in a standard broadcast WAV format. A compact, lightweight frame with a user-friendly front panel makes the Nagra V ideal for over-the-shoulder operation. The Nagra V has four analog inputs (two mic and two line), each routable to either audio track, as well as two AES channels. With a convenient pre-roll / pre-record feature, selectable for up to 20 seconds, you will never be too late to start a recording.

Nagra USA, Inc.
(800) 813-1663
www.nagrausa.com

PCM-7040 DAT RECORDER | By Sony Electronics

Ideally suited for interchanging audio between recording studios and video postproduction facilities, Sony's PCM-7040 DAT recorder offers high-quality two-channel digital recording with SMPTE time code. This high-end recorder is useful for a wide range of audio recording applications where time code synchronization and external control are required.

PCM-MI 2-MOTOR PROFESSIONAL PORTABLE DAT RECORDER | By Sony Electronics

For the audio professional who needs to record on the run, Sony's PCM-MI Professional Portable DAT Recorder is the company's smallest and lightest DAT unit. Some features include up to 3.5 hours of continuous recording, record margin indication, start ID level select, and a high-quality microphone circuit.

Sony Electronics
One Sony Drive
Park Ridge, NJ 07656
(800) 686-7669
www.sony.com/professional

DA-P1 PORTABLE
DAT RECORDER | By Tascam

TASCAM's DA-P1 is a sturdy portable DAT deck with a feature set you'd expect to find on a full-sized studio centerpiece. The DA-P1

features include a switchable 48V phantom power, built-in limiter with 20dB pad for confidence in recording without worrying about clipping, SCMS free recording, SPDIF I/O, and quick-charge battery system with a two-hour play/record time. Of course it can handle recording and playback at 48, 44.1, or

TASCAM America
TEAC America, Inc.
7733 Telegraph Rd.
Montebello, CA 90640
(323) 726-0303
www.tascam.com

32kHz. The DA-P1's mic/line inputs and phantom power are very unique; it's like taking the power of the mixing board with you out on the job. The DA-P1 also has an optional external charger, battery pack, and carrying case, to take it with you wherever you might go. It's the perfect setup for recording interviews, gathering Foley FX, or just recording.

DEVA MULTI-DISK, MULTI-FORMAT
LOCATION RECORDER | By Zaxcom, Inc.

Direct to hard disk recording with back-up to DVD is the most reliable way to record location audio. Only the Deva records to multiple disks at the same time. This allows you to record all disk copies required by post at the same time as the original recordings, saving hours of disk space. Only the Deva system allows you to keep your recorded audio on the set, allowing production to instantly reference previous recordings. And because one size does not fit all, there are three, new versions of Deva. Six-track, eight-track and ten-track models fit the technical requirements and budget of every professional sound mixer.

Zaxcom, Inc.
230 West Parkway, Unit 9
Pompton Plains, NJ 07444
(973) 835-5000
www.zaxcom.com

If you have used this gear and want to share your own experiences, comments, and suggestions in our next edition, send an e-mail to Catherine Lorenze at *DREAMGEAR@cox.net*. We are particularly interested in innovative ways you have used the gear that will help inspire other film, video, and TV professionals.

CAMCORDERS
DIGITAL VIDEO

Canon:	XL1s Camcorder
Hitachi:	Z3000/CR-D10 DVD-RAM Camcorder
Ikegami:	DNS-21W/DNS-201W "The Editcam II" Camcorder
JVC:	GY-DV300U "StreamCorder" Camcorder
	GY-DV550U Studio DV Camcorder
	GY-5000U 3-CCD Professional DV Camcorder
Sony:	DSR-390L DVCAM Camcorder
	DSR-570WSL Wide Screen DVCAM Camcorder
	MSW-900 IMX Wide Screen Digital Camcorder
Thomson/Grass Valley:	LDK 120 DPM Camcorder
	LDK 150 DPM Camcorder

XL1S DIGITAL CAMCORDER | By Canon

The Canon XL1s is not one, but many different cameras. Interchangeable lenses and viewfinders allow the XL1s to be tailored for any shooting condition. Incorporating manual control, and features top-end, professional gear, standard for others to follow: and IEEE1394, interchangeable shooting modes and aspect shooting enhancements, stabilization, picture adjustments, video inputs and outputs, and optimal performance in high-precision optics, full found only previously on the XL1s raises the Features include digital video format lens system, 3-CCD system, multiple ratios, programmed auto exposure, SuperRange optical image audio adjustments, audio and custom keys and presets.

Canon USA
One Canon Plaza
Lake Success, NY 11042
(800) OK-CANON
www.canondv.com

Z-3000/CR-D10 DVD-RAM CAMCORDER | By Hitachi

As the world's first completely tapeless professional recorder, the CR-D10 provides excellent picture quality. Using Hitachi's digital signal processing cameras, the Z-3000 series, along with the CR-D10 recorder and third-party, nonlinear editing software for field applications makes this an extremely flexible, mobile, and cost-efficient field acquisition system. The CR-D10 records digital video from the Z-3000 series professional DSP cameras directly as computer files on the DVD-RAM or DVD-R disk. Projects can be produced completely from a remote location, easily edited in the field, and processed for transmission. Computer operating systems such as Microsoft's Windows, Apple's OS/X, Linux, and Unix can read and write to DVD-RAM and are compatible with DVD-VR specifications.

Hitachi Denshi Ltd. USA
150 Crossways Park Drive
Woodbury, NY 11797
(516) 682-4429
www.hdal.com

DNS-21W/DNS-201W "THE EDITCAM II" CAMCORDER WITH HARD DISK DRIVE | By Ikegami Electronics

The Editcam II, both DNS-21W (FIT CCD) and DNS-201W (IT CCD), is a newly designed compact camcorder in the Avid/Ikegami DNG family, employing hard disk drives as a recording medium in a digital nonlinear environment. The newly designed pocket-sized FP-S4 FieldPak and newly designed circuits allow the camcorder body to be compact and lightweight without sacrificing the many useful features of the Editcam system, such as: instant preview through random access, intelligent recording, good picture quality of 4:2:2, 5MHz sampling at 8-bit quantization, retroloop function, and time-lapse recording. The editing action can be performed with an externally connected laptop computer.

Ikegami Electronics (U.S.A.), Inc.
Brook Avenue
ywood, NJ 07607
0) 368-9171
w.ikegami.com

GY-DV300U DV "STREAMCORDER" CAMCORDER | By JVC

Built to meet the needs of today's broad-band information distribution networks, JVC's new "StreamCorder" is the ideal choice for webcasting. This high-quality, 1/3-inch, 3-CCD camera not only boasts powerful 12-bit A/D, 12-bit digital signal processing and high-quality mini-DV recording with professional functions, but also comes fully equipped to connect to the Internet so you can distribute your images in real time over the Web or local intranets.

GY-DV550U STUDIO DV CAMCORDER (HEAD ONLY) | By JVC

This is the world's first and only studio DV camcorder, operable up to 330 feet from CCU with multicore cable. It offers the features and performance of a studio camera with the added flexibility of a camcorder. The GY-DV550U is perfect for broadcasters but priced within easy reach of webcasters, corporate studios, high schools, universities, cable access studios, and churches. It has all of the features, performance, and accessories expected from a CCU controllable camera, plus the ability to operate in an iso-cam environment. Add to that the fact that it works superbly as a stand-alone camcorder and you have a JVC world's first. This is not just another camcorder with studio add-ons. The GY-DV550U is designed as a full-bandwidth (800+ line) studio camera from the ground up! Plus, it's a full-blown ENG camcorder. Its recordings are compatible with DVCAM and DVCPRO.

JVC Headquarters
1700 Valley Road
Wayne, NJ 07470
(973) 317-5000
www.jvc.com/pro

GY-DV5000U
3-CCD PROFESSIONAL
DV CAMCORDER | By JVC

Advanced 1/2-inch imagers, 12-bit ADC/DSP, and a dual size cassette mechanism make this the most advanced high-performance camcorder available. JVC's next generation 3-CCD Professional DV Camcorder carries the legacy of our enormously popular GY-DV500U. We redesigned the camera from the ground up, giving it features and performance that put it in a league with the most expensive production cameras on the market. Some features include: new double-tension tape transport that accepts full and mini cassettes (up to 276 minutes of recording time), professional DV record/play, DVCAM playback, 400% dynamic range, 800 TV lines (camera), high-resolution frame mode and 2XLR with phantom power, and left eye and Z axis adjustments standard.

JVC Headquarters
1700 Valley Road
Wayne, NJ 07470
(973) 317-5000
www.jvc.com/pro

DSR-390L DVCAM CAMCORDER
WITH STUDIO CAPABILITY | By Sony Electronics

The DSR-390L features three new type 1/2-inch 410K pixel Power HAD CCDs that result in high-quality acquisition with increased sensitivity plus "FIT-like" reduced vertical smear ratio of -115dB, 65dB S/N, and a sensitivity of F13 at 2,000 lux. In addition, the DSR390L comes with a fully operational i.Link port. The i.Link provides video, audio, and data OUT and VTR control IN, allowing transfer from the camcorder to any editing or storage device. This provides extraordinary field capabilities when combined with DSR-DU1 HDD. The optional CA-370 Intercom Adaptor includes the Studio VF Mounting Kit. Otherwise a mounting kit P/N A-8274-968-B is required from Sony parts to attach a DXF-51 viewfinder. The DSR-390L is capable of operating in a studio environment when connected to CCU-D50 at a distance of up to 300 meters (1,000 feet).

Sony Electronics
One Sony Drive
Park Ridge, NJ 07656
(800) 686-7669
www.sony.com/professional

DSR-570WSL 3-CCD WIDE SCREEN DVCAM CAMCORDER WITH STUDIO CAPABILITY | By Sony Electronics

The DSR-570WSL shares the same accessories as the DSR-500WSL, and continues to offer its exceptional performance level and technical benefits, such as three 2/3-inch 16:9 Power HAD CCDs, full DSP processing, and dual (mini and standard) cassette size capability, to name just a few. The DSR-570WSL camcorder adds cost-effective studio operation via CCU control with the Sony CCU-M5A or the new CCU-D50 camera CCU. In addition, via the new CA-370, studio intercom functionality using Sony's DR-100 headset is also added. The new DSR-570WSL is the pinnacle of our renowned DVCAM camcorder lineup.

MSW-900 IMX WIDE SCREEN DIGITAL CAMCORDER | By Sony Electronics

The MSW-900 is a 2/3-inch type 16:9/4:3 wide-screen camcorder for the MPEG IMX format, recording 50Mbs MPEG 4:2:2P@ML, I-frame video. Interlace or progressive recording, switchable to 60i or 30P. Telefile shot metadata system and four channels of 20-bit audio recording. Options available include: video cache recording , SDI output, and "Pool Feed" composite input.

Sony Electronics
One Sony Drive
Park Ridge. NJ 07656
(800) 686-7669
www.sony.com/professional

LDK 120 DPM CAMCORDER

A Grass Valley product by Thomson Broadcast & Media Solutions

Our LDK 120 DPM camcorder is perfect for documentaries, features, and other high-quality DVCPRO productions. Featuring Dynamic Pixel Management™ (DPM) sensors, it offers easy switching between 16:9 and 4:3 aspect ratios, 12-bit A-to-D converters, 22-bit digital signal processing to preserve all of the nuances in colors and grays, and excellent audio processing capabilities.

LDK 150 DPM CAMCORDER

A Grass Valley product by Thomson Broadcast & Media Solutions

Our LDK 150 DPM camcorder offers uncompromising picture quality and a full range of features to ensure maximum creative freedom and superb DVCPRO50 tape recording. Featuring Dynamic Pixel Management™ (DPM) sensors, it offers easy switching between 16:9 and 4:3 aspect ratios, DVCPRO50 4:2:2 recording, 12-bit A-to-D converters, 22-bit digital signal processing, and excellent audio processing capabilities.

Thomson Broadcast & Media Solutions
400 Providence Mine Road
Nevada City, CA 95959
(530) 478-3000
www.thomsongrassvalley.com

CAMERAS | CAMCORDERS
ELECTRONIC
CINEMATOGRAPHY

6

JVC: GY-DV700WU 16:9 CineLine Pro-DV Camcorder

Panasonic: AG-DVX100 24P DV Cinema Camera
                     AJ-HDC27 "VariCam" HD Cinema Camera
                     AJ-SDX900 DVCPRO50 Cinema Camera

Sony: HDW-F900 HDCAM CineAlta Camcorder

Thomson/Grass Valley: Viper FilmStream Camera

GY-DV700WU 16:9 CINELINE PRO-DV CAMCORDER | By JVC

JVC introduces the digital solution that offers the missing factor to the digital cinema equation — the outstanding image quality of the GY-DV700WU CineLine Pro-DV Camcorder. Without question, this is the highest quality DV camcorder for filmmaking, optimized for digital transfer to film. This powerful DV camcorder is ready to handle the sophisticated requirements of the most demanding feature production, yet it's priced within reach of virtually everyone. Developed in cooperation with the BBC, the CineDV DV700 combines three state-of-the-art 2/3-inch, true 16:9 CCDs with JVC's original high-performance dual-pipeline 14-bit DSP (Digital Signal Processing) for truly exceptional image quality. The camcorder body itself weighs only 3 kg (6.6 lb.). Even when you add lens, viewfinder, battery pack, and tape, it is still surprisingly light — weighing in at 5.5 kg (12.1 lb.) or less.

JVC Headquarters
1700 Valley Road
Wayne, NJ 07470
(973) 317-5000
www.jvc.com/pro

AG-DVX100 3-CCD 24P DV CINEMA CAMERA | By Panasonic

2002 Vidy Award Winner   *2002 Best Product of the Year* — Videomaker magazine

The AG-DVX100 is the world's first handheld camera designed with cinema specifications. With its superb, filmlike picture quality, the AG-DVX100 stands as a revolutionary development for independent filmmakers and anyone who produces short movies or streaming video for online distribution. The AG-DVX100 gives you a choice of three shooting modes. Select 24p (24fps, progressive) for images with a movie filmlike look and motion, 30p (30fps, progressive) or 60i (60fps, interface).

> *"The AG-DVX100 does exceptionally well in an interview setting, so it's ideal for this surfing documentary project. It's lightweight, fast and doesn't have the usual video news looks. And I'm delighted that I can shoot 60 minutes at this quality level for about $6.00. The camera bridges the gap between the high cost of film production and the usual news look of video."*

— **Executive Producer/Director Eric Jordan with Aquatic Concept**

Quote obtained from a Panasonic press release 5/15/03

Panasonic Broadcast & Television
Systems Co.
1 Panasonic Way
Secaucus, NJ 07094
(800) 528-8601
www.panasonic.com/broadcast

CAMERAS/CAMCORDERS: ELECTRONIC CINEMATOGRAPHY | 41

AJ-HDC27 "VARICAM" VARIABLE FRAME RATE 16:9 HD CINEMA CAMERA | By Panasonic

"...there are a lot of cinematographers in Hollywood who are really worried that for their next project it will be mandated that it be shot on HD, and they're wondering if they will be able to achieve the same standards they have set with their film work. With this camera, the answer is a resounding — yes."

— Victor Goss, ASC

Quote obtained from Panasonic's Web site

"We purchased the VariCam largely as a replacement for film in product shooting, specifically photographing automobiles. I really liked its variable frame rate shooting — there's a lot of call for off-speed work in the automotive industry. The VariCam material handled a lot of manipulation in post. We'd shot a black car outdoors at night in Detroit. We'd been anxious about the night shooting, but the dark car looked beautiful."

— Director Rick Yarmy, Owner & President of Video Design in Detroit

Quote obtained from a Panasonic press release 3/25/03

The AJ-HDC27 VariCam serves a triple role: 1.) as a 24fps camera, 2.) as a standard 60fps video camera, and 3.) as a variable frame rate special effects camera. This is the first High-Definition production camera that is capable of variable frame rate at the touch of a button. Individual frame rates may be selected from: 4fps to 60fps in single frame increments. Frame rates may be changed during recording. Designed as a high-quality pro-duction camera, this native 720p camcorder can be used for 60fps or the filmlike 24fps acquisition. When acquiring for 24fps projects, higher than 24fps operation can be processed for slow-motion effects while slower than 24fps operation can be processed to speed up motion. Additionally, the variable frame rates and related variable shutter speeds create some very interesting ghostlike motion blur effects, warp-speed zoom effects, and long-exposure still shots typical of what one might see in music videos, sci-fi dramas, and dream sequences.

Panasonic Broadcast & Television Systems Co.
1 Panasonic Way
Secaucus, NJ 07094
(800) 528-8601
www.panasonic.com/broadcast

AJ-SDX900 3-CCD DVCPRO50 CINEMA CAMERA | By Panasonic

NAB Pick Hit 2003 by Millimeter magazine

The AJ-SDX900 combines advanced DVCPRO and DVCPRO50 imaging technology with a compact, lightweight body designed for easy mobility. In designing the AJ-SDX900, Panasonic solicited a host of feedback comments from video professionals. The result is a fully mobile unit that is ideally balanced, easy to maneuver, and rugged enough for the field. Image quality is excellent thanks to a 2/3-inch 520,000-pixel 3-CCD imaging system with progressive scanning capability and new 12-bit DSP circuit. A 24p or 30p progressive shooting mode combines with a cine-like gamma curve to create video that closely replicates the appearance and quality of film. The AJ-SDX900 is an outstanding solution for everything from the production of TV programs and commercials to news gathering and music videos.

HDW-F900 HDCAM CINEALTA CAMCORDER | By Sony Electronics

The HDW-F900 is capable of record/playback of 1080 line 24/25/30 frame progressive or 50/60 interlace images. Memory Stick setup system memorizes various parameter settings and provides instant recall at any time. The CineAlta Camcorder produces picture with astonishing color reproduction accuracy. The Multi Matrix function also offers unique possibilities for creative intervention by allowing selective color enhancement or alteration. Multi Matrix allows a particular color to be selected and its hue changed over a range of approximately 20 degrees. Paint functions also permit color levels to be adjusted on set according to the cinematographer's creative needs. This feature can be used very creatively, particularly with scenes with mixed color lighting.

Sony Electronics
One Sony Drive
Park Ridge, NJ 07656
(800) 686-7669
www.sony.com/professional

VIPER FILMSTREAM CAMERA |

A Grass Valley product
by Thomson Broadcast
& Media Solutions

Our Viper FilmStream™ Camera has no equal. With three 9.2-million-pixel Frame Transfer CCDs, it delivers an RGB 4:4:4 10-bit log output, which has not been compromised by electronic camera signal processing. When your digital cinematography project demands the highest quality, this compact and versatile camera is the only one to use. Some key features include: captures raw data directly from CCDs; unique 4:4:4 RGB Dual Link FilmStream output; native 16:9 or 2.37:1 aspect ratios without resolution loss using Dynamic Pixel Management technology; multiple format support; 1080p @ 23.98, 24, 25, and 29.97 frames per second (fps); 1080i @ 50 and 59.94Hz; and 720p @ 23.98, 24, 25, 29.97, 50, and 59.94fps.

Thomson Broadcast &
Media Solutions
400 Providence Mine Road
Nevada City, CA 95959
(530) 478-3000
www.thomsongrassvalley.com

CAMERAS | CAMCORDERS
FIELD AND
STUDIO PRODUCTION

Ikegami:	HL-DV7AW One-Piece Digital Camera/Recorder
	HL-V79W DVCPRO50 Digital Camera/Recorder
	HL-60W Full Digital Broadcast Camera
Sony:	DVW-790WS Digital Betacam for EFP
	DSR-250ENGN1 Digital Camcorder ENG Package
Thomson/Grass Valley:	LDK 110IT(W) Digital DVCPRO Camcorder
	LDK 140IT(W) Digital DVCPRO Camcorder

HL-DV7AW ONE-PIECE DIGITAL CAMERA/RECORDER | By Ikegami Electronics

Ikegami's HL-DV7AW meets the exacting standards of today's DVCAM shooter with broadcast-standard image quality courtesy of a new digital process LSI (ASIC) that includes a six-axis linear matrix system for finely tuned color. Multiple gamma settings, lens and scene data files, Smartmedia card slot for full camera setup, and a low center of gravity make the HL-DV7AW unmatched for versatility and convenience in the field. Some features include: 16:9 wide-screen type switchable to 4:3 aspect ratio, and +48dB Hyper Gain for very low light conditions.

HL-V79W DVCPRO50 DIGITAL CAMERA/RECORDER (FIT CCD) | By Ikegami Electronics

In addition to the worldwide best-selling DVCPRO, now DVCPRO50 with 4:2:2 encoding is ideally suited for high-end productions. Ikegami's state-of-the-art camera technology enhances the quality of DVCPRO. Various models will satisfy every professional's requirements. The camera section features digital processing from Ikegami's next-generation ASICs. It is designed for maximum camera performance inherited from the HL series, while taking full advantage of DVCPRO's characteristics. DVCPRO all-in-one digital portable cameras are tailored to cover various applications, from news gathering to production, with operating versatility and outstanding picture quality.

Ikegami Electronics (U.S.A.), Inc.
37 Brook Avenue
Maywood, NJ 07607
(800) 368-9171
www.ikegami.com

HL-60W FULL DIGITAL BROADCAST CAMERA | By Ikegami Electronics

"I'm sure the service engineers at Ikegami feel like the Maytag repairman — the cameras just don't break down. That's very important to me, because a camera in the shop can cost me hundreds of dollars in revenue per day."

— Gary Snyder, President, Engineer and CEO of Clark Media

Quote obtained from an Ikegami press release 3/26/03

Combining newly developed digital signal processing features with a compact size (camera head weight is just 5.1 lb.) and low power consumption (10W), the switchable 16:9/4:3 HL-60W brings outstanding image quality and value to a wide range of studio and ENG/EFP applications. The new HL-60W extends Ikegami's long history of digital television advances with the debut of the three-chip AIT 520,000-pixel CCD, and using Ikegami's latest DSP ASIC with 0.18 micron design, in an SD camera.

DVW-790WS ONE-PIECE SWITCHABLE 4:3/16:9 DIGITAL BETACAM CAMCORDER FOR EFP | By Sony Electronics

The DVW-790WS One-Piece Switchable 4:3/16:9 Digital Betacam Camcorder for EFP uses three 16:9 Hyper HAD 1000 CCD FIT imagers to produce more than 700-line resolution while maintaining f9.0 @ 2,000 lux sensitivity. Twelve-bit A/D utilizing 36MHz digital signal processing ensures the highest picture quality for SDTV field capture.

Sony Electronics
One Sony Drive
Park Ridge, NJ 07656
(800) 686-7669
www.sony.com/professional

DSR-250ENGN1 DVCAM 1/3" 3-CCD DIGITAL CAMCORDER ENG PACKAGE | By Sony Electronics

The DSR-250ENGN1 DVCAM 1/3" 3-CCD Digital Camcorder, with standard DV recording capability, accepts both mini and large cassettes. The basic package includes the DSR-250 camcorder, RMT-811 Remote Commander, 4MB Memory Stick, Picture Gear 4.1 Lite, USB driver for PC and Mac, directional monaural microphone (ECM-NV1), DXF-801 viewfinder, lens hood, and lens cap. The DSR-250ENGPAC allows the event, wedding, or news videographer to begin shooting right out of the box, and includes a convenient carry case for safely stowing the gear.

Sony Electronics
One Sony Drive
Park Ridge, NJ 07656
(800) 686-7669
www.sony.com/professional

LDK 110IT(W) DIGITAL DVCPRO CAMCORDER | A Grass Valley product by Thomson Broadcast & Media Solutions

With the LDK 110IT(W) Digital DVCPRO Camcorder, a new standard is set in digital ENG. Combining our reputable skills in camera design with DVCPRO, the LDK 100IT(W) has become today's standard choice for digital program production. It is ideal for news gathering and general program production in the field, and its switchable Interline Transfer CCDs let you move between 4:3 and 16:9 productions easily. You can easily customize its settings to suit your preferences. And its lightweight, durable, and ergonomic design gives you the freedom to work quickly.

LDK 140IT(W) DIGITAL DVCPRO
CAMCORDER | A Grass Valley product by Thomson Broadcast & Media Solutions

For camera operators who work on everything from news programs to soap operas, our LDK 140IT(W) digital camcorder provides superb 4:2:2 recording to DVCPRO50 tape — and can switch between 4:3 and 16:9 formats as well as DVCPRO and DVCPRO50 easily. It also features dual Emmy award-winning skin-contour circuits and easy-to-adjust matrixing memories to ensure natural skin-color reproduction — even in fluorescent light.

Thomson Broadcast & Media Solutions
400 Providence Mine Road
Nevada City, CA 95959
(530) 478-3000
www.thomsongrassvalley.com

If you have used this gear and want to share your own experiences, comments, and suggestions in our next edition, send an e-mail to Catherine Lorenze at *DREAMGEAR@cox.net*. We are particularly interested in innovative ways you have used the gear that will help inspire other film, video, and TV professionals.

CAMERAS | CAMCORDERS
HIGH DEFINITION

8

Ikegami:	HDK-790E/HDK-79E Full Digital HDTV Camera System
JVC:	JY-HD10U Digital Hi-Vision HD Camcorder
Panasonic:	AJ-HDC20A DVCPRO HD Camcorder
Sony:	HDW-730 HDCAM Power HAD 60i/50i Camcorder
Thomson/Grass Valley:	LDK 6000 mkII WorldCam High Definition Camera

The HDK-790E/79E is designed as a multi-use camera to meet the format requirements of HDTV (1080i/720p) and SDTV (480i/480p). The CCD readout can be switched between interlace and progressive scan modes. The signal can be converted in the CCU to different formats. To meet the format requirements of HDTV and SDTV, the Ikegami HDK-series HDTV cameras have incorporated next-generation 0.18 micron ASICs into a new camera control unit, the CCU-790A. Also, using newly developed ASICs, an optional engine board has been developed to achieve frame and multi-format conversion (24p, 30p, 50p, 720p, 1080i, 480i, etc.). Using a down converter incorporated in the CCU as standard, the HDK-790E/79E can be operated as a high-end NTSC studio camera.

HDK-790E/HDK-79E
FULL DIGITAL
HDTV CAMERA
SYSTEM | By
Ikegami Electronics

Ikegami Electronics (U.S.A.), Inc.
37 Brook Avenue
Maywood, NJ 07607
(800) 368-9171
www.ikegami.com

JY-HD10U DIGITAL HI-VISION HD CAMCORDER | By JVC

JVC has made an enormous leap into the future with the world's first affordable HDTV pro-camcorder. This single-CCD marvel lets you record High-Definition native 16:9 content in the 1280 x 720P mode at 30 frames per second. Your recordings are stored on inexpensive, widely available mini-DV cassettes, capable of up to 63 minutes of recording time per cassette. You can play them back directly from the JY-HD10U camcorder onto an HDTV monitor or projector with component inputs, or dub them to JVC D-VHS machines using the IEEE1394 interface. The results are absolutely startling — like nothing you've ever seen from a camcorder in this price range! The JY-HD10U can also be used to make beautiful 16:9 progressive scan recordings in the 480/60P mode — ideal for viewing on today's high-quality DVD players. And, of course, you are still able to make standard 480i recordings in the mini-DV format compatible with a wide range of systems.

JVC Headquarters
1700 Valley Road
Wayne, NJ 07470
(973) 317-5000
www.jvc.com/pro

AJ-HDC20A 2/3" 3-CCD 16:9 1080I DVCPRO HD CAMCORDER | By Panasonic

Panasonic presents striking images from its new AJ-HDC20A High-Definition Camcorder. This 2.2-million-pixel 3-CCD advanced-performance camera delivers enviable pictures for all types of productions. The AJ-HDC20A High-Definition Camcorder delivers truly outstanding HD images, virtually free of video artifacts typical of older-generation HD cameras. Its sturdy, lightweight package, high mobility, and solid recording capabilities make this new DVCPRO HD flagship camera the extended performance and reliability leader for all types of TV production, including digital cinematography. A wealth of operator conveniences such as video setup controls, numerous scene file storage, and a unique color-correction matrix make the AJ-HDC20A the new High-Definition camera of choice.

Panasonic Broadcast & Television Systems Co.
1 Panasonic Way
Secaucus, NJ 07094
(800) 528-8601
www.panasonic.com/broadcast

CAMERAS | CAMCORDERS
SPECIAL EFFECTS

9

JVC: Zcam Real Time Depth Sensing Camera System

Sony: BVP-9500WS Super Motion Camera

Thomson/Grass Valley: The Microcam System
                                       LDK 23HS mkII Super Slow Motion Camera

ZCAM 3D CAMERA REAL TIME DEPTH SENSING CAMERA SYSTEM | By JVC

ZCAM™ is a revolutionary technology by 3DV Systems, with critical optical components designed by JVC, that captures not only normal two-dimensional video, but also measures the depth of each pixel in the image. The system then supplements every video frame with an additional frame called the "Zbuffer." This additional data can then be used in conjunction with a keyer, digital graphics system, or other device to enable a variety of useful effects. Zbuffer data can be used in real time, or recorded along with normal video as "objects" for later use. When you cover high-profile live events such as the presidential election, the NBA playoffs, or the Super Bowl, competition is intense. Object video gives you an edge. You can enhance your live coverage with the effects and enhancements normally only available for movies that go through a lengthy postproduction editing process. Once you capture live action footage in object video format, you can not only make it more visually engaging, but also sell advertising right in the context of the live event. Object video not only enhances your current programming and opens up new revenue streams; it also adds tremendous value to the delivery of video over the Web.

JVC Headquarters
1700 Valley Road
Wayne, NJ 07470
(973) 317-5000
www.jvc.com/pro

BVP-9500WS NEW SUPER MOTION CAMERA WITH IT POWERHAD CCD | By Sony Electronics

The BVP-9500WS is a digital signal processing, wide-screen, Super Motion camera. The BVP-9500WS is capable of three times and normal speed operation (90fps or 60i). Using the CCU-900 and the CA-950, the BVP-9500WS is the first Super Motion camera to utilize an all-digital signal path. The BVP-9500WS utilizes an included wide-screen IT PowerHAD optical head block and requires a CCU-900, CA-950, and viewfinder to complete a system. The BKP-9330 digital interface is also required (for the CCU-900) to provide a 3x SDI output for recording on a MAV-555 storage system.

Sony Electronics
One Sony Drive
Park Ridge, NJ 07656
(800) 686-7669
www.sony.com/professional

THE MICROCAM SYSTEM | A Grass Valley product by Thomson Broadcast & Media Solutions

Supporting our LDK 1657D camera as well as our LDK 1707 camera with its detached optical block, the Microcam™ system features a compact camera head to enable shooting angles that would be impossible with a conventional camera. Yet it preserves all camera features to get the best out of your tightest shots. Some key features include: supports LDK1657D or LDK 1707 with detached optical block, preserves all camera features, and is available in 16:9 switchable to 4:3 and fixed 4:3 aspect ratio.

LDK 23HS MKII SUPER SLOW MOTION CAMERA | A Grass Valley product by Thomson Broadcast & Media Solutions

Our LDK 23HS mkII is the most widely used and demanded super slow motion broadcast camera. Shooting at three times the rate of standard cameras, it offers superb resolution and is compatible with virtually any disk-based slow-motion system. And because it supports standard frame rates, there's no need to double up a camera position to add its capabilities. Some key features include: triple-speed scanning for superb slow-motion replay, 75 frames per second (PAL), 90 frames per second (NTSC), instant replay via virtually any disk-based slow-motion system, and camera pre-sets accommodating various indoor/outdoor lighting situations.

Thomson Broadcast &
Media Solutions
400 Providence Mine Road
Nevada City, CA 95959
(530) 478-3000
www.thomsongrassvalley.co

CAMERAS | CAMCORDERS
NIGHT VISION AND
IMAGE INTENSIFIERS

B. E. Meyers & Co. Inc.:	"OWL" Multi-Purpose Night Vision Pocketscope
Electrophysics:	Astroscope 9350 Night Vision System
	9300 ENG Night Vision Module
OpTex:	Series 3000-XL Image Intensifier

"OWL" 3RD GENERATION +
MULTI-PURPOSE NIGHT VISION
POCKETSCOPE | By B. E. Meyers & Co. Inc., Electro Optics

DREAM GEAR | LORENZE | 60

ASTROSCOPE 9350 NIGHT VISION SYSTEM | By Electrophysics Corp.

Astroscope is a modular night vision system that converts film and digital cameras and camcorders into a powerful nighttime image capture system. Electrophysics offers a wide range of image intensifiers and camera-specific adaptors designed for Canon's EOS and Nikon's AF lens mounts. Mechanical and electronic compatibility ensure the seamless integration of image intensifiers with your existing cameras and lenses. In addition, we offer specialized assemblies for today's most popular fixed-lens camcorders and CCD cameras.

9300 ENG NIGHT VISION MODULE | By Electrophysics Corp.

The broadcast night vision modules are designed for ENG/EFP 1/3-inch, 1/2-inch, and 2/3-inch cameras and deliver the highest-quality nighttime video images available to professional broadcasters. Mounted between the camera and the lens, the module amplifies low-light scenes so they are easily viewed and recorded by the host camera. Designed for B4 and B3 bayonet-mount ENG/EFP cameras, Astroscope is easy to use and requires no setup, calibration, or training.

Electrophysics Corp.
373 Route 46 West
Fairfield, NJ 07004-2442
(973) 882-0211
www.electrophysics.com

SERIES 3000-XL
IMAGE INTENSIFIER | By OpTex

The new generation of image intensifiers from OpTex offer high-resolution images at the lowest light levels. They should NOT be confused with "surveillance" or CCTV night sights or night vision devices. Based on OpTex's Emmy award-winning Mini Image Intensifier so successfully used by both UK and US news crews during the Kuwait crisis, the original unit has been augmented by higher levels of performance with the new Series 2000. The high-performance SuperGen image intensifiers provide virtually blemish-free, low-noise, high-resolution images at a level below starlight. The 3000-XL model is for use on the Canon XL1 and is located between the lens and camera body. It is powered from the camera's onboard battery. Lens functions, such as auto-iris and auto-zoom, are brought forward to the XL mount on the front of the module, thus enabling these functions to be retained. Auto-focus is disabled as this facility is unable to operate at the very low light levels under which the intensifier works.

OpTex
20-26 Victoria Road, New Barnet
N. London EN4 9PF UK
+44 (0)2 084-412-199
www.optexint.com

CAMERAS
35MM/16MM, SUPER 35MM/SUPER 16MM FILM

11

Aaton:	A-Minima Super16 Camera
	35-3Perf 35/Super35 Camera
	XTRprod System — Switchable 16/Super16 Camera
Arri:	Arricam Studio and Arricam Lite 35mm Camera System
	Arriflex 435 Advanced
	Arriflex 16SR3 Advanced
Panavision:	Millennium Panaflex 35mm Camera System
	Platinum Panaflex Camera System
Photo-Sonics:	16mm-1PL Actionmaster 500 High Speed Camera
	16mm-1VN Super 16mm High Speed Camera
	35mm-4C High Speed Camera

A-MINIMA SUPER16 CAMERA

By Aaton & Distributed by Abel Cine Tech NY/LA

"I was able to handhold the camera and shoot while I was riding in the back of a rickshaw. In the street I could shoot pretty covertly from a street corner. The unobtrusiveness was what I loved more then anything about this camera."

— Cinematographer Declan Quinn

Leaving Las Vegas, One True Thing, Monsoon Wedding

Quote from the Abel Cine Tech Web site

The Aaton A-Minima camera is light (5 lb., 10" x 4.5" in size), noiseless (ca. 27dB), and features ultra-accurate AatonCode-II in-camera time recording. A-Minima is meant to be the second camera on well-endowed productions, and is often used as "the one and only camera" in the hands of independent filmmakers. Some features of the A-Minima include: economical design — a simple, uncompromising mechanism design and competitive pricing makes A-Minima the world's most efficient HD-compatible image capture device; lens choice — PL or Nikon mount gives you access to practically all professional motion picture and still lenses; built-in features — an incident meter, time-code masterclock, and intervalometer are built right in; distant-eye viewing — put your eye to the finder or take it away in midshot for the creative flexibility of a camcorder.

Aaton S.A.
bp 3002
38816 Grenoble
cdx1 France
+33 (0)4 76-42-95-50
www.aaton.com
www.a-minima.com

Abel Cine Tech
66 Willow Avenue
Suite 201
Staten Island, NY 10305
(888) 223-1599
www.abelcine.com

35-3PERF 35/SUPER35
CAMERA
By Aaton & Distributed
by Abel Cine Tech NY/LA

The Aaton 35-III, with its absolute image stability and hair-free gate, ensures perfectly clean, archivable images that will remain with us for generations. The practical and ergonomic design of the Aaton 35-III is the reason why it is the most comfortable and versatile handheld 35mm camera available for commercials, documentary, live events, wildlife, run-and-gun operation, or features. And now, thanks to its new 3Perf option, it becomes so quiet it can be used as the "A" camera in all situations. All Aaton 35-III cameras record AatonCode on the side of each and every image; eliminating the need of slates for audio sync. The Aaton 35-III is the only camera offering Instant Magazines.

AATON XTRPROD
SYSTEM
By Aaton & Distributed
by Abel Cine Tech NY/LA

The XTRprod Super16 camera offers such quiet and steady movement that we call it "the ultimate filming machine." Aaton's XTRprod is designed to combine Aaton's renowned camera features such as AatonCode-II, superior image registration, an ultra-luminous viewfinder, and integrated CCD video assist, along with additional integral high-end studio elements. The system also features 16/Super16 switchability, internal light meter, Var-11 shutter, Aatonite illuminated viewing, 800-foot magazine compatibility, and an illuminated LCD panel to control time code, footage, ASA selection, voltage reading, speed selection, and phasing.

ARRICAM STUDIO AND ARRICAM LITE 35MM CAMERA SYSTEM | By Arri Inc.

With the Arricam Studio and the Arricam Lite, Arri introduces an innovative and modular 35mm camera system that combines maximum operating comfort with dependable Arri precision and reliability. Both cameras offer easy and flexible configuration for any operating situation. A three-perforation movement is optionally available for both camera versions. For the first time, a lens control system has been integrated into the camera body that reads and controls all data of the lens. The in-camera slate function marks each take legibly and provides economical advantages in postproduction and reduced use of film stock. The Arricam Studio is distinguished by its low noise level and many advanced features. The Arricam Lite is particularly useful when low weight, small camera size, and operating freedom are required — i.e., remote, Steadicam, or shoulder operation.

Arri Inc.
617 Route 303
Blauvelt, NY 10913
(845) 353-1400
www.arri.com

ARRIFLEX 435 ADVANCED | By Arri Inc.

Comprehensive accessories and new interfaces allow the 435 Advanced camera to be
perfectly integrated in a large variety of applications — from motion control to in-camera
effects with speed ramps, not to mention classic second-unit applications. Using the electronically adjustable mirror shutter, exposure programs can be created and, with the push
of a single button, recalled. A newly designed, high-performance shutter drive cuts adjustment time in half, allowing for much quicker speed ramps. The new minimum frame rate
has been reduced to 0.1fps. Additionally, a Single Frame/Capping Shutter is available that
can also be accessed and controlled directly through the motion control software. The
reworked IVS II defines the new standard of quality for video taps. The Arriflex 435 body
weighs in at only 6.5 kg. Without special preparation, the camera can easily be handheld
with the standard 400-foot magazine.

ARRIFLEX 16SR3 ADVANCED | By Arri Inc.

Arri's 16SR3 Advanced weighs approximately 7 kg (15.4 lb.) with loaded 400-foot magazines and
on-board battery. Other features include: noise level — standard version, 20dB(A) + 2dB(A), high-
speed version, 27dB(A) + 2dB(A); shutter opening sector — 180°, 172.8°, 144°, 135°, 90° , 45°;
lens mount — 54mm pl-mount, retrofit to super 16; viewfinder magnification — 10X (10/17X with
viewfinder extension); filming speeds — standard version, 5 to 75fps (crystal accurate to
0.001fps), high-speed version, 10 to 150fps;
power supply — 24V; temperature range —
-20°C/+50°C (- 4°F/+122°F); dimensions —
L 264mm/W 172mm/H 195mm
(viewfinder in horizontal position),
L 264mm/W 100mm/H 298mm
(viewfinder in vertical position).

MILLENNIUM PANAFLEX 35MM CAMERA SYSTEM | By Panavision

The Millennium is the latest addition to the Panavision tradition of Panaflex 35mm film cameras. Fully compatible with our existing camera systems, this studio-quiet camera incorporates new mirror, movement, and drive components, motorized speed shutter dissolve (11 1/2 to 180°), remote control receiver, faceplate connectors for focus, t-stop, and zoom control — yet it is lighter in weight for the most demanding handheld work. New camera optics include a brilliant, full-field viewfinder that is quickly detachable for conversion to Steadicam, video finder, or video only applications. Frame rate from 3 to 50fps in 1/1000 frame increments, with the latest in motor technology and controls. The Millennium accepts 400-foot and 1,000-foot lightweight composite magazines.

PLATINUM PANAFLEX 35MM
CAMERA SYSTEM | By Panavision

The Platinum Panaflex 33mm system represents the industry standard. Features include: 19db quiet, variable, in-shot focal plane shutter 50 to 200°; microprocessor monitoring of all critical camera functions; full-fitting dual registration pins; crystal controlled in 1/10 frame stops at all speeds from 4 to 36fps forward and reverse (to run in reverse requires reversing magazine); extension and intermediate high-performance color-corrected viewfinders; external, variable Panaglow control.

Panavision
6219 De Soto Avenue
Woodland Hills, CA 91367
(818) 316-1000
www.panavision.com

16MM-1PL ACTIONMASTER 500 HIGH SPEED CAMERA

By Photo-Sonics, Inc.

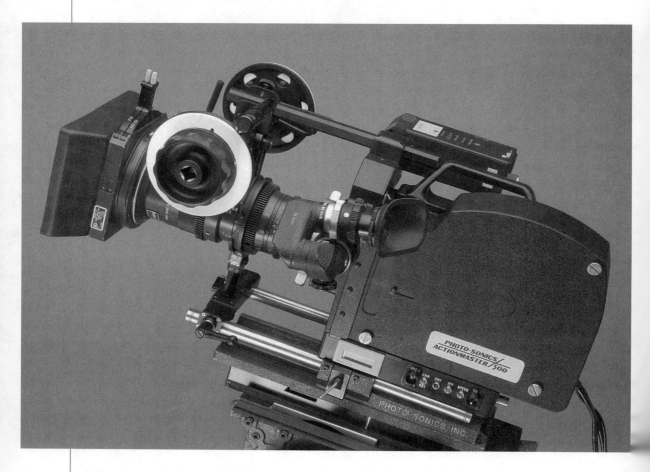

Simply put, the Photo-Sonics 16mm-1PL camera is the best-selling high-speed instrumentation film camera of all time! The 16mm-1PL utilizes state-of-the-art electronics to accurately control its speed between the selectable ranges of 10 to 500 pictures per second. All camera functions are controlled by programmable logic arrays and a highly accurate, temperature-compensated crystal. This new servo utilizes the latest surface-mounted technology and custom flex circuitry for reliability, even in the most severe environments. The design of the film magazine enables users to change magazines on the camera within a few seconds.

16MM-1VN SUPER 16MM HIGH SPEED CAMERA | By Photo-Sonics, Inc.

The 16mm-1VN is the world's smallest film camera, offering superb image quality guaranteed through the use of the intermittent, or pin-registered, movement. Its compact size, 1.5-lb. body weight, and rugged construction have led to it being used in a wide variety of applications, from nature and sports documentation, to being fitted in an AIM 9 missile pod for military flight testing, to being used in vehicle certification crash test work. The 16mm-1VN has optional FDRS and/or phase-lock capability, uses surface mount device (SMD) technology throughout, and offers 24 to 200fps with high resolution.

Photo-Sonics, Inc.
820 S. Mariposa Street
Burbank, CA 91506
(818) 842-2141
www.photosonics.com

35MM-4C HIGH SPEED CAMERA | By Photo-Sonics, Inc.

The Photo-Sonics 35mm-4B and 35mm-4C are precision 35mm, rotating prism, high-speed motion picture cameras operating over the range of 85 to 3.250 frames per second. The two models are operationally identical and vary only in the configuration of film magazine mounting. The 35mm-4C magazine is mounted at an angle to accommodate the use of larger lenses or telescopes. Both cameras are designed for high-speed photography on a full 35mm format. A rotary prism is utilized for image compensation on the film while the film is in continuous motion. The rotary prism operates in sync with a disk shutter positioned between the prism and the film. By using the prism/shutter combination, an even exposure over the full 35mm format is obtained, resulting in high-resolution and greater shutter efficiency.

Photo-Sonics, Inc.
820 S. Mariposa Street
Burbank, CA 91506
(818) 842-2141
www.photosonics.com

CAMERAS

UNDERCOVER AND SURVEILLANCE PRODUCTION

12

OpTex:
Button Cam
Glasses Cam Type 1 and Type 2
Micro Digital Recorder
Miniature Radio Color Camera
Pen Cam

BUTTON CAM | By OpTex

The Button Camera is a miniature CCD color or black-and-white camera with a 3.6mm pinhole lens built into the back of a shirt button. With the front aperture of the lens no more than 1mm in diameter, the Button Cam is ideally suited for covert surveillance, slipping neatly through the buttonhole of most shirts. To keep the front of the shirt flat, press studs are provided for sewing into the shirt above and below the camera. For better concealment, 10 matching buttons are supplied, allowing the camera to easily blend into the clothing being worn. The color version is powered by four AA batteries located in a battery pack holder supplied with the camera. The black-and-white version is powered by a 12V NiCad battery pack. For increased personal security, both cameras are fitted with a single power-in/video-out cable measuring less than 2mm in diameter.

GLASSES CAM TYPE 1 AND TYPE 2 | By OpTex

The Glasses Cam Type 1 is a revolutionary way of covertly recording live events. Designed to blend in with standard commercial glasses, the Glasses Cam incorporates a 3.7mm pinhole lens, a 1/3-inch inter line color CCD camera and an FET amplified microphone. The main feature of the system is that the lens is fitted in the nose bridge, so "What you see is what you take," and virtually no front element exposure makes the camera an ideal tool for covert surveillance. As an added measure of realism the glasses use UV-protected and photosensitive lenses that automatically adjust their tint to the ambient brightness. The recording cables run through a pair of permanent lanyards that can run undetected down the user's back to a box containing audio and video outputs and the camera's 12V NiCad battery power supply.

The Glasses Cam Type 2 is mounted in a superthin wire frame and uses digital signal processing video camera technology. They are lighter, more comfortable, and give a more natural look to the wearer. As a result of these improvements, the color Glasses Cam Type 2 are now virtually indistinguishable from normal spectacles.

MVR-007 MICRO
DIGITAL RECORDER | By OpTex

Marginally larger than a pack of cigarettes, the OpTex MVR-007 is
a MicroMV video recorder that will capture up to one hour of video
at a resolution of approximately 500 TV lines. The MVR-007 can
be body worn, making it very suitable for covert video applications.
Accepting analog video and audio inputs, the recorder can be
connected to a wide range of mini and covert video cameras. Also
supplied is a micro LED, which can be pinned discreetly inside a
pocket to give a visual confirmation.

OpTex
20-26 Victoria Road,
New Barnet
N. London EN4 9PF UK
+44 (0)2 084-412-199
www.optexint.com

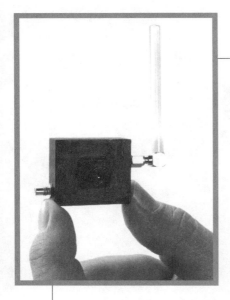

MINIATURE RADIO COLOR CAMERA | By OpTex

The OpTex Miniature Radio Color Camera is the smallest of its type in the world and is designed to provide a link using the MPT1349 UK license-exempt frequency band with effective radiated power level not greater than 100mW. (*Note: 1349 is license-free only in the UK and parts of Europe. This does not conform with United States standards.*) It is ideal for investigative journalism or work of a covert nature. The radio camera provides a simple plug-in link requiring no operator intervention. The 6V DC power supply to the transmitter is via an SMC miniature connector and on the receiver a miniature two-pin Lemo connector. Located next to this is a BNC socket for video input/output. These units are supplied with a short whip antenna, which should achieve a link of about 500–1,000 ft./150–300m.

PEN CAM | By OpTex

The Pen Camera features the same equipment as the Glasses Cam Type 1, but the camera is now inserted in a chunky ballpoint-pen casing, with the lens next to the pocket clip and the microphone on the top of the cap. The output signal travels down a cable attached to the bottom of the pen casing, which can be passed through a hole in the pocket where the pen is placed, allowing it to be concealed inside the lining of the jacket. The video and audio signals can be fed directly into a recorder or for remote simultaneous surveillance and/or recording via one of the OpTex microwave transmission systems.

OpTex
20-26 Victoria Road, New Barnet
N. London EN4 9PF UK
+44 (0)2 084-412-199
www.optexint.com

CAMERA 13
ACCESSORIES

Arri:	Arrimotion
Barber Tech Video Products:	EZ Flag
Datavideo:	Intervalometer and DV Bank System
NCS Products:	"Revolution" Intervalometer
Preston Cinema:	F/X Module
16x9 Inc./Band Pro:	Sim Time-Frame Intervalometer
Tiffen:	Tele2X Wide Angle Viewfinder

ARRIMOTION MOTION CONTROL SYSTEM | By Arri Inc.

Arri's main intention was to develop an easy-to-operate, user-friendly motion control system that allows the director and camera operator to create and execute perfect, high-quality visual-effects shots without the need of highly specialized equipment and complicated setups. The system, based on an Arrihead camera head, covers most motion control applications and is as easy to operate as a tape recorder. Some key advantages include: can replay recorded sequences at any speed; can be programmed via keyframes; can import data from CGI systems and can export to CGI systems; and supports all combinations of iris speed and shutter ramps in connection with the Arriflex 435 ES Motion Control.

Arri Inc.
617 Route 303
Blauvelt, NY 10913
(845) 353-1400
www.arri.com

EZ FLAG | By Barber Tech Video Products

EZ Flag camera flags are available with either 1/20 screw mount, shoe mount, or clamp mounts and come in three sizes — 14", 18", and 20".

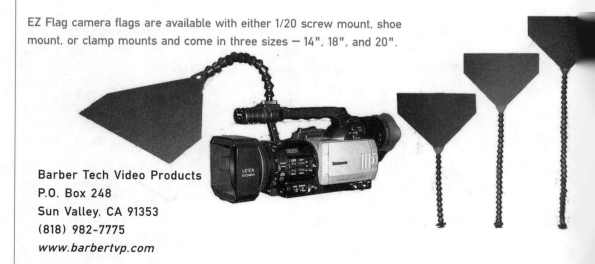

Barber Tech Video Products
P.O. Box 248
Sun Valley, CA 91353
(818) 982-7775
www.barbertvp.com

INTERVALOMETER AND DV BANK
SYSTEM FOR TIME LAPSE | By Datavideo

With Datavideo's DV Bank and TL-1 Intervalometer system, producers can creatively animate the operation of machines, maps and charts, storyboards, games, titles, or anything else that an assignment requires. You can create unique, compelling, animated, real-object video images without having to resort to complex computer animation programs. The technical producer can use the system to effortlessly make traditional time-lapse images of sunsets, sunrises, plant growth, construction sites, traffic flow, etc. The DV Bank is a DV-in/DV-out 60-Gigabyte hard-drive recorder capable of recording up to 4.5 hours of live video. When combined with the Intervalometer, it can record any combination of live and time-lapse video up to 486,000 frames.

Datavideo Corporation
12300-U East Washington Blvd.
Whittier, CA 90606
(562) 696-2324
www.datavideo-tek.com

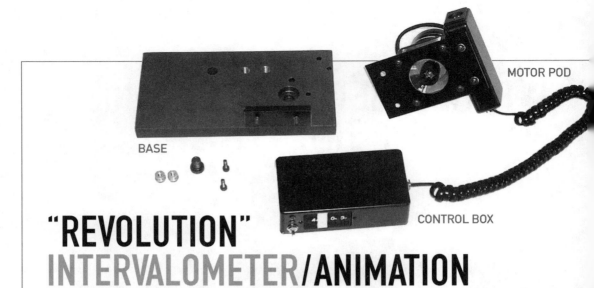

BASE

MOTOR POD

CONTROL BOX

"REVOLUTION" INTERVALOMETER/ANIMATION MOTOR FOR THE ARRI II | By NCS Products

NCS Products designs and manufactures time-lapse and sync motors for 16mm and 35mm motion picture cameras. Models are available for the Bolex, Beaulieu, Krasnogorsk, Arriflex II, and Eyemo cameras. Motors can also be adapted to other cameras.

NCS Products
P.O. Box 177
Albertson, NY 11366
(888) 333-1666
www.intervalometers.com

F/X MODULE | By
Preston Cinema Systems

What do the camera crews from *007, Matrix 2, Minority Report, Ali, Human Stain, Terminator 3, The Hunted* (and the list goes on) know that you don't? Perhaps that our new F/X unit provides an unparalleled combination of creative control and ease of use. Camera speed ramping with exposure compensation via iris, shutter, or iris/shutter in combination leads the list of features. In addition, depth of field can be controlled using the shutter for exposure compensation. The lens library stores data for more than 100 lenses. Each of the lenses can be calibrated and named by the user in prep, so that lens changes on the set only take moments. Storing and repeating moves is a snap. Up to 11 minutes of camera speed, camera shutter, and lens data can be stored and played back. A wide variety of cameras from most of the major manufacturers can be controlled, from Arriflex and Aaton to Panavision.

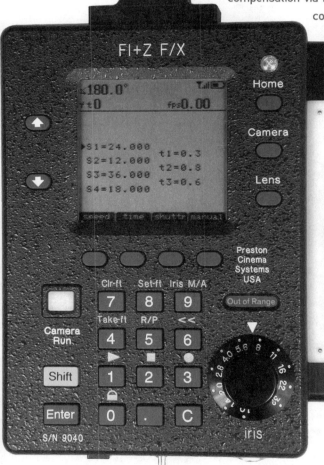

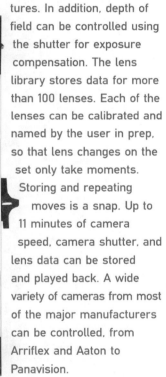

Preston Cinema Systems
1659 Eleventh Street, Suite 100
Santa Monica, CA 90404
(310) 453-1852
www.prestoncinema.com

SIM TIME-FRAME INTERVALOMETER FOR THE SONY'S CINEALTA 24P CAMCORDER | Distributed by 16x9 Inc./Band Pro

The new F-900 Intervalometer is built to work with the Sony CineAlta 24P HDW-F900's single frame record feature, allowing various time-lapse effects. The F-900 Intervalometer allows record intervals to be set from four seconds (minimum allowed by the HDW-F900) up to 18 hours. The unit requires no modification to the camera. Control is achieved through a supplied 12-pin cable connected to the lens servo zoom interface connector found on all HD ENG-style lenses with servo zoom control. ENG-style lenses are preferred because of the need for auto iris when interval recording. Additional custom interface cables allow the use of the F-900 Intervalometer with Cine-style lenses, without a built-in servo zoom control. 12V power is provided on a 4-pin Hirose connector.

Band Pro Film/Video, Inc.
3605 West Pacific Avenue
Burbank, CA 91505
(818) 841-9655
www.bandpro.com

16x9 Inc.
3605 West Pacific Avenue
Suite B
Burbank, CA 91505
(866) 800-1699
www.16x9inc.com

TELE2X WIDE ANGLE VIEWFINDER FOR SONY AND IKEGAMI CAMERAS | By Tiffen

The Tele2X Wide Angle Viewfinder is available for Sony or Ikegami camera models. The Tele2X magnifies your viewfinder image, alleviates eyestrain, prevents injury from close-up viewing, and allows you to adjust the camera while keeping the full frame in view.

The Tiffen Company, LLC
90 Oser Avenue
Hauppauge, NY 11788-3883
(631) 273-2500
www.tiffen.com

If you have used this gear and want to share your own experiences, comments, and suggestions in our next edition, send an e-mail to Catherine Lorenze at *DREAMGEAR@cox.net*. We are particularly interested in innovative ways you have used the gear that will help inspire other film, video, and TV professionals.

CAMERA
AERIAL SYSTEMS
AND STABILIZATION

14

Coptervision: CVG-A Remote Control Helicopter

FLIR Systems: UltraMedia III ENG Stabilized Aerial Camera System

Flying-Cam: Flying-Cam II Remote Control Helicopter

Tyler: Major Mount Helicopter Camera Mount
                             Middle Mount II Helicopter Camera Mount
                             Nose Mount II Helicopter Camera Mount
                             Super Nose Mount Helicopter Camera Mount
                             Video Ball Mount

Wescam: 35mm Gyrostabilized Film Systems

CVG-A REMOTE CONTROL HELICOPTER | By Coptervision

"The primary shot at JPL's Pasadena facilities was in the Mars Yard with the Mars rover. Coptervision's helicopter was able to hover directly above the rover, creating the point of view of being on Mars looking at the rover when, all of a sudden, the helicopter lifted up, revealed the shadow of a person and then tilted up, and panned to reveal the buildings around JPL. It was exactly what I was looking for."

— Jack Dawson, Live Shot Coordinator for NASA's Jet Propulsion Laboratory

Quote obtained from a Coptervision press release 3/22/02

Since 1997, Coptervision has provided state-of-the-art remote-control helicopters for film and video production. Manufactured and designed by an in-house team of experts, the helicopters are five feet in length with a six-foot blade span and weigh a total of 45 lb. Most recently, the company has unveiled the CVG-A, the most technologically advanced helicopter of its kind. By incorporating the latest in unmanned technology, the CVG-A is more precise, robust, and versatile than its predecessors. The helicopters include a three-axis, gyro-stabilized camera system, which features 360° roll, 360° pan, and 120° tilt. Super 35mm/35mm, super 16mm/16mm, and digital video cameras also come with the package, which consists of a three-person crew, two helicopters (one as back-up), and two cameras of the same format. The ready-to-shoot package is available on a per-project basis and is easily transported anywhere in the world.

Coptervision
7625 Hayvenhurst Ave., #41
Van Nuys, CA 91406
(818) 781-3003
www.coptervision.com

ULTRAMEDIA III ENG STABILIZED AERIAL CAMERA SYSTEM | By FLIR Systems

The UltraMedia III is the latest in an award-winning series of ultra high performance aerial broadcast camera systems from FLIR Systems. Totally digital, the UltraMedia III uses the industry-standard Sony BVP-570 camera. Mated to the Sony camera is a 1,000mm Canon lens, enabling you to get those really close shots, and to stand off when air traffic control limits your air crew's access to the scene of newsworthy events. To make these longer focal lengths possible, FLIR has equipped the UltraMedia III with advanced stabilization technology, which means the image your audience sees is virtually jitter free, even at maximum zoom.

FLIR Systems
16505 SW 72nd Avenue
Portland, OR 97224
(800) 322-3731
www.flir.com

"We were shooting at low levels and I wanted to use the Zeiss superspeed lens. Producer Todd Hallowell explained to the City (NYC) that we would use this mini-helicopter for the shot. The equipment does not function under the FAA rulings, so we could bring it in and fly it either in front of or behind the cars, as they passed through the repeated archways of the bridge... the shot was safe and exciting."

— Dave Dunlap, 2nd Unit Cinematographer
for *A Beautiful Mind*

Quote obtained from *ICM* magazine, Dec. 2001, in an article by Bonnie Goldberg

FLYING-CAM II REMOTE CONTROL HELICOPTER | By Flying-Cam, Inc.

In order to achieve impeccable, quality photography, every movement of the Flying-Cam II gyro-stabilized head is remotely controlled by the camera operator. This ensures creative and accurate composition. Our unique remote head permits pan, roll, and tilt movements simultaneously. The Flying-Cam II is the sole system that can offer you 360° unlimited pan capability. Utilizing technology known as Body-Pan, we integrate the visions of both the camera operator and the pilot in a completely unique manner. This technology, protected by patent, allows for complete and precise control not available in any other system in the world. The Flying-Cam II weighs 30 lb., is 6.5 ft. in length, and has a main rotor diameter of 6 ft. Flight height ranges from 6 in. to 300 ft. above the ground. Among Flying-Cam's credits are *Harry Potter and the Chamber of Secrets*, *Ocean's Eleven*, *Mission Impossible 2*, and many others.

Flying-Cam, Inc.
3100 Donald Douglas Loop North, #203
Santa Monica, CA 90405
(310) 581-9276
www.flying-cam.com

MAJOR MOUNT HELICOPTER CAMERA MOUNT FOR CAMERA PACKAGES UP TO 120 LB. | By Tyler Camera Systems

The Major Mount is a helicopter camera mount designed to capture an aerial perspective from the side of the helicopter, providing 100° of pan, tilt, and roll movements, making it ideal for air-to-ground or air-to-air scenic aerials or fast action sequences. Straight-forward or straight-back shots can be made by crabbing the helicopter up to 40 mph. And, with the optional Gyro Assist, the Major Mount performance is enhanced, allowing greater focal lengths to be achieved with the same ease of operating. Major Mounts are used by your operator and AC and can utilize your camera and lenses or Tyler's 35mm camera package.

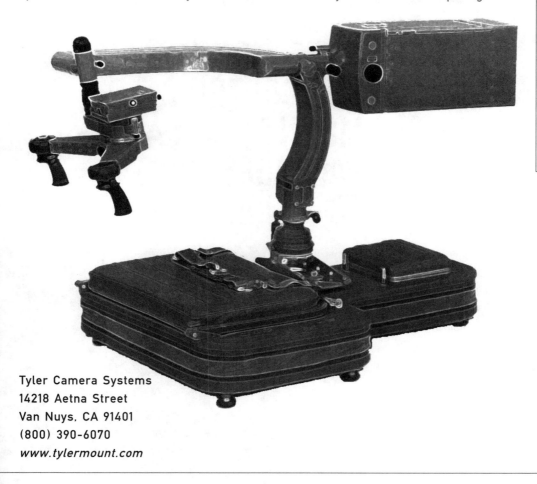

Tyler Camera Systems
14218 Aetna Street
Van Nuys, CA 91401
(800) 390-6070
www.tylermount.com

MIDDLE MOUNT II HELICOPTER CAMERA MOUNT FOR CAMERA PACKAGES UP TO 60 LB. | By Tyler Camera Systems

The Middle Mount is a helicopter camera mount designed to capture an aerial perspective from the side of the helicopter, providing 100° of pan, tilt, and roll movements, making it ideal for

air-to-ground or air-to-air scenic aerials or fast action sequences. Straight-forward or straight-back shots can be made by crabbing the helicopter up to 40 mph. And, with the optional Gyro Assist, the Middle Mount performance is enhanced, allowing greater focal lengths to be achieved with the same ease of operating. Middle Mounts are used by your operator and AC and can utilize your camera and lenses or Tyler's 35mm camera package.

NOSE MOUNT II HELICOPTER CAMERA MOUNT FOR CAMERA PACKAGES UP TO 39 LB. | By Tyler Camera Systems

The Nose Mount is a helicopter camera mount designed to capture a forward-looking "flight of the helicopter" point of view in which the horizon rolls as the helicopter banks, providing 200° of remotely controlled tilt movement, making it ideal for approach, reveal, chase, vertical scenic aerials or fast action sequences. Nose Mounts are used by your operator and AC and can utilize your camera and lenses or Tyler's 35mm camera package.

SUPER NOSE MOUNT HELICOPTER CAMERA MOUNT FOR CAMERA PACKAGES UP TO 120 LB. | By Tyler Camera Systems

The Super Nose Mount is a helicopter camera mount designed to capture a forward-looking "flight of the helicopter" point of view in which the horizon rolls as the helicopter banks, providing 200° of remotely controlled tilt movement, making it ideal for approach, reveal, chase, vertical scenic aerials or fast action sequences. Nose Mounts are used by your operator and AC and can utilize your camera and lenses or Tyler's 35mm camera package.

CAMERA AERIAL SYSTEMS AND STABILIZATION | 91

The UltraMedia II Video Ball Mount is a laptop-controlled helicopter mount designed to capture an aerial perspective from the front or side of the helicopter, providing 360° pan, 125° tilt movements with a constant level horizon. Images remain steady, even in tightly banked turns. This advanced gyro system cannot be unseated by extreme aircraft maneuvers. The active gyro stabilization also provides extreme focal length capability.

Tyler Camera Systems
14218 Aetna Street
Van Nuys, CA 91401
(800) 390-6070
www.tylermount.com

VIDEO BALL MOUNT | By Tyler Camera Systems

35MM GYROSTABILIZED FILM SYSTEMS | By Wescam

Wescam's 35mm Gyrostabilized Film Systems provide smooth, crystal-clear, accurate images. Mount the 35mm system to any type of moving platform, including but not limited to helicopters, fixed-wing aircraft, boats, camera cars, cranes, tracks, dollies, and cables. All of these platforms have been equipped with the Wescam 35mm film system and have provided outstanding service to the motion picture industry. Capabilities of the stabilized 35mm system include: 360° continuous pan in either direction; tilt up to 30° or down to 90° from the horizon; all camera, lens, and steering functions remotely controlled and monitored from the operator's console; variable frame rate from 0.5 to 60fps continuous and remotely selectable crystal sync for any speed, including TV sync; speed aperture control system yields constant exposure when varying frame rate while retaining a rock-solid image.

Wescam
7150 Hayvenhurst Avenue
Van Nuys, CA 91406-3823
(818) 785-9282
www.wescam.com

CAMERA
GROUND SYSTEMS
AND REMOTE HEADS
15

Coptervision:	Remotevision
	Rollvision Wireless Remote Head
Doggicam Systems:	Sparrow Head
Innovision Optics:	Radcam Omni Remote Control Camera Car
	Super Shuttle
Microdolly Hollywood:	Power Head
Telemetrics:	CTS-S2 Robotic Camera Trolley System
	PT-HP-S2 Servo Pan and Tilt Head
	PT-CP-S2 Servo CP Pan and Tilt Head
VariZoom:	VZ-MC100 Portable Remote Head
Wescam:	XR Pan, Tilt, and Roll Head

REMOTEVISION AND ROLLVISION | By Coptervision

Remotevision is a newly developed "4-in-1" radio control created to work in conjunction with the Rollvision system. It features a 5.6-inch color monitor and controls the pan, tilt, roll, zoom, and iris of the camera. Designed to be portable, the Remotevision radio can be handheld or placed on a tripod.

Rollvision, the most groundbreaking technology from Coptervision, is a portable and wireless three-axis camera system that is revolutionizing film and video production in Hollywood and around the world. Measuring 19

inches in diameter and weighing 16 lb., the dynamic Rollvision remote head can be placed on various camera platforms including cables, Steadicam, camera cars, cranes, dollies, tracking and rail systems and more. It features 360° roll, pan, and tilt and comes with universal mounts for hassle-free installation. In addition, the system can accommodate many types of cameras ranging from the Arri 435 with a 400-ft. magazine to numerous HD cameras. The Rollvision/Remotevision package is available for rent or sale.

Coptervision
7625 Hayvenhurst Ave., #41
Van Nuys, CA 91406
(818) 781-3003
www.coptervision.com

SPARROW HEAD | By Doggicam Systems

The Sparrow Head provides the opportunity to remotely operate in situations previously unimagined. At 16.5 lb. (30 lb. with camera), the Sparrow Head is the smallest, lightest, and lowest 35mm remote head available. One of the unique features built into the head is an integrated rigging system. This is the only remote head ever designed specifically to be mounted to fast-moving objects as well as standard crane operations. The head has frequently operated at speeds in excess of 120 mph with no problem. The rigging system allows quick and secure applications to vehicles like motorcycles, karts, cars, and anything that moves, offering shots that have, up to now, only been a director's dream.

"Whether it was on the camera car, a boat, mounted underneath a tractor-trailer rig during a stunt, inside a car crashing through a fireball, on a motorcycle, or just quickly and efficiently thrown up on a crane, the Sparrow Head was the most used piece of equipment on the set of Fast and Furious 2."

— Terry Lennard, 2nd Unit Director on *Fast and Furious 2*

Quote provided by Doggicam Systems

Doggicam Systems
1500 W. Verdugo Ave.
Burbank, CA 91506
(818) 845-8470
www.doggicam.com

RADCAM OMNI REMOTE CONTROL CAMERA CAR WITH UNIVERSAL MOUNT

| Distributed by Innovision Optics, Inc.

Completely wireless, Radcam is capable of moving fast enough to keep pace with a sprinting dog and has a turning radius of 60". Fully adjustable four-wheel independent suspension lets it move just as quickly over rough or uneven terrain. Speed and steering are controlled by a radio controller. The Radcam accepts a variety of video and film cameras, including Panavision and HD cameras. The Radcam has been used on features such as *Home Alone 3, The Big Lebowski,* and *Small Soldiers*.

Innovision Optics, Inc.
1719 21st Street
Santa Monica, CA 90404
(310) 453-4866
www.innovision-optics.com

SUPER SHUTTLE

Distributed by Innovision Optics, Inc.

Super Shuttle

Super Shuttle, Innovision's top-of-the-line shuttle system, offers high-speed capability, programmable positions, longer range of travel, focus and zoom control, and an attractive slim-line design. This remote-controlled camera platform is capable of traveling along a straight or curved track and comes complete with a Pan & Tilt Head and Controller with eight

preset memory positions. Shuttle systems are installed at CNN Headline News in Atlanta, E! Entertainment in New York City, Rede Globo in Brazil, TV Globo in Brazil, and KB Films in Sweden.

Innovision Optics, Inc.
1719 21st Street
Santa Monica, CA 90404
(310) 453-4866
www.innovision-optics.com

POWER HEAD

By Microdolly Hollywood

This new power head provides remote control of pan and tilt movement for cameras weighing up to 40 lb. (18kg). It can be mounted on the microdolly jib arm or a suction mount. A unique, fully adjustable clutch system allows the power head to be driven with super-smooth, hi-tech cables. Pan and tilt are both controlled by a simple rotating handlebar. This allows an operator to make professional shots even with very limited experience. Setup time is less than five minutes. Built to run in extreme weather conditions, the power head is designed to travel and comes in an attaché-size hard case.

Microdolly Hollywood
3110 W. Burbank Blvd.
Burbank, CA 91505-2313
(818) 845-8383
www.microdolly.com

CTS-S2 ROBOTIC CAMERA TROLLEY SYSTEM | By
Telemetrics Inc.

Features of the CTS-S2 Robotic Camera Trolley System include: smooth operating variable speed, light-weight aluminum track, in-line cable trolleys or companion cable track option for cable looping, upright mounting or upside down (overhead ceiling mounted), straight or curved configurations, direct drive trolley, compatibility with Telemetrics pan/tilt mechanisms and controllers, and custom lengths.

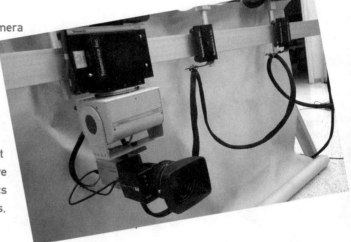

PT-HP-S2 SERVO PAN AND TILT HEAD | By
Telemetrics Inc.

The Telemetrics PT-HP-S2 is a precision pan/tilt head with smooth variable operating speed. Heavy-duty cross roller bearings and swiss motors with isolation mounts provide quiet operation. The lens connector provides direct connection and interface to lens functions. Manual smooth motion is accomplished using velocity servo controls. Sixty-four presets are available. Some key features include: smooth slow- or high-speed "camera operator" like moves, programmable timed presets that start and stop all axes simultaneously, and serial camera control interface for most Sony, Panasonic, Ikegami, and Hitachi cameras.

PT-CP-S2 SERVO CP PAN AND TILT HEAD | By Telemetrics Inc.

Telemetrics Inc.
Camera Control Systems
6 Leighton Place
Mahwah, NH 07430
(201) 848-9819
www.telemetricsinc.com

The Telemetrics PT-CP-S2 is a precision pan/tilt head with smooth variable operating speed. Heavy-duty cross roller bearings and swiss motors with isolation mounts provide quiet operation. The lens connector provides direct connection and interface to lens functions. Lens interface options are also available and the unit is available with either top or side camera mounting platform options. Some key features include: smooth slow- or high-speed "camera operator" like moves, programmable timed presets that start and stop all axes simultaneously, and serial camera control interface for most Sony, Panasonic, Ikegami and Hitachi cameras.

VZ-MC100 PAN AND TILT SYSTEM | By VariZoom

VariZoom has created a brand-new lightweight and extremely portable remote head, weighing only 8 3⁄4 lb. So portable, the new VZ-MC series pan and tilt heads allow for remarkably fast setups. VariZoom has compacted all of the electronics necessary to drive the precision pan and tilt head into one small control housing, allowing for portability and versatility. Just mount the VZ-MC remote head on a tripod or jib or mount it to a wall. You can undersling it as well. Plug into the supplied cord leading to the control handle, power up your control handle by battery or with the supplied AC/DC power supply, and you're ready to go!

VariZoom
P.O. Box 201990
Austin, TX 78720
(888) 826-3399
www.varizoom.com

XR PAN, TILT, AND ROLL HEAD | By Wescam

The Wescam XR is the most stable head in the industry. With precise steering and stabilization working in conjunction and occurring simultaneously, the XR has continuous pan, tilt, and roll capability that is unlimited and unrestricted. The XR is the only remote head that incorporates three-axis technology, precise steering, and uncompromised stability together in one package. Working from a 100% digital control system, the XR is stabilized at any altitude and is perfect for all ground applications including boat, camera car and cable, standard Technocranes, Super Technocranes, and Strata Cranes. The XR's open architecture is fully compatible with most camera and lens combinations. Interchangeable between film and HD systems, the XR can even be integrated with VistaVision, IMAX, and other large-format films.

Wescam
7150 Hayvenhurst Avenue
Van Nuys, CA 91406-3823
(818) 785-9282
www.wescam.com

CAMERA
SLATING AND
SYNCING TOOLS
16

Aaton:	OriginC+ Masterclock
	GMT-S Timecode Generator
	InDaw-MX Audio-Sync Station
	HD-Keylink
Professional Sound Corp.:	DigiSlate

ORIGINC+ MASTERCLOCK |

By Aaton & distributed by Abel Cine Tech NY/LA

OriginC+ is Aaton's six-hour masterclock designed to provide reliability and peace of mind to AatonCode shoots. Flexible and simple to use, OriginC+ can interface with cameras, audio recorders, and other time code devices in both ASCII and SMPTE formats. Most importantly, OriginC+ can be used as a time code comparator on-set, checking and monitoring drift between all time code devices. The unit can also be used as a highly stable 1ppm SMPTE generator for time code recorders, slates, and other accessories.

GMT-S TIMECODE GENERATOR | By Aaton & distributed by Abel Cine Tech NY/LA

The perfect companion to the OriginC+, GMT-S is a miniature, high 1ppm precision SMPTE generator designed to add frame-accurate time code capability to digital audio recorders, time code slates, laptops, and other related devices. The unit can receive time code in ASCII or SMPTE form and can send out time code in ASCII and at 24, 25, 29.97df, or 30 SMPTE frame rates.

INDAW-MX NETWORKABLE WORKSTATION FOR FILM/VIDEO AUDIO SYNCING | By Aaton & distributed by Abel Cine Tech NY/LA

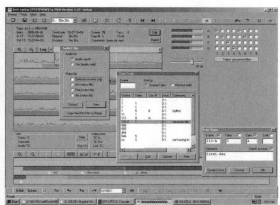

InDaw made a name for itself by speeding up the image and sound syncing that video dailies require; anticipating the coming availability of CantarX, Deva3, PD6, Portadrive on-location, multitrack recorders, the new InDaw MX (Windows 2000) converts all recording forms — analog tapes, digital tapes, and multitrack files — into the two tracks that image editors require. This "mixdown" is a real-time process happening while dubbing two AES tracks onto a video cassette, and can be performed at a tenth of real time for CD burning or hard-disk copy to Keylink-Instasync and image-editing stations.

HD-KEYLINK |

By Aaton & distributed by Abel Cine Tech NY/LA

Aaton's HD-Keylink makes HD and SD in one pass easy with three unique features: 1) simultaneous HD & SD, 2) vigilant monitoring through six miniature video cameras that can read all 16 and 35 codes with no contact at all with the film, and 3) contact-free head ensures a freshly processed negative with no dust generation — ever.

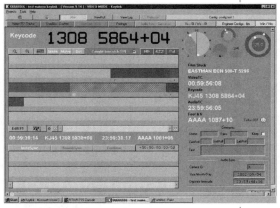

Aaton S.A.
bp 3002
38816 Grenoble
cdx1 France
+33 (0)4 76-42-95-50
www.aaton.com

Abel Cine Tech
66 Willow Avenue, Suite 201
Staten Island, NY 10305
(888) 223-1599
www.abelcine.com

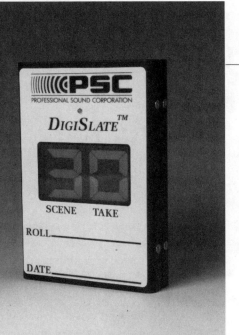

DIGISLATE | By Professional Sound Corporation

The new PSC DigiSlate was developed for use by the documentary-style recordist. This small and rugged device contains a large, sunlight-readable liquid crystal display for scene and take numbering from 1 to 99. The PSC DigiSlate also contains an internal tone oscillator and slate microphone for use in both clap syncing and voice slating. Additionally, the PSC DigiSlate outputs a regulated 5Vdc for use in triggering of external devices such as the clap oscillator of a Nagra recorder.

Professional Sound
Corporation
28085 Smyth Drive
Valencia, CA 91355
(661) 295-9395
www.professionalsound.com

CAMERA
STABILIZATION
AND RIGGING TOOLS

17

Barber Tech:	Steddiepod
CamMate:	Steady-Shot
Canada Camera Car:	Car Mount Kit
Cinekinetic:	Cinesaddle and Minisaddle Marsupial Cinesaddle Miracle Mount
Doggicam Systems:	Doggicam Handheld Camera System Doggimount Bodymount
Glidecam:	Body-Pod Accessory for the 4000 Pro Stabilizer V-8 Professional Stabilization System V-16 and V-20 Professional Stabilization Systems
GPI:	PRO System Camera Stabilizer
Hollywood Lite:	GT Series Camera Stabilizer The Low-Rider The Running Rig
Microdolly Hollywood:	Suction Mount Kit
ProMax:	SteadyTracker Ultralite and SteadyTracker Xtreme
Sachtler:	Artemis Cine/HD Camera Stabilizing System Artemis DV Camera Stabilizing System
16x9 Inc./Band Pro:	EasyRig2 TörtleRig Camera Support
SpyderCam:	SpyderCam Specialty Rigging System
Tiffen/Davis & Sanford:	Steady Stick
Tiffen/Steadicam:	Mini Camera Stabilizing System ProVid2, ProVid2+ Camera Stabilizing Systems Steadicam Jr. Steadicam Ultra Cine Camera Stabilizing System
VariZoom:	FlowPod MediaPro Shoulder Support System VZ-LSP Shoulder Support System VZ-1 Shooter Camera Stabilizer

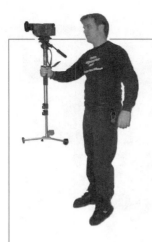

STEDDIE**POD** | By
Barber Tech Video Products

Steddiepod is the redevelopment of a device developed more than 20 years ago by multiple Emmy award-winning creator Eddie Barber. Steddiepod is ideal as a handheld camera stabilizer. You can walk with the Steddiepod, creating shots that are as smooth as silk. It can be used as a monopod, or to boom up and over objects. Bottom mounted, the Steddiepod makes great Kitty/Doggy/Monkey cam shots. And as a body camera mount, the Steddiepod allows operators to film/tape themselves as they walk, talk, dance, or perform.

Barber Tech Video Products
P.O. Box 248
Sun Valley, CA 91353
(818) 982-7775
www.barbertvp.com

STEADY-SHOT | By
CamMate Systems

When you can't get the shot with our world-famous crane system, try the all-new CamMate Steady-Shot. Get those smooth tracking moves that you see in all the high-dollar productions with a low-budget pocketbook. Features include: double-padded vest, roller-bearing movement, double bubble level, Anton Bauer battery, and a load of up to 20 lb.

CamMate Systems
425 E. Comstock
Chandler, AZ 85225
(480) 813-9500
www.cammate.com

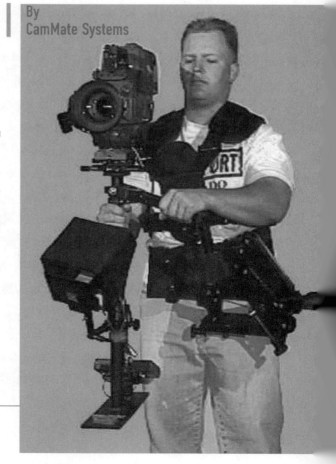

CAR MOUNT KIT | By Canada Camera Car

Canada Camera Car
1025 Stacey Court
Mississauga, Ontario
Canada L4W 2X7
(905) 602-6996
www.canadacameracar.com

Canada Camera Car's camera mount system is fast, secure, safe, and compatible with standard "Grip" equipment. The side mount includes a head-locking system with full 360° rotation and a total of 50° of tilt. The average "ready for camera" rigging time is about five minutes for a moderately experienced technician. The hood mount rigging time is about eight minutes for a moderately experienced technician.

CINESADDLE AND MINISADDLE | By Cinekinetic

If you want to maximize the setups you can fit into a tight schedule, get Cinekinetic's most popular product, the Cinesaddle. Many cinematographers use the Cinesaddle primarily as a replacement for their tripod but it may also be used to attach your camera to any moving object. Packed within its pockets is a car-mounting kit and full instructions for its use. The Cinesaddle weighs only 1.5 lb. and will support all professional Betacam video cameras as well as 35mm and 16mm cine cameras. The Minisaddle is a small version of the Cinesaddle, weighing an unbelievable 1 lb., and it is designed to accommodate the new range of consumer DV cameras and all domestic camcorders.

"The most interesting place I've used the Cinesaddle was from the bow of a boat. We wanted a beauty shot of the river while the boat was really moving fast. Obviously, a tripod was not the answer. Using the Cinesaddle, the shot turned out even better than we had imagined."

— Rochelle Olson, DP for Lockheed Martin, U.S.A.
Quote obtained from Cinekinetic's Web site

MARSUPIAL
CINESADDLE | By Cinekinetic

Cinekinetic's product line also includes the Marsupial Cinesaddle. It comes complete with a pouch that is used as a storage compartment to store your DV-size camera when you're not using it as a camera mount. When not being used to support your camera, the hi-tech filling surrounds and protects your camera from damage

MIRACLE
MOUNT | By Cinekinetic

Mount your camera outside a window, attach it to a lamppost, hang it from a lighting grid, or suspend it from an overhanging highway barrier. This revolutionary device makes it easy to get that special shot without prior rigging experience. Just pull up to your location and secure your camera to any stable horizontal or vertical surface. The jaws can be adjusted to any thickness, whether a one-inch table or a 50-foot house. The Miracle Mount comes with enough extension tubes to fit across a three-foot span. If you need to span a larger area, order extra extension tubes from Cinekinetic. Special straps are included so you can clamp this mount to any regular or irregular surface such as a pillar in a building, a tree, or a boulder.

Cinekinetic U.S.A.
1405 Vegas Valley Drive, #177
P.O. Box 73063
Las Vegas, NV 89170
(702) 731-4700
www.cinekinetic.com

DOGGICAM HANDHELD CAMERA SYSTEM | By Doggicam Systems

The Doggicam system is a self-contained, lightweight, and fully balanceable handheld camera system. The equipment allows any operator to make smooth moves with the camera in low or high mode. Its modular design allows easy adaptation of the system to the demands of any shot. The Doggicam system supports various Arri, Aaton, and mini-DV camera models. No special operation training is required.

DOGGIMOUNT | By Doggicam Systems

For 100 years, the film industry has mounted cameras by bolting in the bottom of the camera body. Doggicam Systems rethinks the entire approach with the Doggimount. The Doggimount system quickly secures the camera to an object, providing uniquely dynamic shots.

BODYMOUNT | By
Doggicam Systems

Bodymount offers uniquely dynamic shots by attaching the camera to a person to be photographed. The vest and bracketing allow easy and comfortable placement of the camera from any angle. The vest can be hidden with wardrobe to allow framing to the middle of the chest. Bodymount supports various Arri, Aaton, and mini-DV camera models.

Doggicam Systems
1500 W. Verdugo Ave.
Burbank, CA 91506
(818) 845-8470
www.doggicam.com

BODY-POD ACCESSORY FOR THE 4000 PRO STABILIZER | By Glidecam Industries, Inc.

The Glidecam Body-Pod is a lightweight rigid support system that, when used with either the Glidecam 2000 Pro or 4000 Pro handheld stabilizers, allows all the weight of the system to be supported by your body. The Body-Pod allows you to shoot in cushioned comfort for indefinite periods of time. It takes the stabilizer's weight out of your hands and arms and displaces the weight onto your waist and shoulders. Stress and fatigue are virtually eliminated, allowing you the freedom to shoot events that require uninterrupted shooting.

V-8 PROFESSIONAL CAMERA STABILIZATION SYSTEM | By Glidecam Industries, Inc.

The Glidecam V-8 Professional Camera Stabilization System allows you to walk, run, go up and down stairs, shoot from moving vehicles, and travel over uneven terrain without camera instability or shake. The Glidecam V-8 is designed primarily for use with lightweight video camcorders and 8mm motion picture cameras. The V-8 instantly adds high production value to every scene, and because it is body mounted, it allows you to shoot for long periods of time with very little fatigue.

V-16 AND V-20 PROFESSIONAL CAMERA STABILIZATION SYSTEMS | By Glidecam Industries, Inc.

The Glidecam V-16 and Glidecam V-20 Professional Camera Stabilization Systems are both designed to allow you to walk, run, go up and down stairs, shoot from moving vehicles, and travel over uneven terrain without any camera instability or shake. The Glidecam V-16 and Glidecam V-20 are designed primarily for use with professional video cameras and 16mm motion picture cameras. The V-16 stabilizes cameras weighing from 10 to 20 lb., and the V-20 stabilizes cameras weighing from 15 to 26 lb.

Glidecam Industries, Inc.
Camelot Industrial Park
130 Camelot Drive Bldg. #4
Plymouth, MA 02360
(800) 600-2011
www.glidecam.com

THE PRO CAMERA STABILIZING SYSTEM | By GPI

Designed and built by operators to meet the critical demands and requirements of today's filmmakers, the PRO system is configured easily to meet various shot requirements. Components and modules are interchangeable and the simplicity of the system reduces the amount of setup time. As a modular system, the PRO is designed to incorporate state-of-the-art developments in camera stabilization technologies and supporting accessories. Upgrades and components allow the operator to tailor the package to his or her needs and market. As newer technologies are developed, they can easily be incorporated into the PRO system.

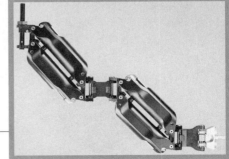

GPI — George Paddock, Inc.
7306 Coldwater Canyon, Unit 5
North Hollywood, CA 91605
(818) 982-3991
www.pro-gpi.com

GT SERIES CAMERA STABILIZER | By Hollywood Lite

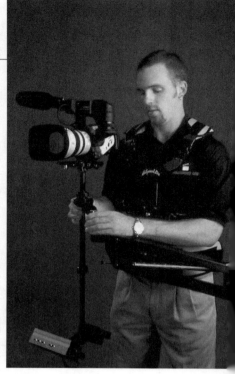

This state-of-the-art stabilizer is the most solid and robust of its kind, made out of lightweight T6 aluminum. All parts are machined to precise dimensions to ensure dynamic balance of the sled, fluid motion of the arm, and a snug fit of the vest. The dynamically balanced sled is fully adjustable and comes with a five-inch TFT, color LCD monitor. Its easy tilt makes viewing more convenient. An expandable post and sliding gimbal give you many configurations on the height you desire for your camera.

THE LOW-RIDER CAMERA STABILIZER | By Hollywood Lite

The new and exciting Low-Rider stabilizer is for the videographer who is striving for that low-to-the-ground video shot, especially on moving things, such as snakes, reptiles or insects, animals, or even crawling babies! Capture the beauty of flowers and foliage, or snow-covered grass. Movement close to the ground has never been easier than this. You simply mount your camera inside the low-mode cage and hold onto the grip. The monitor gimbal on the top is also adjustable for easy viewing. All wires are hidden inside the post and can be easily changed or replaced if a larger monitor is needed.

Hollywood Lite
(310) 871-7386
www.hollywoodlite.com

THE RUNNING RIG | By Hollywood Lite

The Running Rig is the top-of-the-line video stabilizer from Hollywood Lite. This stabilizer is equipped to handle dockable video cameras weighing 15 to 25 lb. An enhanced camera-mounting platform allows accurate adjustments to your camera, fore and aft as well as side to side, without complicated locking procedures. Two easily accessible knobs allow immediate fine adjustments. The gimbal represents precision design and construction, which guarantees a precise intersection of all three axes; six precision bearings provide a smooth, deflection-free pan, roll, and tilt.

SUCTION MOUNT KIT | By Microdolly Hollywood

The Suction Mount Kit uses three strong suction cups, six universal joint clamps, and a set of rods to connect in seconds to mount a camera or light almost anywhere, even on the corner of a glass building. The mount weighs just 6 lb. (2.6kg) and is ideal for positioning a camera or light on a moving vehicle. The camera-plate and light-stand attachments are included. The mount comes in a heavy-duty metal-reinforced case that doubles as a camera platform for low shots. A large base plate provides a mounting surface if needed. Total holding force of the Suction Mount is 200 lb. (90kg).

Microdolly Hollywood
3110 W. Burbank Blvd.
Burbank, CA 91505-2313
(818) 845-8383
www.microdolly.com

STEADYTRACKER ULTRALITE AND STEADYTRACKER XTREME | By ProMax

This lightweight steady device is easy to operate while taking amazing footage. The SteadyTracker Ultralite gives you the ability to shoot subject matter that is impossible to shoot otherwise. Take amazing footage as you walk, run, travel up stairs, or even out of a moving car. Expand the creativity of your production by engaging the viewers when making them a part of the action. With the SteadyTracker, you can accelerate and decelerate when panning, quickly start/stop, reverse directions while flying, tilt smoothly at the start or end of a boom, or dutch off the axis during a flying move. The SteadyTrackers have been designed for handheld use, body-supported use, and self-supported use.

ProMax
16 Technology Drive, Suite 106
Irvine, CA 92618
(800) 977-6629
www.promax.com

ARTEMIS CINE/HD CAMERA STABILIZING SYSTEM | By Sachtler Corporation

The new camera stabilizing system Artemis Cine/HD features a modular construction that suits it to almost every film or HD video camera. Its compact design, which features a 180° pivoting battery backpack, allows perfect positioning of the posterior batteries for standard-mode, low-mode, and high-mode operation. Unlike its competitors, it is configurable for any application — whether film or HD video. The setup is amazingly fast and requires hardly any tools.

ARTEMIS DV CAMERA STABILIZING SYSTEM | By Sachtler Corporation

This extremely mobile system ensures fluid camera work and offers operators enormous advantages — including a full range of completely tool-free setups! The self-tightening spindles in the side-to-side mechanism enable users to position the camera perfectly. Its state-of-the-art design features upper and lower clamps that are molded from the same piece of aluminum. This ensures exceptional stability and tortional strength, and prevents vibration. The Artemis DV camera plate is compatible with Sachtler fluid heads, ensuring fast changeover from the tripod to Artemis DV. And because the system's total height is easy to adjust, the vertical weight distribution can be specifically set to suit the camera being used.

Sachtler Corporation of America
55 North Main Street
Freeport, NY 11520
(516) 867-4900
www.sachtler.com

EASYRIG2 CAMERA SUPPORT

Distributed by 16x9 Inc./Band Pro

The EasyRig2 gives you the speed and mobility of a handheld camera, while still achieving steady shots from the shoulder and hip. Specially designed suspension lines with shock absorbers accept the weight of your camera and redistribute the majority to your hips, where it is more efficiently supported. The EasyRig is ideal for news broadcasts, sport events, documentaries, commercials, and many other handheld situations where stability is crucial and where the freedom to move is essential. EasyRig accepts loads from 13 to 35 lb. (6 to 16kg) and folds into a specially designed carrying bag.

"It was indispensable in running down a four-block street at a parade trying to keep up with a trotting miniature horse and carriage. I was drenched in sweat, but I couldn't have done it without the EasyRig."

— Mark Schulze, of Crystal Pyramid Productions, on his use of the EasyRig2 for shooting Animal Planet's *That's My Baby*

Quote obtained from 16x9 Inc.'s Web site/Reviews

TÖRTLERIG CAMERA SUPPORT | Distributed by 16x9 Inc./Band Pro

Like its big brother, EasyRig, the ergonomically designed TörtleRig reduces static load to the arm and shoulder muscles by redistributing camera weight to the hips, where it is easily supported. Designed by a Swedish cinematographer, TörtleRig utilizes an overhead support arm, back support bar, hip belt, and integral padded backpack capable of carrying all necessary camera gear. Combining the speed and mobility of handheld shooting with the increased steadiness provided by a support system, TörtleRig was designed specifically for DV cameras, which by virtue of their light weight are susceptible to shakiness when used handheld. TörtleRig also makes it easy for shooters to conduct interviews without assistance, thanks to nearly hands-free operation of the camera.

16x9 Inc.
3605 West Pacific Ave., Suite B
Burbank, CA 91505
(866) 800-1699
www.16x9inc.com

Band Pro Film/Video Inc.
3403 West Pacific Ave.
Burbank, CA 91505
(818) 841-9655
www.bandpro.com

SPYDERCAM SPECIALTY RIGGING SYSTEM | By SpyderCam

More than just a camera on a cable, SpyderCam is actually a highly specialized system of rigging components, combined on a location-by-location basis to best fit the unique needs of any specific shot. This computer-controlled system of synthetic ropeways, load carriers, travelers, high-speed winches, and top-notch crew gives motion control-like repeatability to payloads (cameras, props, or even stunt people!) in complex, 3-D paths through space at speeds and distances that have to be seen to be believed. It's truly a "flying carpet" that allows you to film long dolly shots with no track, soar effortlessly over rivers and lakes, race through tunnels, glide between buildings, and more. Because SpyderCam can be configured to operate in a variety of modes, it has quickly become the preferred tool for filmmakers wanting to cover the zone between camera cranes and helicopters. SpyderCam can utilize the following remote heads: Libra Head, Stab-C, Spacecam, Wescam, FLIR, and Cam Remote, and fly anything from the smallest video packages to IMAX.

SpyderCam
28130 Ave. Crocker #322
Valencia, CA 91355
(661) 775-9058
www.spydercam.com

DAVIS & SANFORD STEADY STICK

| A Davis & Sanford product
by Tiffen

Perfect for in-the-field situations, Steady Stick provides you with relief from the strain of extended periods of handheld shooting by removing the weight of the camera from your shoulder and back. Steady Stick gives you a steady shot every time, from any height or any angle. Highlights include: cameras up to 30 lb. supported; evenly distributes the weight of the camera from your shoulders to your hips so you aren't fatigued; easily holds 400mm lens and gets a steady shot at 1/4 second; lightweight, versatile, and portable; quick release coupler easily disconnects to attach your camera to a tripod; lets you pan low or hold camera high over a crowd.

MINI CAMERA STABILIZING SYSTEM

| A Steadicam product
by Tiffen

The Steadicam Mini is built for today's ENG cameras and produces the same fluid and dynamic motion as our larger systems. The Mini is designed to be used with lightweight video camcorders weighing 5 to 15 lb. This system gives the operator the flexibility of a handheld camcorder with the precision and smoothness of a dolly. The Mini is ideal for documentaries, weddings and events, local cable origination, industrial training and communications.

The Tiffen Company, LLC
90 Oser Avenue
Hauppauge, NY 11788-3886
(631) 273-2500
www.tiffen.com
www.steadicam.com

PROVID2 AND PROVID2+ CAMERA STABILIZING SYSTEMS | A Steadicam product by Tiffen

The ProVid2 and ProVid2+ are popular systems for broadcasting, independent teleproduction studios, and new, digital, lightweight camera applications. The vest spreads the system's weight comfortably across your hips and torso. The no-tools, iso-elastic arm enables your camera to float evenly and freely in any position throughout the arm's entire range. The system weighs a mere 20 lb. and fits neatly into the trunk of a car. And because it's modular, you can upgrade your system as you grow.

STEADICAM JR. CAMERA STABILIZER | A Steadicam product by Tiffen

The Steadicam Jr. is ideal for virtually all 8mm, Hi8, VHS-C, mini-DV, and digital camcorders weighing 2 to 4 lb. It's lightweight and affordable. Features include: an integral 2.9-inch high-resolution monitor, adjustable stage, and patented quick-release gimbal and handle.

STEADICAM ULTRA CINE CAMERA STABILIZING SYSTEM | A Steadicam product by Tiffen

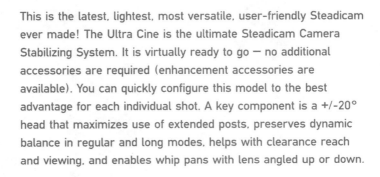

This is the latest, lightest, most versatile, user-friendly Steadicam ever made! The Ultra Cine is the ultimate Steadicam Camera Stabilizing System. It is virtually ready to go — no additional accessories are required (enhancement accessories are available). You can quickly configure this model to the best advantage for each individual shot. A key component is a +/-20° head that maximizes use of extended posts, preserves dynamic balance in regular and long modes, helps with clearance reach and viewing, and enables whip pans with lens angled up or down.

The Tiffen Company, LLC
90 Oser Avenue
Hauppauge, NY 11788-3886
(631) 273-2500
www.tiffen.com
www.steadicam.com

FLOWPOD | By VariZoom

This uniquely styled device is the most versatile piece of support gear on the market. Designed to work perfectly with or without a VariZoom control, the FlowPod merges our popular StealthPod monopod with this patent-pending stabilizing system. Our unique multipurpose handle features a telescoping pin that can be either locked in-line for use as a monopod or unlocked to allow free-floating action shots. The slim design allows for ease of use in the tightest of shooting situations.

VariZoom
P.O. Box 201990
Austin, TX 78720
(888) 826-3399
www.varizoom.com

MEDIAPRO SHOULDER SUPPORT SYSTEM | By VariZoom

Varizoom's MediaPro is the counterbalanced solution for the Canon XL1 and XL1s. Features include: multi-axis gimbal, adjustable chest pad, quick-release camera platform, and it holds up to three belt packs.

VZ-LSP PROFESSIONAL SHOULDER SUPPORT SYSTEM FOR DV AND HI8 CAMCORDERS | By VariZoom

The VZ-LSP is designed specifically for the popular "prosumer" camcorders that are smaller than traditional shoulder-mount cameras, including the Sony VX-1000, DSR-200, TRV-900, and Canon's XL1 and GL1. The VZ-LSP ensures a stable shooting platform by providing three points of body contact: shoulder, hand, and abdomen. The LSP may also be configured with or without the ab support depending on shooter preference. Attach your camcorder to the shoulder-brace camera platform using the camera's tripod-mounting receiver with the included knurled screw. Then position the camera platform (forward, back, up, or down) so that the viewfinder or LCD monitor meets the eye comfortably.

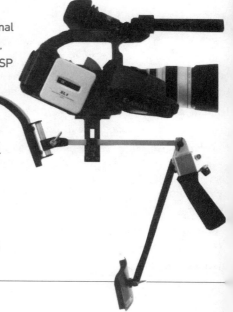

VZ-1 SHOOTER PROFESSIONAL SHOULDER SUPPORT SYSTEM FOR MINI-DV AND HI8 CAMCORDERS | By VariZoom

The VZ-1 Shooter ensures a stable shooting platform by resting easily on your shoulder, keeping most of the weight of the camera off your arm. The VZ-1 Shooter simply adjusts to fit your body. Bend it and forget it! Attach your camcorder to the shoulder-brace camera platform using the camera's tripod-mounting receiver with the included knurled screw. Position the camera platform (forward, back, up, or down) so that the viewfinder or LCD monitor meets the eye comfortably.

VariZoom
P.O. Box 201990
Austin, TX 78720
(888) 826-3399
www.varizoom.com

If you have used this gear and want to share your own experiences, comments, and suggestions in our next edition, send an e-mail to Catherine Lorenze at *DREAMGEAR@cox.net*. We are particularly interested in innovative ways you have used the gear that will help inspire other film, video, and TV professionals.

CASES, COVERS, BAGS, AND VESTS

18

HydroFlex: Splash Bags

Kata: ABBA-5 Anti-Bullet Body Armor
                        Banana Heavy-Duty Camera Case
                        Camera Gloves
                        Exo-33 DV Camera Case
                        Grizzly-3 (CBP-3) Camera Backpack
                        Hexabag Soft Case Stand Organizer
                        Panda Multipurpose Backpack for DV Production
                        RC-10 and CRC-11 Rain Cover

Lowepro: DryZone 100 Waterproof Camera Backpack
                        Linx 240 Camera and Laptop Bag
                        Super Trekker AW Backpack

Portabrace/K&H Products: Field Editor Case
                        Hiker Pro Backpack
                        Polar Bear
                        Polar Mitten Heated Camera Case
                        Rain Slicker
                        Storm Coat

SPLASH
BAGS | By
HydroFlex, Inc.

HydroFlex splash bags, made for a variety of cameras, are not just rain covers, but sealed units incorporating custom dry suit-type zippers, which allow easy access to the camera with full confidence of protection. They can easily be handheld or mounted on a tripod or crane. Combining a splash bag with our HydroHead remote pan and tilt head affords the ideal solution to remote camera use in rain, dump tank, or boat situations. *(Splash bags are for surface use only: They are not submersible.)* All of our splash bags have integral spray deflector systems built in to prevent water drops from staying in front of the lens. Either the HydroFlex air-powered spray deflector system or the spinning disk-type system can be accommodated. Internally, a defogging system keeps condensation from forming in front of the lens.

HydroFlex, Inc.
5335 McConnell Ave.
Los Angeles, CA 90066
(310) 301-8187
www.hydroflex.com

ABBA-5 ANTI-BULLET BODY ARMOR | By Kata Ltd.

This armored vest was designed to protect the videographer or film-maker when shooting in high-risk situations. The ABBA-5 offers protection against shrapnel and knives, as well as pistol, submachine-gun, and high-velocity bullets, while providing optimal weight distribution. Unlike other anti-bullet vests, Kata's Body Armor offers protection for the sides of the torso as well as the chest and back.

PRESS

BANANA HEAVY-DUTY CAMERA CASE | By Kata Ltd.

The Banana is a roomy, heavy-duty production case built to hold lots of equipment, large and small. Its ergonomic, contoured shape (patent pending) provides greater comfort when carrying heavy loads by bringing the center of gravity closer to the body. The opening of the Banana faces toward your body in carry mode, allowing you a complete view of its contents and easy access to your gear. The Banana comes in three sizes.

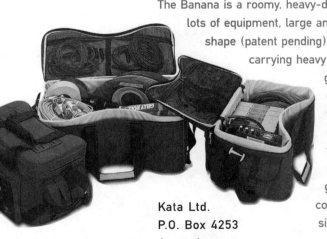

Kata Ltd.
P.O. Box 4253
Jerusalem
91042 Israel
+972-25-38-88-45
www.kata-bags.com

CAMERA
GLOVES | By Kata Ltd.

"We were shooting in 40 mph wind and blowing sand. It was so bad you could not see. I thought that my camera was ruined because it was packed with sand. After thorough cleaning, I removed the Kata camera glove and found that the camera was not even dusty. The critical areas like the tape compartment were completely clean."

— Jack Quirk, Owner of KJ Productions in Oklahoma
Quote obtained from Kata

Kata's Camera Gloves are tailored to fit your camera like a glove, snugly with no loose ends, and offering ultimate protection from dust, extreme elements, dirt, bumps, and scratches. Intelligent product design allows full and easy access to all controls. Made of neoprene material, the non-fray lamination allows you to cut open additional slots to fit your exact working camera configuration.

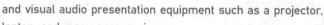

EXO-33 DV
CAMERA CASE | By Kata Ltd.

Exo-33 is Kata's ultimate case for DV production fieldwork. It's designed to fit a range of equipment used by the DV market: medium-size camcorders such as the Canon XL1 and the Pansonic DVC-15 with standard accessories; small camcorders such as the Sony PD-150, Panasonic DVX-100, and JVC's GY-DV300 with many accessories; and visual audio presentation equipment such as a projector, laptop, and many accessories.

GRIZZLY-3 (CBP-3) CAMERA BACKPACK | By Kata Ltd.

Grizzly-3 is a large camera backpack that can also be used as a daily camera case. This unique design fits a large range of cameras, from compact cameras with many accessories to a full-size professional camera with battery and lens installed. The Grizzly-3 is ergonomically engineered to ease the burden when carrying heavy equipment under rough conditions and offers four carrying options: on your back, on your shoulder, by hand, or wheeled (Insertrolley System not included).

HEXABAG SOFT CASE STAND ORGANIZER | By Kata Ltd.

The sturdy, protective Hexabag unfurls to reveal six deep cylindrical pockets for packaging and organizing light stands, gel rolls, microphone stands, or other long accessories. Its innovative design makes it possible to retrieve items by simply opening the padded lid.

Kata Ltd.
P.O. Box 4253
Jerusalem
91042 Israel
+972-25-38-88-45
www.kata-bags.com

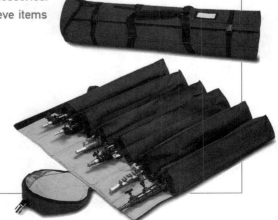

PANDA MULTIPURPOSE BACKPACK FOR DV PRODUCTION | By Kata Ltd.

Kata's Panda is the perfect solution for the needs of DV field production work. It meets the strict new airline regulations for carry-on bag size, and can be used either as a backpack or a shoulder case by utilizing the Omega concealment system. The case easily accommodates and protects DV camera, laptop, accessories, and personal effects.

Kata Ltd.
P.O. Box 4253
Jerusalem
91042 Israel
+972-25-38-88-45
www.kata-bags.com

RC-10 AND CRC-11 RAIN COVER | By Kata Ltd.

The Kata Rain Cover is fabricated from waterproof material with crystal-clear vinyl panels on the camera's control side. The cover slips quickly over a camera to protect it from sudden showers and is secured by a quick pull of drawstrings. The Rain Cover successfully protected equipment during Weather Laboratory testing in severe weather conditions. It is designed for efficiency down to the smallest detail.

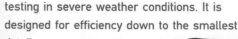

DRYZONE 100 WATERPROOF CAMERA BACKPACK | By Lowepro

DryZone 100 is a brand-new, smaller version of our innovative and highly popular DZ 200, the first completely waterproof, soft-sided camera backpack.

Like its big brother, DryZone 100 has three components: a waterproof drypod with a hi-tech patented TIZIP™ zipper; a heavy-duty camera compartment (customizable for a number of systems); and the backpack, which includes a tuck-away tripod holder, self-draining outer mesh pockets, generous inner mesh pockets, drain hole, ergonomic backpack harness with contoured shoulder straps, a sternum strap, and a rubber handle.

LINX 240 CAMERA AND LAPTOP BAG | By Lowepro

Not your average camera-and-notebook bag, this designer-style sling bag wraps around the body for carrying comfort and security, then slides quickly to the front for easy access. Linx 240 capacity: a mid-size notebook, small digital or 35mm point-and-shoot camera, cell phone, memory cards in cases, CD, four AA batteries, PDA, and other personal accessories.

Lowepro
3171 Guerneville Road
Santa Rosa, CA 95401
(707) 575-4363
www.lowepro.com

SUPER TREKKER AW BACKPACK | By Lowepro

The Super Trekker AW is our largest photo backpack for photographers who carry substantial loads. This great-looking, virtually new pack boasts new hi-tech materials and lots of extra features, including an improved harness system, the most advanced technical harness system of any camera pack; revolutionary water-resistant, quick-access YKK zippers; three totally redesigned accessories (Trekker DayPack, Trekker Lens Pouch, and Trekker Accessory Pouch); a travel cover; rubber handle; and an All Weather Cover™ for protection against extreme weather, dust, and sand.

Lowepro
3171 Guerneville Road
Santa Rosa, CA 95401
(707) 575-4363
www.lowepro.com

FIELD EDITOR CASE | A Portabrace product by K&H Products, Ltd.

The Field Editor Case is designed to protect and carry portable field editors. The sides are heavily padded while the bottom has an additional armored layer to protect vulnerable connectors. The padded exterior pocket accommodates power supply and cables. Heavy-duty HB-40 shoulder strap and leather handle included.

Portabrace/K&H Products, Ltd.
Box 249
North Bennington, VT 05257
(800) 442-8171
www.portabrace.com

HIKER PRO
BACKPACK

**A Portabrace product
by K&H Products, Ltd.**

The Hiker is designed for videographers who have to travel long
distances or just want to keep their hands free. The case has a
plastic frame, making it strong and light. The camera is securely
held in place by a tie-down strap and an adjustable shelf. The
backpack has pockets for the tripod plate, extra tape, and batteries.

POLAR BEAR

**A Portabrace product
by K&H Products, Ltd.**

*"At one point, when the weather closed in and the helicopters could not get in to get us out, the entire
equipment package had to be abandoned. The equipment (inside the Portabrace cases) was placed in
survival tents and weighted with rocks against the tremendous winds. This was in the Dry Valleys where
the winds can reach 200 mph. After an overnight without the chemical heaters, the lenses were a little
stiff, but we retrieved the entire package without the smallest problem."*

— **Filmmaker Ron Gardner, on shooting in the Antarctic for PBS's science series** *Nova*
Quote obtained from Portabrace/K&H Products, Ltd.

The Polar Bear case is designed to keep your camcorder warm in cold temperatures. It is
thickly padded with insulation. The interior is lined with mylar fabric to reflect heat back into
the camera chamber. Air-activated warmers placed inside the case maintain interior temperatures to keep battery, recorder, lens, and hands warm. Tested at -50° Fahrenheit. Two hand
openings at the lens are enclosed with fleece cuffs for warm access. Suede
leather handles make it comfortable to carry. Attached insulated lens
hood protects the lens in transport. It also prevents condensation
from forming when bringing Polar Bear in from the cold.
The hood stores conveniently inside a pocket when
shooting.

Portabrace/K&H Products, Ltd.
Box 249
North Bennington, VT 05257
(800) 442-8171
www.portabrace.com

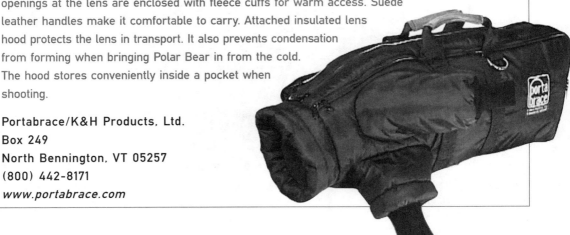

POLAR MITTEN HEATED CAMERA CASE | A Portabrace product by K&H Products, Ltd.

The Polar Mitten, designed for the mini-DV camera, is a smaller version of our popular Polar Bear case. It keeps your camcorder warm in cold temperatures. It is thickly padded with a high-loft insulation material. The interior is lined with mylar fabric to reflect heat back into the camera chamber. Air-activated warmers placed inside the case maintain interior temperatures to keep battery, recorder, lens and hands warm. Tested at -50° Fahrenheit, Polar Mitten is supplied with four heat packs.

RAIN SLICKER | A Portabrace product by K&H Products, Ltd.

The Rain Slicker is constructed with a waterproof, multiple-layer nylon fabric. Zippers, flaps, Velcro, and vinyl windows allow you to reach critical controls and view meters and readouts. The Rain Slicker is easy to put over the camera, mic, windscreen, batteries, and pistol grip. A rain fly covers the entire top of the camera to seal the handle opening. The Rain Slicker fabric is constructed of laminations of water-repellent nylon, a waterproof film, and a soft nylon interior protecting the camera. Designed to work on a tripod as well as on your shoulder.

STORM COAT | A Portabrace product by K&H Products, Ltd.

The Storm Coat was developed with extreme weather conditions in mind. We were particularly mindful of ENG configurations where multiple microphones and accessories need extra room. It is made from a newly designed fabric that withstands extremes in temperatures and has a waterproof factor that significantly exceeds Coast Guard specifications. A special lens hood protects both conventional and internal-focus lenses (please specify lens type, round or square, when ordering). Clear vinyl windows let you easily view controls and displays. A rain fly on top sheds water efficiently while allowing protected access to the tape door.

Portabrace/K&H Products, Ltd.
Box 249
North Bennington, VT 05257
(800) 442-8171
www.portabrace.com

If you have used this gear and want to share your own experiences, comments, and suggestions in our next edition, send an e-mail to Catherine Lorenze at *DREAMGEAR@cox.net*. We are particularly interested in innovative ways you have used the gear that will help inspire other film, video, and TV professionals.

CRANES, CAMERA CARS, BOATS, AND PROCESS TRAILERS

19

Boom Audio & Video:	Cool Cam Revolutionary Camera Crane
CamMate Systems:	2000 Series Crane
Canada Camera Car:	22' Raven Deck Boat
	Insert Car Type 1 and Type 2
Chapman/Leonard:	Maverick Mobile Arm Vehicle
	Raptor Mobile Arm Vehicle
	Titan II Mobile Crane
Filmair International:	Giraffe Classic Crane
	Giraffe Long Ranger Crane
Glidecam:	Camcrane 200
Panther:	Foxy Crane System
	Galaxy Crane
ProMax:	Cobra Crane
Sachtler:	CamCrane DV
	CamCrane EFP
Shotmaker:	Classic Camera Car
	Elite Camera Car
	Enlouva IV Crane
	Motorcycle Process Trailer

COOL CAM PRO AND COOL CAM DV REVOLUTIONARY CAMERA CRANE | By Boom Audio & Video

Cool Cam DV — NAB 2001 Editor's Pick of Show

Boom Audio & Video
18, avenue Jules Tricault
35170 Bruz, France
+33(0)2 99-05-35-83
www.boom-audio.com

Cool Cam enables movement that has not been possible before. It allows perfect fluidity, from 15cm (0.5ft.) to 4m (13 ft.) height in all axes. The Cool Cam can be set up by one person in a few minutes. The Cool Cam can even be operated in tight, indoor spaces. Both the Cool Cam Pro and the Cool Cam DV are adjustable in length from 1.7m (5.5 ft.) to 4m (13 ft.). The Cool Cam Pro weighs about 15kg (32 lb.) with camera. The Cool Cam DV weighs under 13kg (29 lb.) with camera.

2000 SERIES CRANE | By CamMate Systems

The versatility of setup and operation make the CamMate 2000 Series Crane the ideal tool for both studio and remote locations. For applications requiring extended camera height and reach, the new 2000 Series will provide quality, precision moves with lens heights up to 50 ft. Constructed with our high-strength 6-ft. extensions, the 2000 Series gives you more combinations with greater weight limits. With all the same electronics features as our famous Travel Series, combined with up to 50 ft. of camera reach, the 2000 Series can't be beat!

CamMate Systems
425 E. Comstock
Chandler, AZ 85225
(480) 813-9500
www.cammate.com

22' RAVEN DECK BOAT | By Canada Camera Car

This very stable, deep "V" tri-hull has a whopping 1,600-lb. load capacity. The ride at all speeds is excellent and it handles rough water (2-ft. waves) with ease. Handling brings rails to mind with very little lean on cornering. Hydraulic trim planes counter any uneven load distribution. A 3 x 7 ft. tower platform can be installed to a height of up to 8 ft. above the deck and is available upon request. The 2 x 7 ft. rear platform is only 12 inches from the water and has been used for both stationary "water box" and high-speed filming.

INSERT CAR TYPE 1 AND TYPE 2 | By Canada Camera Car

Features of our Insert Car Type 1 and Type 2 include: purpose-built 7.5-liter V8 engine producing 385 horsepower at 3,000 rpm, 7 Link stabilized, fully automatic air-ride suspension, offset towing capability, tow bar and tool package, front mount filming platform, open loop Clear Com communications system, two camera rails and leveling heads, and a complete selection of pipes, clamps, straps, and rigging equipment.

Canada Camera Car
1025 Stacey Court
Mississauga, Ontario
Canada L4W 2X7
(905) 602-6996
www.canadacameracar.com

MAVERICK MOBILE ARM VEHICLE | By Chapman/Leonard

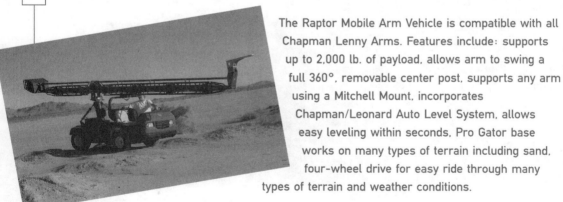

The Maverick Mobile Arm Vehicle can be used with
most types of arms, including Lenny Arms and
Technocranes. Features include: remote-controlled power steering
for rear wheels, heavy-duty braking applied to all four wheels, battery-powered
hydraulic arm brakes, gasoline engine or electric motor capabilities, hydraulic leveling in less than
five seconds, hand- or foot-operated camera turrets, qualified driver sent with every order, cruises
at 50 mph, four-wheel steering, defies any terrain, partial crabbing ability, swings 360°. Many
accessories are available.

RAPTOR MOBILE ARM VEHICLE | By Chapman/Leonard

The Raptor Mobile Arm Vehicle is compatible with all
Chapman Lenny Arms. Features include: supports
up to 2,000 lb. of payload, allows arm to swing a
full 360°, removable center post, supports any arm
using a Mitchell Mount, incorporates
Chapman/Leonard Auto Level System, allows
easy leveling within seconds, Pro Gator base
works on many types of terrain including sand,
four-wheel drive for easy ride through many
types of terrain and weather conditions.

Chapman/Leonard Studio Equipment, Inc.
12950 Raymer Street
North Hollywood, CA 91605
(888) 88-DOLLY
www.chapman-leonard.com

TITAN II MOBILE CRANE | By Chapman/Leonard

The Titan II Mobile Crane features remote-controlled power steering for rear wheels, heavy-duty braking applied to all six wheels, battery-powered hydraulic arm brakes, gasoline engine or electric motor, hydraulic leveling in less than 10 seconds, hand- or foot-operated camera turrets, qualified driver sent with every order, cruises at 50 mph, six-wheel steering and six-wheel drive, defies most terrain, partial crabbing ability, swings 360°, silent operation and push-button balancing. Many accessories are available.

GIRAFFE CLASSIC CRANE | By Filmair International

With its ultra-light modular design, either manned or remote, the Giraffe Classic was designed for space efficiency. Tapered sections nest inside each other, making it easily transportable in light vans, small planes, helicopters, and boats. The Giraffe Classic can be hand-carried up mountains and other hard-to-reach locations. This modular flexibility is also easy on the budget. Fast and versatile, the Giraffe Classic is the backbone of our fleet and has a maximum lens height of 31 ft.

Filmair International
1040 Islington Avenue
Toronto, Ontario
Canada M8Z 6A4
(416) 207.2051
www.filmairinternational.com

GIRAFFE LONG RANGER CRANE | By Filmair International

Ultralight, the Giraffe Long Ranger has the longest reach of all our cranes. Either manned or remote, the Long Ranger was designed for space efficiency. Tapered sections nest inside each other, making it easy to transport in cube vans, planes, and boats. Fast and versatile, the Giraffe Long Ranger is the pride our fleet, with a maximum lens height of 44' 2".

Filmair International
1040 Islington Avenue
Toronto, Ontario
Canada M8Z 6A4
(416) 207.2051
www.filmairinternational.com

CAMCRANE 200 | By Glidecam Industries, Inc.

The Camcrane 200 is a tripod-mounted, boom-arm camera crane system designed to allow you to smoothly boom your camera up, boom your camera down, and move your camera in an infinite number of 360° arcs. When balanced and used correctly, the Camcrane 200 moves with such tremendous precision and fluidity that the results can only be called "picture perfect."

Glidecam Industries, Inc.
Camelot Industrial Park
130 Camelot Drive Bldg., #4
Plymouth, MA 02360
(800) 600-2011
www.glidecam.com

FOXY CRANE SYSTEM

| By Panther and distributed by Ste-Man, Inc. in Hollywood

The Foxy Crane System is an unmatched crane concept. No matter which length is required, with the Foxy you have all possibilities. Setup or change can be done by only one person in just a few minutes. The Foxy Crane serves as a platform crane or as a remote crane. The Foxy's base has been designed as wide base and can thus be used for both the 62cm (24.5 in.) and the safe 100cm (39.5 in.) track gauge. The air, studio, or track wheels enable using the Foxy's base as a transport cart, as a tracking dolly, and even as a lightweight dolly.

GALAXY CRANE

| By Panther and distributed by Ste-Man, Inc. in Hollywood

The concept and the design of the new Galaxy Crane incorporated ideas and suggestions from rental houses, crane operators, and Panther's long experience in building cranes. Safety and stability as well as easy, comfortable handling were the prime objectives for the development of this crane system. The Galaxy sets new standards and opens a new dimension not only with regard to crane arm length.

Panther GmbH
Raiffeisenallee 3
82041 Oberhaching-Munich
Germany
+49-89-61-39-00-01
www.panther.tv

Ste-Man, Inc.
10663 Burbank Blvd.
North Hollywood, CA 91601
(818) 760-8240
www.ste-man.com

COBRA CRANE | By ProMax

Cobra Cranes are very easy to set up and break down because they mount right on top of your tripod's head. There is no reason to remove the head and reattach it for every setup and breakdown. With our Cobra Cranes, you can achieve very smooth and beautiful moves. All Cobra Cranes use a cable-and-pulley parallelogram leveling system, with a unique tilting feature built in. Cobra Cranes are extremely smooth in all directions, booming up and down, boom panning side to side, and tilting. Use regular barbell weights for counterbalance.

ProMax
16 Technology Drive, Suite 106
Irvine, CA 92618
(800) 977-6629
www.promax.com

CAMCRANE DV | By Sachtler Corporation

This lightweight crane, designed for DV camcorders up to 5.5kg (12.1 lb.), is ideal for any standard tripod with a bowl diameter of 100mm. The crane features tool-free setup and dismantling, and ensures fast camera positioning. Camera movement can be pre-set either at horizontal or to deliver top/bottom views at a selected angle. And using the lever arm, camera position can even be adjusted throughout operation. The crane's weight of 6.5kg (14.3 lb.) and transport length of 1.1m (3' 7") make it a standard part of the luggage.

Sachtler Corporation of America
55 North Main Street
Freeport, NY 11520
(516) 867-4900
www.sachtler.com

CAMCRANE EFP | By Sachtler Corporation

Sachtler offers the CamCrane EFP, designed to meet field production needs. A unique feature of the new CamCrane EFP is that it performs damping inside the camera console. This minimizes vibration and guarantees the best possible picture quality. The CamCrane EFP can easily be set up by one operator. With its low weight, the new CamCrane EFP is ideal to transport. Easy and fast to set up, the crane is also telescopable to five different lengths, plus an optionally available maximum extension length of 650cm (21' 4"). These features make the crane flexible enough for any application.

Sachtler Corporation of America
55 North Main Street
Freeport, NY 11520
(516) 867-4900
www.sachtler.com

Shotmaker Camera Cars &
Cranes
10909 Vanowen Street
North Hollywood, CA 91605
(818) 623-1700
www.shotmaker.com

CLASSIC CAMERA CAR | By Shotmaker

The reliable Shotmaker Classic features rugged, three-axle construction coupled with a wide stance for maximum stability. The front camera platform is detachable and can be reattached, high or low, on either side of the vehicle. The platform is designed to carry two cameras and four people in complete safety. Additional camera platforms are located over the cab and on the rear of the vehicle. Self-correcting rear air suspension gives you chatter-free running shots every time.

ELITE CAMERA CAR | By Shotmaker

The Academy Award-winning Shotmaker Elite combines a powerful yet smooth-running camera car with a ready-to-use crane in one hardworking vehicle. Take command of an Elite on your next production and discover why it's been called the most significant moviemaking tool in a generation! The Shotmaker Elite features a crane arm that reaches a lens height of 23 ft. (higher with risers). The arm can rotate through 360° without cable wrap-up, with the vehicle in motion or stationary.

ENLOUVA IV CRANE | By Shotmaker

Manufactured from lightweight, extruded aluminum, the new Enlouva IV crane is easy to assemble and operate. When used with a Shotmaker Enlouva base or Mammoth base the crane can achieve a maximum lens height of 23' 8" and a minimum lens height of -15', for a total lift range of 38' 8". The new Enlouva IV crane features a redesigned, lightweight fulcrum for faster setup time. The counterweight bucket has been redesigned to accept more counter-balance weights, allowing the crane to carry a heavier camera package. The Enlouva IV crane can also be mounted on a Shotmaker Classic or Shotmaker Premier Plus camera to achieve great moving shots.

MOTORCYCLE PROCESS TRAILER | By Shotmaker

With a surface area of 7' 2" W x 8' 6" L, the motorcycle process trailer is ideal for shooting traveling shots of motorcycles or push-bikes — even snowmobiles! The trailer can carry up to three bikes side by side at a height of nine inches above the ground and is often used for close-up shots where no rotating wheels are seen in frame.

Shotmaker Camera Cars & Cranes
10909 Vanowen Street
North Hollywood, CA 91605
(818) 623-1700
www.shotmaker.com

If you have used this gear and want to share your own experiences, comments, and suggestions in our next edition, send an e-mail to Catherine Lorenze at *DREAMGEAR@cox.net*. We are particularly interested in innovative ways you have used the gear that will help inspire other film, video, and TV professionals.

DOLLIES, TRACKING, AND ACCESSORIES

20

Chapman/Leonard:

Hustler IV Hydraulic Lift Camera Dolly
Super Peewee III Hydraulic Lift Camera Dolly
Super Peewee IV Hydraulic Lift Camera Dolly

Gillard Industries:

G I Track

J. L. Fisher:

Model 9 Dolly
Model 10 Dolly
Model 11 Dolly
Dolly Driver Portable Lift Beam Charging Kit

Losmandy:

Spider Dolly
Losmandy FlexTrak

Microdolly Hollywood:

Basic Dolly Kit

Panther:

Evolution Dolly
Husky Folding Dolly

Shotmaker:

Minislider Dolly
Tow Dolly

HUSTLER IV HYDRAULIC LIFT CAMERA DOLLY | By Chapman/Leonard

Chapman/Leonard's new Hustler IV Dolly includes a new sliding sideboard system with both high and low positions. The Hustler IV Dolly accommodates conventional, crab, and round steering modes and has a built-in heater system for constant arm speed, even in cold weather conditions. Working on standard straight or curved 24.5-inch track without auxiliary wheels, the Hustler IV features a new track wheel design for improved performance. Greater payload means the Hustler IV can also carry many types of jib arms, and a new hydraulic system permits smoother, more precise camera moves.

SUPER PEEWEE III HYDRAULIC LIFT CAMERA DOLLY | By Chapman/Leonard

The Super Peewee III Dolly includes a universal head mount (dolly arm nose attachment) and features new, X O X leveling that locks into four different positions.

The built-in riser can be adjusted without camera removal, and the system is lightweight for travel and storage. Other features include a universal stop valve and a new control valve design for faster, quieter, and smoother stopping.

Chapman/Leonard Studio Equipment, Inc.
12950 Raymer Street
North Hollywood, CA 91605
(888) 88-DOLLY
www.chapman-leonard.com

SUPER PEEWEE IV HYDRAULIC LIFT CAMERA DOLLY | By Chapman/Leonard

Chapman/Leonard's Super Peewee IV features a new arm design that provides greater operator clearance, while assuring greater rigidity, smoothness, speed, and added vertical travel. The new valve concept gives the operator much improved control, while providing for greater speed with added precision. Other features include improved universal head performance and improved arm performance. Also, the Super Peewee IV now comes with built-in heat control for the hydraulic system.

G I TRACK | By Gillard Industries, Inc.

This revolutionary dolly track system is equipped with a removable and replaceable PVC plastic-capped smooth riding surface. Designed by both a key grip and a dolly grip, G I Track is appreciated by film technicians, camera operators, and directors of photography for its innovative design, features, and quality components. Patented extruded 6005AT61 structural aluminum rails and PVC plastic capping form together for the ultimate smooth tracking surface. Time takes its toll on other manufactured precision track, and bumps and nicks can make the rails unusable, but that's not the case with the G I Track's PVC cap system. If the cap gets damaged, simply replace it at a fraction of the cost.

Gillard Industries, Inc.
157 April Road
Port Moody, BC
Canada V3H 3M4
(604) 328-2052
www.gillardindustries.com

MODEL 9 DOLLY | By J. L. Fisher, Inc.

The Model 9 is our largest camera dolly. It is a stable, reliable camera platform with a variety of features and accessories. This dolly is widely known for its use in television production and has provided the industry with a long history of reliable service. A new feature of the Model 9 Dolly is a smoother hydraulic system that includes a dampening valve that cushions the top and bottom of the lift. The Model 9 Dolly is easy to maneuver, dependable, requires low maintenance, and continues to meet the needs of professionals in the motion picture, television, and video industries.

MODEL 10 DOLLY | By J. L. Fisher, Inc.

Recognized as the industry standard, the Model 10 Dolly is manufactured from the highest-quality materials and components to meet the demanding needs of the motion picture, television, and video industries. This stable, reliable dolly offers operators versatile features and a wide variety of accessories. The Model 10 Dolly is smooth, quiet, and easy to use, with a reputation for being safe, well made, and low maintenance.

J. L. Fisher, Inc.
1000 Isabel Street
Burbank, CA 91506
(818) 846-8366
www.jlfisher.com

MODEL 11 DOLLY | By J. L. Fisher, Inc.

The Model 11 is our smallest dolly. Lightweight and compact, it is built with the same high-quality standards found in all J. L. Fisher products. The Model 11 Dolly shares the same controls and characteristics of the Model 10 Dolly and has a complete line of its own accessories. It operates effortlessly on square or round track, making the Model 11 and Model 10 an excellent two-dolly combination. The Model 11 Dolly is engineered and manufactured to meet the demanding production needs of the motion picture, television, and video industries. Compact size, three-way steering, and a solid lift beam give operators a wide variety of options. The reliable, quiet, smooth, and safe Model 11 requires minimal maintenance.

DOLLY DRIVER PORTABLE LIFT BEAM CHARGING KIT | By J. L. Fisher, Inc.

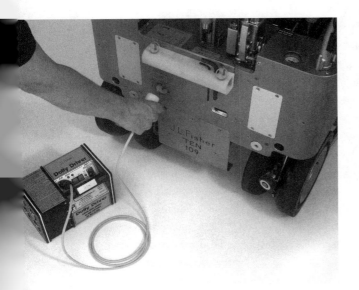

The J. L. Fisher Dolly Driver is a portable AC power source that lets you recharge the lift beam numerous times when no AC outlet is available. The Dolly Driver has enough power to recharge the lift beam system more than 16 times on the Model 11 Dolly and more than seven times on the Model 9 and 10 Dollies. This means you can get more than 100 lift cycles on a Model 11 and more than 60 on the Model 9 and 10 Dollies before you need access to an AC outlet.

SPIDER DOLLY
| By Losmandy for Hollywood General Machining, Inc.

The Losmandy Spider Dolly is the most portable professional dolly on the market. Combined with a piece of FlexTrak, the simple 3-Leg Spider converts your tripod into an inexpensive, extremely portable tracking dolly. Add a fourth leg, and you can further accessorize it to be a fully ridable dolly with adjustable center column, foot platforms, and push bar. Three small cases allow it to be checked through as luggage on an airline. Also, the Spider, when combined with floor wheels and the LWT Tripod, creates an easy and safe way to position heavy cameras and jib arms. Supports 400 lb. (182kg). The legs fold up for shipping.

LOSMANDY FLEXTRAK
| By Losmandy for Hollywood General Machining, Inc.

This amazing seamless dolly track can be configured in straight runs that can suddenly curve in any radius or direction. The basic unit is 40 feet, which will loop to make one 17-foot run. Two pieces side by side will create a 40-foot run. Each section rolls up into a two-foot-diameter bundle and weighs 40 lb., creating unprecedented portability for a track rigid enough to support an operator, yet flexible enough to curve into a 90° turn with a two-foot radius. The key to FlexTrak's success lies in the unique capability of our Spider Dolly's track wheels, which are designed with double articulating arms that create the ability to negotiate sharp radius turns. It can also work with other dolly systems because the outer diameter of the FlexTrak is the same as that of standard steel track. However, other manufacturers' dollies may not work as well on our FlexTrak.

Hollywood General Machining, Inc.
1033 N. Sycamore Avenue
Los Angeles, CA 90038
(323) 462-2855
www.porta-jib.com

BASIC DOLLY KIT
By Microdolly Hollywood

The Microdolly Basic Kit Camera Dolly and Dolly Track System weighs only 10 pounds (4.5kg) and fits into a soft-case bag only 34 inches (86cm) long. The track is spring-loaded and snaps together as it is unfolded. The dolly with 13 feet (4m) of track can be set up on almost any surface in less than two minutes. It is designed to carry up to 100 pounds of camera gear. Silent, smooth, bump-free camera moves can be accomplished much quicker than with conventional dolly equipment.

Microdolly Hollywood
3110 W. Burbank Blvd.
Burbank, CA 91505-2313
(818) 845-8383
www.microdolly.com

EVOLUTION DOLLY
By Panther and distributed by Ste-Man, Inc. in Hollywood

This completely newly constructed camera dolly, Panther Evolution, was developed in cooperation with grips and cameramen. This is the first time a dolly has a patent-pending crab and steer shift box, where the wheels can be steered from two sides and can be rotated by 360°. The perfect steering geometry enables circular drives without any noise from the wheels. For longer, straight drives, the dolly is very stable. With only one movement, the Evolution Dolly can be switched into crab mode. The height-adjustable steering rod can be mounted on all four wheel arms to permit play and shock-free steering maneuvers.

Panther GmbH
Raiffeisenallee 3
82041 Oberhaching-Munich
Germany
+49-89-61-39-00-01
www.panther.tv

Ste-Man, Inc.
10663 Burbank Blvd.
North Hollywood, CA 91601
(818) 760-8240
www.ste-man.com

HUSKY FOLDING DOLLY

By Panther and distributed by Ste-Man, Inc. in Hollywood

Succeeding the legendary lightweight dolly, the new Husky Folding Dolly combines state-of-the-art design and manufacturing. Thus, it was possible to reduce the weight by 11kg (24 lb.). More than this, the Husky Dolly can fold for transport into such an ingenious folding position that it serves as a transport cart for your camera case or other bulky equipment. The Husky is also a stable base for your tripod and can also accommodate Bazooka risers, turnstile attachment, or mounted seats.

Panther GmbH
Raiffeisenallee 3
82041 Oberhaching-Munich
Germany
+49-89-61-39-00-01
www.panther.tv

Ste-Man, Inc.
10663 Burbank Blvd.
North Hollywood, CA 91601
(818) 760-8240
www.ste-man.com

MINISLIDER DOLLY | By Shotmaker

The Minislider Dolly glides within black anodized-aluminum channel beams, enabling you to make smooth camera moves within a confined area. The Minislider Dolly can be positioned on the back seat of a car (with room for a cameraman), on boats and trains, in a booth or on a counter, out of a window or balcony, off a building or bridge, or anywhere you need to make a short camera move and you have limited space for setup. An adjustable wheel tension allows for controlled slider flow and a locking brake for secure camera positioning. Beam and clamps have 1 1/4-inch speedrail flanges mounted to facilitate easy rigging. (Speedrail, elbows, and tees are included). The Mitchell plate supplied with the Minislider can be secured to the dolly base, allowing lower mounting of a fluid head. It can also be secured to the underside of the dolly base for use with a remote or Weaver Steadman head.

Shotmaker Camera Cars & Cranes
10909 Vanowen Street
North Hollywood, CA 91605
(818) 623-1700
www.shotmaker.com

TOW DOLLY | By Shotmaker

The Shotmaker Tow Dolly can be towed from 11 different hook-on points around the Elite, Classic, or Premier camera car, offering the director a variety of shots from which to choose. The tow dolly suspends the front wheels of the picture vehicle just one inch above the ground. The picture car is secured to the dolly with nylon straps around the front wheels, preventing any damage to the towed vehicle.

If you have used this gear and want to share your own experiences, comments, and suggestions in our next edition, send an e-mail to Catherine Lorenze at *DREAMGEAR@cox.net*. We are particularly interested in innovative ways you have used the gear that will help inspire other film, video, and TV professionals.

FILTERS AND MATTE BOXES 21

Canon:

FS-72U Filter Set for the Canon XL1s

Century Optics:

Century DV Matte Box

Schneider Filter Kit

Tiffen:

Black Diffusion Filter

Black Pro-Mist Filter

Gold Diffusion Filter

Pro-Mist Filter

Special Effects DV Filter Kit

Ultra Pol Filters

Video Essentials DV Filter Kit

Warm Pro-Mist Filter

FS-72U FILTER SET FOR THE CANON XL1S | By Canon

Canon USA, Inc.
One Canon Plaza
Lake Success, NY 11042
(800) OK-CANON
www.canondv.com

Canon's FS-72U Filter Set includes Neutral Density (ND8), polarizing, and ultra-violet filters; 72mm thread size. This filter set is for use on all XL lenses except the 3-D lens.

CENTURY DV MATTE BOX FOR 4 X 4 AND 3 X 3 FILTERS | By Century Precision Optics

Century proudly presents the most exciting advance in light control for DV cameras: the Century DV Matte Box. Packed with features that protect your camera and enhance your creativity, the Century DV Matte Box mounts directly to most DV cameras. Only a soft rubber lens ring contacts your lens barrel, so you don't have to worry about your lens during the bumps and grinds of capturing exciting footage. The system comes with six rubber lens rings to fit most cameras.

Century Precision Optics
11049 Magnolia Blvd.
North Hollywood, CA 91601
(800) 228-1254
www.centuryoptics.com

SCHNEIDER
FILTER KIT | By
Century Precision Optics

Century Optics is pleased to present three of the most useful Schneider Filters now packaged together in a single kit. The Schneider 4 x 4 Filter Kit consists of three Schneider glass filters, including: a Circular True-Pol, which has an extraordinary ability to reduce glare and reflections, saturate colors, deepen blue skies, improve contrast, and penetrate haze; a Black Frost 1/2 that takes the edge off video for a filmlike look and can be used for styling or mood modifying, and; a Neutral Density filter designed to control exposure or depth of field under various lighting conditions without affecting color or contrast.

Century Precision Optics
11049 Magnolia Blvd.
North Hollywood, CA 91601
(800) 228-1254
www.centuryoptics.com

BLACK
DIFFUSION
FILTER | By
Tiffen

The Black Diffusion/FX filter gives a silky-smooth look to textured surfaces. It does a spectacular job of suppressing facial blemishes and wrinkles, while maintaining a clear, focused image.

The Tiffen Company, LLC
90 Oser Avenue
Hauppauge, NY 11788-3886
(631) 273-2500
www.tiffen.com

BLACK PRO-MIST FILTER | By Tiffen

Tiffen's Black Pro-Mist filter offers similar characteristics to our Pro-Mist filter, but provides a more subtle effect; less lightening of shadows, and reduction of contrast. Our Black Pro-Mist filter is available in several grades.

GOLD DIFFUSION FILTER | By Tiffen

The Gold Diffusion/FX filter takes the effect of the Black Diffusion/FX a step further. It adds a soft, golden tint to shadows, and infuses images with a special warmth. Yet it still manages to balance any mix of skin tones. Neutral colors appear minimally affected, while cool colors and skin tones are slightly warmed and softened with beautiful results.

The Tiffen Company, LLC
90 Oser Avenue
Hauppauge, NY 11788-3886
(631) 273-2500
www.tiffen.com

PRO-MIST FILTER | By Tiffen

Tiffen's Pro-Mist filter is our most popular motion picture effect. The Pro-Mist filter creates a special "atmosphere" by softening excess sharpness and contrast and creating a pearlescent glow around highlights. The Pro-Mist filter is great for portraits and landscapes and is available in several grades.

No Filter

With UltraPol Filter

No Filter

With UltraPol Filter

SPECIAL EFFECTS DV KIT | By Tiffen

Tiffen's Special Effects DV Kit is designed primarily for professional shooters using prosumer DV cameras to produce results that are pleasing, less harsh, and less brassy. The Special Effects DV Kit includes: Color-Grad ND 0.6 — balances sky to foreground; Pro-Mist 1/4 — tones down excessive sharpness and reduces contrast by lightening shadow areas somewhat; Enhancing — makes reds, rust browns, and oranges "pop" and is ideal for fall foliage; Gold Diffusion/FX 1/2 — gives a silky-smooth look to textured surfaces and adds a warm, gold tone to the scene.

No Filter

With UltraPol Filter

ULTRA POL FILTERS FOR SATURATING COLOR AND REDUCING GLARE | By Tiffen

Tiffen's Linear Ultra Pol and Circular Ultra Pol filters offer the best polarization effects available for professional motion picture and television work. They extract the maximum of unwanted glare from the scene and render crisp, white clouds against a dramatically dark blue sky, like never before. Distracting reflections from water and windows become invisible with the magic of the Ultra Pol filter. Ultra Pols get the most from any scene that requires a polarizer.

The Tiffen Company, LLC
90 Oser Avenue
Hauppauge, NY 11788-3886
(631) 273-2500
www.tiffen.com

VIDEO ESSENTIALS DV KIT | By Tiffen

Tiffen's Video Essentials DV Kit is designed primarily for professional shooters using pro-sumer DV cameras to produce results that are more pleasing, less harsh, and less brassy. The Video Essentials DV Kit includes: Clear Filter to help protect your lens from dirt and damage; Circular Polarizer to increase color saturation while reducing reflection and glare; Warm UV17 that removes 97% of the ultraviolet light.

WARM PRO-MIST FILTER | By Tiffen

Tiffen's Warm Pro-Mist filter is a combination of our Pro-Mist filter and 812 warming filter. The Warm Pro-Mist warms (for color imaging) and softens, giving skin a healthy, natural glow. The Warm Pro-Mist is available in several grades.

If you have used this gear and want to share your own experiences, comments, and suggestions in our next edition, send an e-mail to Catherine Lorenze at *DREAMGEAR@cox.net*. We are particularly interested in innovative ways you have used the gear that will help inspire other film, video, and TV professionals.

FURNITURE 22
ERGONOMIC
AND STORAGE

Biomorph:

HAG Capisco Ergonomic Chair
HAG HO4 Ergonomic Chair
HAG HO5 Ergonomic Chair
Maxo and Pro Biomorph Interactive Ergo Desks

Herman Miller:

Aeron Ergonomic Chair
Ergon 3 Ergonomic Chair
Mirra Ergonomic Chair

Marketec:

ARC Series Ergonomic Desk
BodyBilt Big and Tall Series Ergo Chair
Crescent Series Ergonomic Desk
Therapod Ergonomic Chair

Russ Bassett:

Slidetrac Storage Shelves

Winsted:

Slim-Line Uplite Console

HAG CAPISCO ERGONOMIC CHAIR | By Biomorph

The HAG Capisco is an ergonomically designed task chair and stool. It is ideal for sit-to-stand applications as it adjusts from chair height to stool height instantly. The unconventional design allows for multiple sitting positions. Adjustments can be made in chair height, seat pan forward and back, seat back up and down, and tilt.

HAG H04 ERGONOMIC CHAIR | By Biomorph

The HAG H04 is an ergonomically designed command chair. Sleek and subtle, this chair has the most adjustments and includes a high-contoured back with arms, casters, and optional headrest. Adjustments can be made in chair height, seat pan forward and back, seat back up and down, arms up and down, and tilt.

Biomorph
11 Broadway, Suite 905
New York, NY 10004
(888) 302-DESK
www.biomorph.com

HAG H05 ERGONOMIC CHAIR | By Biomorph

The HAG H05 is an ergonomically designed command chair. It has a revolutionary design with only one wheel and lever for all adjustments. With its hard-wearing nylon fabric upholstery, the HAG H05 also features a high-contoured back with arms that rotate behind you. Adjustments can be made in seat depth, back height, chair height, armrest height, and tilt.

MAXO AND PRO BIOMORPH INTERACTIVE ERGONOMIC DESKS | By Biomorph

Biomorph Interactive Desks are ergonomically designed, precision-crafted, tilt-action, height-adjustable furniture for today's technology and the people who use it. The result of extensive research and development, Biomorph's patented, revolutionary surface designs and range of flexible options complement the human body, creating a healthy and comfortable environment for people who use computers. Both the Maxo and Pro models provide maximum workspace and multiple-monitor support for professional and console applications.

AERON
ERGONOMIC
CHAIR | By Herman Miller, Inc.

Combining distinctive looks with pioneering ergonomics, the Aeron performs like no other chair. It adapts naturally and adjusts precisely to fit people of all sizes and postures doing all kinds of activities. Aeron chairs come in three sizes and offer the PostureFit solution. This next-generation breakthrough provides natural, custom-fitted lower-back support below the beltline for healthier posture and outstanding lower-back comfort. The high-back design also takes weight off the lower spine, and the strong, meshlike Pellicle suspension system distributes weight evenly over the seat and back.

ERGON 3
ERGONOMIC
CHAIR | By Herman Miller, Inc.

The Ergon 3, thickly cushioned for long-term work, cradles the user to align the body in the most comfortable posture. The standard-feature high backrest maintains the spine's natural curve and supports the upper back. And soft edges and a waterfall seat front help maintain proper circulation.

MIRRA ERGONOMIC CHAIR | By Herman Miller, Inc.

Mirra is an innovative blend of passive and active adjustments that provide a new reference point in performance, aesthetics, and value. Mirra automatically shapes itself to each user, while a few simple adjustments fine-tune the fit and feel. The pliable, elastic TriFlex back supports the entire spine and conforms to size, posture, and movements. A camber shape at the base of the back gives healthy, comfortable support to the lower back below the beltline.

Herman Miller, Inc.
855 East Main Avenue
P.O. Box 302
Zeeland, MI 49464-0302
(888) 443-4357
www.hermanmiller.com

ARC SERIES ERGONOMIC DESK | By Solutions Furniture for Marketec

If you're using multiple monitors, then the ARC is made for you. Accommodating up to three 20-inch monitors, the ARC's curved design positions all three monitors for optimal viewing. On the ARC, the height-adjustable monitor stand on wheels has been modified to make room for as many as three monitors. Designed to be adapted to your needs, the separate pieces can be mixed and matched.

Marketec
4417 West Magnolia Blvd.
Burbank, CA 91505
(800) 557-8861
www.marketec.com

BODYBILT BIG AND TALL SERIES S2504 ERGONOMIC CHAIR | By ErgoGenesis and distributed by Marketec

The only fully adjustable line of Big and Tall chairs on the market, the Big and Tall Series offers unprecedented comfort and adjustability for larger workers. Like all BodyBilt chairs, each Big and Tall model features 10 standard adjustments and BodyBilt's unique pressure-reducing seat contour.

CRESCENT SERIES ERGONOMIC DESK | By Solutions Furniture for Marketec

The Crescent Series ergonomic desk is the most versatile furniture solution on the market, with style and options that are built to last! A height-adjustable monitor stand on wheels helps to eliminate back and neck strain. And the curved design of the desk and monitor bridge pulls your equipment toward you, placing it all within line of sight and easy reach.

Marketec
4417 West Magnolia Blvd.
Burbank, CA 91505
(800) 557-8861
www.marketec.com

THERAPOD ERGONOMIC CHAIR | By All Seating and distributed by Marketec

Like everyone, your upper, middle, and lower back regions are affected by how you sit. Yet each region has requirements for support that are unique to you alone. Therapod's patented design accommodates every region of your back using body-specific strap adjustments. The net result is a comfortable fit superbly suited to your entire back.

SLIDETRAC STORAGE SHELVES | By Russ Bassett Corporation

The Slidetrac Storage Shelving System is an above-the-floor system that features side-to-side shelving, ease of motion on heavy-duty ball-bearing wheels, and filing control accessories that retain media. Products are organized by what they store: 4mm, 8mm, audiocassette, mini-DV, small and large DVCPRO, mini and large DVCAM, VHS, DVHS, DV, small Beta, small D2, large Beta, 3/4" U-matic, large D2, CD, and DVD. When your collection involves multiple formats, we encourage you to contact the factory for assistance specific to your unique application.

Russ Basset Corporation
8189 Byron Road
Whittier, CA 90606
(562) 945-2445
www.russbassett.com

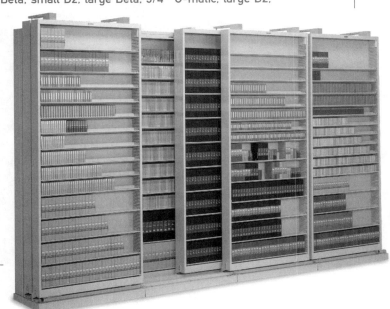

SLIM-LINE UPLITE
CONSOLE | By
The Winsted Corporation

A unique feature of the Slim-Line Uplite Console is its indirect lighting system. Two pendant (hanging) fluorescent lighting fixtures direct soft, ambient light on the spacious work surface. The perforated grill on the underside of the fixtures allows a portion of the reflected light to reach the work surface, eliminating any shadows cast from the ceiling. The attractive cabinets include rounded filing-cabinet enclosures with lockable doors on each end of the console.

The Winsted Corporation
10901 Hampshire Ave., SO.
Minneapolis, MN 55438-2385
(800) 447-2257
www.winsted.com

HEADS
FLUID, PAN, AND TILT

23

Cartoni:	Alfa Fluid Head
	Beta Fluid Head
	C20 S Fluid Head
	Lambda Fluid Head
Manfrotto:	516 Pro Video Head
Sachtler:	Dutch Head 35
	DV 2 II
	DV 4 II
	DV 15
	Horizon Plus 35/16
	Panorama Plus
	Studio 9+9
	Video 18 Dutch
	Video 90 FB
Vinten:	Vision 3 Pan and Tilt Head

ALFA LIGHTWEIGHT FLUID HEAD FOR DV AND ENG PROFESSIONAL VIDEO CAMERAS | By Cartoni and distributed by Ste-Man, Inc. in Hollywood

This is the Cartoni for the new generation of DV and lightweight ENG professional video cameras. The Alfa provides for fast dynamic counterbalance of camera loads up to 8kg (17 lb.). For heavier cameras weighing up to 10kg (22 lb.) an upgraded version, Alfa II, is also available. On both versions, Alfa and Alfa II, the camera weight is counterbalanced by a double spring group that can be disengaged while shooting with ultralight equipment by simply flipping a lever. The quick-release sliding plate allows the camera to be perfectly balanced and easily mounted.

Ste-Man, Inc.
10663 Burbank
N. Hollywood, CA 91601
(818) 760-8240
www.ste-man.com

Cartoni S.p.A.
Via Giuseppe Mirri, 13
01159 Rome, Italy
+39 (0)6 438-2002
www.cartoni.com

BETA FLUID HEAD FOR ENG CAMCORDERS | By Cartoni and distributed by Ste-Man, Inc. in Hollywood

The Cartoni Beta Fluid Head is the ideal mate for today's on-the-move compact ENG camcorders. The camera weight is counterbalanced by two groups of springs operated by two easy-action levers, allowing three stepped balance weights plus "free" position. Cameras of 5kg (11 lb.) are easily counterbalanced with the first spring module. The second module allows support of an 8kg (18 lb.) video camera. With both spring modules engaged together, the system is ready to counterbalance a 10kg (22 lb.) camcorder.

C20 S FLUID HEAD FOR EFP CAMCORDERS AND SUPER 16MM FILM CAMERAS | By Cartoni and distributed by Ste-Man, Inc. in Hollywood

The Cartoni C20 S Fluid Head is designed to provide an extremely stable support system for either standard EFP camcorder configurations or super 16mm film cameras. By simply presetting the differential spring reactive elements, its unique counterbalance system is ready to support a wide range of cameras weighing from 5 to 25kg (11 to 55 lb.). A 55mm sliding base, combined with a quick-release plate, allows the cameraperson to fine-tune the balancing of any camera and lens combination, while an eight-position easy grip selector provides for the most suitable dynamic compensation.

LAMBDA NODAL SWING HEAD FOR FULLY EQUIPPED 35MM CAMERAS

By Cartoni and distributed by Ste-Man, Inc. in Hollywood

The Cartoni Lambda is a Nodal Swing Head ideally suited for 35mm film cameras that are fully equipped with long lenses, matte box, and extra-large magazines. Designed to provide a high level of operational flexibility, this fluid head can be easily fitted to a wide range of supports, such as tripods, dollies, cranes, and camera cars. The mounting can be inverted for low-line lens positioning, allowing the camera to be moved all the way to the ground. With the Lambda, there is no need to change or disassemble a variety of additional platforms or risers to suit the optical center of the camera. Simply adjust the center of gravity by turning the two independent wheels. The vertical sliding platform will immediately rise or lower with a precise, positive movement.

Ste-Man, Inc.
10663 Burbank
N. Hollywood, CA 91601
(818) 760-8240
www.ste-man.com

Cartoni S.p.A.
Via Giuseppe Mirri, 13
01159 Rome, Italy
+39 (0)6 438-2002
www.cartoni.com

516 PRO VIDEO HEAD | By Manfrotto and distributed by Bogen Photo Corp.

Specifically designed for the latest DV camcorders, the 516 Pro Video Head is compact, light, and can support cameras up to 10kg (22 lb.) The 516 is a cost-effective high-performance video head equipped with fluid cartridges that provide continuous adjustable drag control. This system gives quite a wide range of friction control down to zero drag and operates in both pan and tilt axes. Other features include separate pan and tilt locking mechanisms, a fixed counterbalance spring of 16.5-lb. load capacity at a center of gravity of 5 inches, two telescopic pan handles, and a bubble level. The 516 can be mounted on a flat base tripod with a 3/8-inch female thread attachment, or by attaching the 500MVBALL to the head base, allowing it to fit a 100mm bowl.

Bogen Photo Corp.
565 East Crescent Avenue
P.O. Box 506
Ramsey, NJ 07446-0506
(201) 818-9500
www.bogenphoto.com
www.manfrotto.com

DUTCH HEAD 35 | By Sachtler Corporation

Sachtler Corporation of America
55 North Main Street
Freeport, NY 11520
(516) 867-4900
www.sachtler.com

The Dutch Head 35's features include Sachtler's patented fluid-damping and counterbalance systems. In addition, it has a cross-sliding plate that uses a high-precision dovetailed guidance with a sliding range of 60mm (2.4 in.). This enables the camera's center of gravity to be aligned exactly over the head's swiveling axis. The head is able to tilt the horizon, and features a scale on the right side panel that shows the exact degree of third-axis movement.

DV 2 II FLUID HEAD FOR MINI-DV LIGHTWEIGHT CAMERAS | By Sachtler Corporation

Even the smallest and lightest mini-DV camcorders should be able to shoot blur-free pictures. Ideally, they should be able to shoot films that are barely inferior to those shot by larger models. Sachtler's fluid head DV 2 II, in combination with tripod DA 75 L (System DV 2 II), is designed exactly for this purpose. In short: professional camera support for small budgets.

DV 4 II FLUID HEAD FOR CAMCORDERS WEIGHING UP TO 5KG (11 LB.) | By Sachtler Corporation

Featuring two-step damping and two-step balancing, the fluid head DV 4 II is the ideal choice for use with first-class mini-DV camcorders (e.g., Canon, Sony, and Panasonic). An extensive range of accessories is now available for these camcorders, including lens hoods, lens adapters, etc. Tripod set DV 4 II, made up of tripod ENG 75/2D and fluid head DV 4 II, is also available for these camera configurations.

Sachtler Corporation of America
55 North Main Street
Freeport, NY 11520
(516) 867-4900
www.sachtler.com

DV 15 FLUID HEAD FOR DIGITAL CAMERAS | By Sachtler Corporation

The DV 15 closes the gap between the DV 12 TB and the Video 18. The DV 15 Fluid Head is perfectly designed for the latest generation of digital camera equipment. As with the DV 12 TB, the DV 15's balance plate ensures perfect counterbalance of the camera weight across the vertical plane. Torsion springs enable you to quickly and easily compensate for torque as the camera tilts. And there is no need to hold the camera during tilts, freeing you to concentrate fully on your camerawork.

HORIZON PLUS 35/16 FOR HD PRODUCTIONS | By Sachtler Corporation

This sophisticated fluid head offers High-Definition camera operators all the possibilities of a classical movie shoot. Our Horizon Plus Fluid Head has an 18-step counterbalance system. Fine-tuning is achieved via half steps that are disengageable. Thus, the camera can be balanced in any position. The self-illuminating Touch Bubble even allows you to set up in the dark. An included bracket lets you mount the viewfinder extension on either side of the pan-and-tilt head. With a maximum payload of 35kg (77 lb.) it can easily handle all standard 16 and 35mm cameras.

PANORAMA PLUS FLUID HEAD FOR 16MM LIGHTWEIGHT CAMERAS | By Sachtler Corporation

The Panorama Plus is the ideal companion for any documentary work where weight is of the essence. Ideal for mobile 16mm cameras, the Panorama Plus offers nearly all the advantages of the Studio 9+9: perfected counterbalance, 90° tilt, and a self-illuminating Touch Bubble.

STUDIO 9+9 FLUID HEAD FOR 35MM CAMERAS | By Sachtler Corporation

The head for all 35mm cameras displays state-of-the-art technology: perfected counterbalance, 90° tilt, and a self-illuminating Touch Bubble. The Studio 9+9 is ideal together with the Dutch Head 35, a combination that enables the camera to tilt the horizon. And as the name indicates, there are now nine levels of extra-powerful drag, ensuring perfect counter-balance in 18 steps. Levels 2 to 7 are fairly fine, while the jump from levels 7 to 9 is much greater.

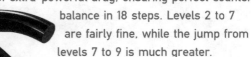

Sachtler Corporation of America
55 North Main Street
Freeport, NY 11520
(516) 867-4900
www.sachtler.com

VIDEO 18 DUTCH HEAD | By Sachtler Corporation

Why not take full advantage of breathtaking scenes and extraordinary settings? With Sachtler's Video 18 Dutch, you can do just that. The head for special effects provides you with seven steps of drag, even in conjunction with lateral tilt. A Dutch Head add-on has been developed for all film, ENG, and DV fluid heads with camera plate 16.

VIDEO 90 FB | By Sachtler Corporation

Professional cameramen have long chosen the Video 90 for OB and studio applications, and for good reason: lightweight but at the same time supporting enormous loads up to 90kg (200 lb.); a simple, sturdy, squeeze-proof construction; and unsurpassed leakproof, frictionless, maximum damping that is identical on the horizontal and vertical planes. The Video 90 FB has maximum damping action for studio and OB applications. A high-performance, jerk-free damping system is indispensable for long focal lengths in OB applications. Broadcasting professionals know they can rely on Sachtler damping systems. It is always at hand in full force.

VISION 3 PAN AND TILT HEAD | By Vinten

The Vision 3 is the smallest and lightest pan-and-tilt head in the Vision range. Designed for the new digital age of smaller, lighter video cameras, the Vision 3, weighing in at just 2.3kg (5 lb.), incorporates many key features you would usually only expect to see in larger, more expensive heads. The Vision 3 comes with an illuminated leveling bubble for quick and easy setup, detented and calibrated drag controls using Vinten's Lubricate Friction (LF) system, plus a full ±90° of smooth tilt movement. To provide balance over a range of payloads from 1 to 10kg (2.2 to 22 lb.), the Vision 3 incorporates a unique and easily interchangeable spring.

Vinten
709 Executive Boulevard
Valley Cottage, NY 10989
(845) 268-0100
www.vinten.com

JIB ARMS AND BOOM BASES 24

EZ FX:	EZ FX Jib
	EZ UnderSling
J. L. Fisher:	Model 2 Boom
	Model 7 Boom
	Model 23 Jib
Losmandy:	Porta-Jib Traveller
	Standard Porta-Jib
Microdolly Hollywood:	Basic Jib Kit

EZ FX JIB | <small>By EZ FX</small>

The EZ FX (Easy Effects) Jib is portable, user-friendly, and the most versatile jib in the industry. A cost-effective way to add production value and get the sophisticated look of moving camera shots, the EZ FX Jib can also save valuable production time by allowing you to set up your static shots very quickly. Accessories like the EZ FX Handle make this the most unique jib on the market. Now extendable with two optional Extension Kits, this system will grow with your needs.

EX FX
324 Maguire Road
Ocoee, FL 34761
(800) 541-5706
www.ezfx.com

DREAM GEAR | LORENZE | 188

EZ UNDERSLING | <small>By EZ FX</small>

For special applications such as getting the camera as low to the ground as possible or dropping the camera into the sunroof of a car, the EZ UnderSling bracket is the right accessory for the job. With both vertical and horizontal adjustments for various-size cameras, using the UnderSling is as easy as 1, 2, 3. Simply invert the camera platform on the jib, attach the UnderSling, then snap your camera in place.

MODEL 2 BOOM | By J. L. Fisher, Inc.

The Model 2 is our smallest microphone boom. This telescopic boom is quiet, smooth, safe, and easy to use on location, in feature films, and in television and video productions. The Model 2 Boom can be mounted overhead on Catwalk Stands (ACS, CS) or on stage flooring using the Model 6 Base (6) or Model 3 Base (3). The Model 2 Boom's compact size and features enable the boom operator to position the microphone in confined areas.

MODEL 7 BOOM | By J. L. Fisher, Inc.

The Model 7 Boom is a quiet, smooth, and easy-to-use telescopic microphone boom with a variety of features and accessories that enable operators to position microphones in nearly any position. This boom is primarily for use in television production and has provided the industry with a long history of reliable service. The Model 7 Boom is available in four different lengths, providing sound personnel with a wide range of flexibility. The Model 7 Boom can be mounted overhead on Catwalk Stands (ACS, CS) or on stage flooring using the Model 6 Base (6). A new feature available on our longer booms is a carbon-fiber inside tube that is lighter, more rigid, and quieter than standard tubes.

J. L. Fisher, Inc.
1000 Isabel Street
Burbank, CA 91506
(818) 846-8366
www.jlfisher.com

STANDARD PORTA-JIB

By Losmandy for
Hollywood General Machining, Inc.

Designed to carry up to 100 lb. (45kg) of camera and fluid-head weight, this is the most versatile of all lightweight jibs. It assembles in less than five minutes, with no tools required. All parts are machined aluminum and stainless steel. Boom and pan lock are included. Front inserts are available for all standard fluid heads: 100mm, 150mm, Mitchell. Base plate is available for standard 150mm and Mitchell tripods, or it can be equipped with our LWTi interface plate that allows it to drop into our Light Weight Tripod. The 17-inch and 36-inch Extension Kits can be used to further the range of the Standard Porta-Jib. Use them either in the traditional front-operated mode or in conjunction with a lightweight remote head to obtain dramatic high-angle or overreaching shots.

BASIC JIB KIT

By
Microdolly Hollywood

The Basic Jib Kit includes the Microdolly Jib and the standard 34-inch Microdolly Soft Case. An adapter plate to attach the jib to almost any professional tripod and a heavy-duty camera plate knob to mount the camera are also part of the kit. The innovative Jib Arm will easily handle most professional film and video cameras. Gym weights may be used, or a sturdy collapsible Weight Cage accessory will hold anything you have for counterweight: rocks, sand, even water! The jib can be set to automatically adjust the camera tilt or Dutch angles as you move. Other features include: adjustable tilt-and-pan friction controls, bubble level on yoke base and on camera plate, and the camera plate is also adjustable for level.

Microdolly Hollywood
3110 W. Burbank Blvd.
Burbank, CA 91505-2313
(818) 845-8383
www.microdolly.com

If you have used this gear and want to share your own experiences, comments, and suggestions in our next edition, send an e-mail to Catherine Lorenze at *DREAMGEAR@cox.net*. We are particularly interested in innovative ways you have used the gear that will help inspire other film, video, and TV professionals.

LENS ACCESSORIES
AND LENSES

Alan Gordon Enterprises:	Mark V Director's Viewfinder
Angenieux:	Optimo 24–290 Lens 26x7.8 AIF.HR Tele Super Zoom Lens
Canon:	16X Mechanical Servo Zoom Lens
Century Optics:	S2000 Mark II T4 Periscope Lens Low Angle Prism
Fujinon:	HA13x4.5 BERM/BERD ENG Lens HA22x7.8 BERM/BERD ENG Lens HA13x4.5B Cine Lens Hae3x5 Cine Super E Series Zoom Lens Hae10x10 Cine Super E Series Zoom Lens
Innovision Optics:	HR Prime Lenses for the Probe II and Probe II+ Probe II Lens System 6000 Series Innovision Tubular Lens System
OpTex:	Canon/OpTex HD and EC Lenses Excellence Periscope/Probe System
Panavision:	Primo Macro Zoom Lens
16x9 Inc./Bank Pro:	Tochigi Nikon Telephoto Lens for Digital Cinematography Zeiss DigiPrime HD Lenses
ZGC:	Cooke S4 HD Zoom Lens Cooke S4 Prime Lenses

Technical Achievement Award from the Academy of Motion Picture Arts & Sciences
Prime Time Emmy Engineering Award from the Academy of Motion Picture Arts & Sciences

MARK V
DIRECTOR'S VIEWFINDER | By Alan Gordon Enterprises

The Mark V Director's Viewfinder accurately defines choice of lenses, angles, and coverage in a wide variety of formats for both film and video. With a 12:1 zoom ratio, the Mark V Director's Viewfinder is an essential tool for today's professional filmmaker. Setting up shots using the 16mm and 35mm direct-reading windows gives you a wide range of film and video formats including 1/2-inch, 2/3-inch, and Super 16. The aspect ratio ring is calibrated for film and video ratios 1.33:1, 1.66:1, 16 x 9, 1.85:1, and 2.40:1.

Alan Gordon Enterprises
5625 Melrose Avenue
Hollywood, CA 90038
(323) 466-3561
www.alangordon.com

OPTIMO 24-290
LENS FOR 35MM
FILMMAKING | By Angenieux

The Optimo 24-290mm features a new optical design that propels its performance above and beyond virtually any lens. In addition, this new design completely eliminates breathing and ramping. The Optimo 24-290mm lens offers constant superior levels of optical performance all across its entire zoom range. This lens also produces impressive contrast and color reproduction that rivals the highest-performing prime lenses. The extremely fast aperture speed of T2.8 offers a larger use of the spectral band and focal range at any position. Color filters are provided in standard, in order to match with the Cooke S4 series and Zeiss Ultra Primes and to make the Optimo fully compatible with these prime lenses.

Thales Angenieux SA
42570 Saint-Heand
France
+33 (0)4 77-90-78-00
www.angenieux.com

26X7.8 AIF.HR TELE SUPER ZOOM LENS | By Angenieux

Angenieux's 26x7.8 Tele Super Zoom Lens has the longest focal range in the industry for an ENG lens. Features include the next generation of advanced-performance optics, the use of sophisticated aspherical polishing technology with extremely tight tolerances, and the lens provides increased resolution and no chromatic aberration.

Thales Angenieux SA
42570 Saint-Heand
France
+33 (0)4 77-90-78-00
www.angenieux.com

16X MECHANICAL SERVO ZOOM LENS FOR THE XL1S | By Canon

This manual lens gives you the flexibility of calibrated manual focus and calibrated power zoom, power iris, and two built-in ND filters.

Canon USA, Inc.
One Canon Plaza
Lake Success, NY 11042
(800) OK-CANON
www.canondv.com

S2000 MARK II T4 PERISCOPE LENS | By Century Optics

Designed to fulfill the demands of 35mm feature and commercial work, the Series 2000 Mark II T4 Periscope represents a remarkable advancement in the optical fidelity and usefulness of periscopic relay systems. While ideal for shooting miniatures and tabletop setups, the Periscope is equally at home on location — where lighting conditions are less easily controlled. The Series 2000 Mark II Periscope utilizes ultra-low dispersion Fluoro-Phosphate glass, dramatically reducing field curvature and chromatic aberrations, which radically improves off-axis resolution. A wide range of camera and lens adapters is available.

Century Precision Optics
11049 Magnolia Blvd.
North Hollywood, CA 91601
(800) 228-1254
www.centuryoptics.com

LOW ANGLE PRISM | By Century Optics

In the past, when the script called for a super low angle shot, the crew had two choices: either dig a hole, or raise the set. Now, many cinematographers have discovered an easy way to get that ultra-low viewpoint with Century's Low Angle Prism. The Super Wide Low Angle Prisms will take you down to points of view as low as two inches above the floor. If the situation calls for a high-angle but restricted shot, such as shooting above a driver's shoulder in a car or off a ceiling, the Low Angle Prism inverts to cover high-angle shots as easily as low angles. The system is fully compatible with the Zeiss 16mm at Academy aperture or the 18mm at full aperture. The Super Wide Low Angle Prism directly couples with Arri bridgeplate rods for rock-solid positioning of Zeiss primes.

HA13X4.5 BERM/BERD AND HA22X7.8 BERM/BERD HD ENG LENSES | By Fujinon, Inc.

The HA13x4.5 BERM/BERD and HA22x7.8 BERM/BERD offer the precise focusing and superior optical quality demanded for HD applications but with the durability and light weight expected by professionals who regularly shoot in the field. The HA13x4.5 BERM/BERD is a 2/3-inch format, wide-angle lens with the widest angle in the market — 4.5mm with a 93.6° horizontal field of view. The BERM version has a 2X extender and manual focus servo zoom, while the BERD version also features a 2X extender, servo focus, and servo zoom. The HA22x7.8 BERM/BERD is a telephoto lens with a 2X extender, making it the longest such lens in the market with a reduced size and weight, improved f-number, maximum relative aperture of f/1.8, and reduced Minimum Object Distance.

HA13x4.5 HD

HA22x7.8 HD

Fujinon, Inc. USA
10 High Point Drive
Wayne, NJ 07470-7434
(973) 633-5600
www.fujinon.com

HA13X4.5B CINE STYLE LENS | By Fujinon, Inc.

HA13x Cine

The new HA13x4.5B is the widest angle Cine Style zoom lens on the market. With a 4.5mm focal length at its widest end, the HA13x4.5B provides a 93.6° horizontal field of view. The lens offers focus rotation up to 280° for easier and more exact focusing, with little focus "breathing" — the tendency of a lens to make an image look bigger or smaller when its focus is changed. A larger barrel diameter and a focus rotation of 280° (almost double that of a standard prime) provides for precise focus follow. Maximum photometric aperture of T1.7 (HaeF5-F) and T1.5 (HaeF8-F) results in more latitude in controlling depth of field. Minimal breathing while focusing and distortion-free, edge-to-edge sharpness set a new standard for digital imaging.

Fujinon, Inc. USA
10 High Point Drive
Wayne, NJ 07470-7434
(973) 633-5600
www.fujinon.com

HAE3X5 AND HAE10X10 CINE SUPER E SERIES ZOOM LENSES | By Fujinon, Inc.

Like all lenses in the Cine Super E series, the new Hae3x5 and Hae10x10 zoom lenses are especially designed for 2/3-inch CCD, High-Definition, digital video cameras and provide precise, aberration-free images for a variety of motion picture applications. The popular Cine Super E series now includes eight fixed focal length prime lenses and four zooms. The new Hae3x5 zoom lens features a 5-15mm focal length and 3X zoom ratio in a highly portable, compact design weighing 11 lb. The Hae10x10 offers a 10-100mm focal lens and 10X zoom ratio and weighs 12 lb.

HR PRIMES FOR THE PROBE II AND PROBE II+ | Distributed by Innovision Optics

Innovision Optics is now introducing a new set of high-resolution prime lenses for our existing Probe II and Probe II+ lens owners. The HR Primes feature all-new optical designs using better quality glass than previously available Probe II lenses. Features include: increased sharpness and contrast; overall image improvement from edge to edge; focal lengths of 12mm, 20mm, 28mm, 40mm, 55mm; all lenses are waterproof; and all lenses have optical flats for protection.

PROBE II LENS SYSTEM | Distributed by Innovision Optics

Innovision's Probe II is developed especially for shooters whose projects require long tubular lenses and higher-resolution images. The Probe II features high-resolution glass elements and relay optics for images with remarkable edge-to-edge sharpness, flat field, and extreme depth of field. State-of-the-art multiple coatings provide sharp, low-dispersion images. The Probe II comes in 35mm film and video/16mm versions. The video/16mm Probe II easily covers Super 16 as well.

Innovision Optics
1719 21st Street
Santa Monica, CA 90404
(310) 453-4866
www.innovision-optics.com

6000 SERIES INNOVISION TUBULAR LENS SYSTEM | Distributed by Innovision Optics

This lens system extends the realm of the tabletop and product shooting by providing access to hard-to-get-to areas never before photographed with conventional film lenses. Get dramatic effects shooting objects as minute as the bristles of a toothbrush or computer chips. The 6000 Series Lens System features a selection of three lens barrels, the Focusing Relay Module, and the Light Source. Interchangeable lens mounts allow compatibility with popular video, 16mm, and 35mm cameras. Fully sealed, the 6000 Series Lens barrels are immersible in liquids such as oil-based fuels, mineral oils, or salt water.

Innovision Optics, Inc.
1719 21st Street
Santa Monica, CA 90404
(310) 453-4866
www.innovision-optics.com

CANON/OPTEX HD AND EC LENSES FOR HD AND ELECTRONICS CINEMATOGRAPHY | By Canon and distributed by OpTex

These high-quality, mid-range prime lenses are suitable for HD, Digital Betacam, DVCPRO, and 2/3-inch ECTV cameras. They produce the kind of differential focus familiar to filmmakers without the image shift associated with many zoom lenses. Canon's HD-EC Primes exhibit high MTF, high resolution, and high contrast from the center of the image to its extreme edges, an important benefit of Canon's new proprietary design techniques. Other features include reduced flare, with an exceptionally sharp, flat picture and virtually no curvature of field.

OpTex
20-26 Victoria Road, New Barne
N. London EN4 9PF UK
+44 (0)2 084-4 12-199
www.optexint.com

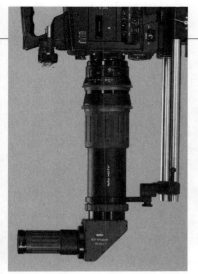

OPTEX EXCELLENCE: MODULAR PERISCOPE/PROBE SYSTEM FOR HDTV AND FILM | By OpTex

The OpTex Excellence offers such a high image quality that you will think you are using a prime lens. This multi-format system can be configured to work on 2/3-inch HDTV/SDTV or film, with interchangeable format modules allowing the film configuration to work with 35mm silent aperture, anamorphic, and Super 16mm. VistaVision and 65mm modules are also in development. The entire system is color matched so whether it is used as a periscope or a probe, and whatever lens is used, color remains constant.

OpTex
20-26 Victoria Road, New Barnet
N. London EN4 9PF UK
+44 (0)2 084-412-199
www.optexint.com

PRIMO MACRO ZOOM LENS | By Panavision

Following the Academy Award-winning Primo primes and zoom series of lenses, Panavision proudly introduces the first Primo Macro Zoom to complement this series. Combining wide-angle zooming and continuous close focusing capability in a compact design makes this lens extremely versatile. Employing two aspherical surfaces in an extremely sophisticated optical/mechanical design has resulted in many technical breakthroughs to give you an extremely unique lens for zooming, variable prime use, and/or close-focus macro work.

Panavision
6219 De Soto Ave.
Woodland Hills, CA 91367
(818) 316-1000
www.panavision.com

TOCHIGI NIKON TELEPHOTO LENS FOR DIGITAL CINEMATOGRAPHY

| Distributed by
16x9 Inc./Band Pro

The Tochigi Nikon 300mm lens is a superior-quality telephoto designed expressly to suit the needs of cinematographers as they move to the digital arena. The 300mm internal-focus lens features oversized dual-sided engravings with large and clear focus marks and a 210° Angular Focus Rotation Scale. Iris and focus gears are integrated. The cine-style support conveniently interfaces directly with Chrosziel and Arriflex bridgeplate systems. The lens also accepts two 52mm internal filters. Cinematographers will also appreciate that the lens features a long 300mm focal length, a fast T2.2 aperture, and a 13-inch MOD (minimum object distance). This unique combination is useful in creating the compressed shallow depth of field shots that are so popular in contemporary film production. Providing optimum performance at maximum aperture, the Tochigi Nikon is also excellent for shooting in low-light situations such as a sunset.

Band Pro Film/Video, Inc.
3403 West Pacific Ave.
Burbank, CA 91505
(818) 841-9655
www.bandpro.com

16x9 Inc.
3605 West Pacific Ave., Suite B
Burbank, CA 91505
(866) 800-1699
www.16x9inc.com

ZEISS DIGIPRIME HD
LENSES | Distributed by
16x9 Inc./Band Pro

The Zeiss DigiPrime lenses, developed by Carl Zeiss, bring Zeiss' superior engineering and unsurpassed manufacturing craftsmanship to the digital cinematography world. The new design is optimized to fully utilize both the creative and technical potential of the best HD cameras utilizing 2/3-inch imagers. Complete with B4 mount, the DigiPrimes offer custom features for film-style production with HD cameras, like no other lenses on the market. Cinematographers have long appreciated the advantages of prime lenses. Their smaller, lighter design makes them ideal for handheld camerawork. Built with fewer optical elements, primes have less glass-to-air surfaces, so images have greater clarity and brilliance and are less prone to flare and ghosting. DigiPrimes have been designed to deliver images far crisper and sharper than those achieved with a zoom. With an unchanging center of gravity (thanks to their internal focus design), DigiPrimes are suited for work requiring critical balance like Steadicam.

COOKE S4 HD ZOOM LENS 8-46MM T1.7 (5.75X8, F/1.4) | Distributed by ZGC, Inc.

The S4 HD Zoom Lens is the first Cooke video lens for the 21st century, created by the pioneers of video lens technology. Award-winning S4 film lens expertise applied to video has produced a High-Definition lens for the traditional cinematographer shooting in video. Cooke incorporated several features for the professional camera including a special cam mechanism for back focus adjustment, clear, calibrated focus scales, interchangeable footage and metric focus rings, and two opposing focus, zoom, and iris scales.

ZGC, Inc.
264 Morris Ave.
Mountain Lakes, NJ 07046
(973) 335-4460
www.zgc.com

COOKE S4 PRIME LENSES | Distributed by ZGC, Inc.

*1999 Academy of Motion Picture Arts & Sciences, Scientific and Engineering
Award for Optical and Mechanical Design*
2000 Two Queen's Awards for Enterprise, Innovation and International Trade

*"For parts of 'Erin Brockovich,' we wanted a very natural, almost documentary look.
On some of the location interiors, and inside cars, I let the windows go four or five
stops over. I had run a lot of tests on the new Cooke primes and I knew what they
could do. I was confident those windows would hold. And I knew veiling glare would-
n't wash out the interiors — I wouldn't lose the blacks. Looking again at the 'Erin'
footage, I still see a smoother transition from in focus to out than I get from any
other high-speed lens out there. And their sharpness is unbeatable."*

— Director of Photography Ed Lachman, ACS

Quote obtained from ZGC

Designed and developed in close technical collaboration with Clairmont Camera and Otto
Nemenz in Hollywood, the Cooke Series 4 Prime Lenses represent a major advance in fixed
focal length lenses for 35mm-format professional cinematography. Features include superb
control of flare, distortion, veiling glare, and spherical aberrations at full aperture. Cooke's
award-winning cam mechanism liberates the lens from a simple thread rotation, giving the
operator an appropriate rate of focus at all distances, and allows for better-spaced and more
detailed and visible index marks. Cooke focal lengths: 14, 16, 18, 21, 25, 27, 32, 25, 40, 50, 65, 75,
100, and 135mm, and a soft-focus attachment for the 65mm lens.

If you have used this gear and want to share your own experiences, comments, and suggestions in our next edition, send an e-mail to Catherine Lorenze at *DREAMGEAR@cox.net*. We are particularly interested in innovative ways you have used the gear that will help inspire other film, video, and TV professionals.

LENS
ADAPTERS, ATTACHMENTS, AND CONVERTERS

26

Century Optics:	Achromatic Diopters for the Canon XL1s
	IF Super Fisheye Adapter
	1.6X Tele-Converter
	2X Tele-Extender
	.6X Wide Angle Adapter for the Canon XL1s
	.7X Wide Angle Converter for the Canon XL1s
OpTex:	XLAnamorphic Adapter for the Canon XL1s
Spintec:	RD Rain and Snow Deflector
ZGC:	P+S Technik Mini35 Digital Adapter
	P+S Technik Pro35 Digital Converter

ACHROMATIC DIOPTERS FOR THE
CANON XL1S | By Century Optics

When the shot calls for an extreme close-up, choose Century Diopters. For maximum magnification and image clarity, these macro zoom attachments give your lenses more close-up range, while preserving zoom capabilities. Available in +2.0, +4.0, and +7.0 magnifications, Century Achromatic Diopters are essential whenever you need to focus tightly on a small object in tabletop, miniature, and flat-field videography. Two or more diopters can be stacked on the front of the lens for even more magnification to shoot exceptionally crisp shots of very small objects.

IF SUPER FISHEYE ADAPTER | By Century Optics

Century Precision Optics
11049 Magnolia Blvd.
North Hollywood, CA 91601
(800) 228-1254
www.centuryoptics.com

The IF Super Fisheye is specifically created for the 20X, 21X, and 22X IF broadcast lenses. Due to the Super Fisheye Adapter's characteristic barrel distortion, extreme low and high angle shots are made more dramatic. An attic crawl space induces heightened claustrophobia. A forest of tall skyscrapers bends menacingly over the audience. Because the Century Super Fisheye takes in a much wider angle of view than the human eye, it may be used to visually plunge audiences into a scene — surrounding them with a noisy crowd or exiling them to a lonely beach. While extreme telephoto shots tend to flatten the subject against the background, the Super Fisheye exaggerates depth, pulling nearby objects closer and causing distant objects to recede into the background.

1.6X TELE-CONVERTER FOR THE CANON XL1S | By Century Optics

Add the 1.6X Tele-Converter to the front of your 16X zoom to shift its focal range in the telephoto direction. It's the perfect tool when it's inconvenient, dangerous, or even impossible to move as close to the subject as you would like. The 1.6X Tele-Converter alters your zoom's focal length range from 5.5-88mm to 56-140mm, with no appreciable light loss. The Tele-Converter is especially effective in run-and-gun shooting situations because it attaches more quickly than rear-mount tele-extenders.

2X TELE-EXTENDER | By Century Optics

In situations that make it difficult, dangerous, or even impossible to move in closer to fill the frame with a distant subject, a Tele-Extender from Century Precision is the perfect solution. Mounted between the camera and video zoom, the Tele-Extender doubles the lens's focal length, enabling a shooter to capture faraway action in close-up. Once attached, the unit yields a two-stop light loss and shallow depth of field. If a zoom ranges from 9-144mm, a 2X Tele-Extender from Century Precision converts it in seconds to an 18-288mm. As a result, subjects that were previously out of range, across a river, a stadium, or a police barricade, now fill the frame.

Century Precision Optics
11049 Magnolia Blvd.
North Hollywood, CA 91601
(800) 228-1254
www.centuryoptics.com

.6X WIDE ANGLE ADAPTER FOR THE CANON XL1/XL1S | By Century Optics

Ideal for shooting situations in which zooming isn't needed, the .6X offers a 40% wider angle of view and minimal distortion. It allows partial zooming up to 8X while in auto-focus (loses focus beyond 8X). The resulting focal length is 3.3-26mm with a 72°-10.33° horizontal angle of view. Century offers a Bayonet Mount version that attaches with a twist to the front of your XL1's standard 16X or manual 14X lens in place of the factory sunshade.

.7X WIDE ANGLE CONVERTER FOR THE CANON XL1/XL1S | By Century Optics

Century's .7X Wide Angle Converter attaches quickly to the front of your XL1's 16:1 zoom, offering a 30% wider angle of view and full zoom-through capabilities. The .7X shifts the focal length range from 5.5–88mm to 3.85-61.6mm — with no appreciable light loss. Canon's 3X lens is compact and useful, but imagine switching those delicate electronic lenses quickly on a wet day at the beach. The .7X Wide Converter slips onto the front of the 16X zoom with a one-handed twist, instead. Yet it results in an effective focal length nearly as wide as the 3X (within half a millimeter) and zooms six times as far.

Century Precision Optics
11049 Magnolia Blvd.
North Hollywood, CA 91601
(800) 228-1254
www.centuryoptics.com

XLANAMORPHIC ADAPTER FOR THE CANON XL1S | By OpTex

This zoom-through Anamorphic Adapter offers XL1s users wide-screen recording while maintaining optical quality. Designed for use with the Canon XL1 6X Manual Lens, the OpTex XLAnamorphic Adapter optically squeezes a 16:9 image onto the 4:3 chips used in the camera. Due to the constraints of the optics, a mechanical zoom stop is provided to limit the minimum focal length to 12mm. The zoom-through capability covers from 12mm to 84mm focal lengths.

OpTex
20-26 Victoria Road, New Barnet
N. London EN4 9PF UK
+44 (0)2 084-412-199
www.optexint.com

RD RAIN AND SNOW DEFLECTOR | By Spintec

Spintec RD is the only lightweight rain and snow deflector. This revolutionary lens accessory is for professional video and film cameras and is used in news, sports, nature, and other field productions to remove the visual interference of rain and snow on the lens. Additional features of the Spintec RD include: no gyro effect when panning and tilting, fits practically all video and film lenses, and low power consumption.

Spintec
Beit Zayit 205
Jerusalem, 90815 Israel
+972-2-579-7999
www.spintec.co.il

P+S TECHNIK MINI35 DIGITAL ADAPTER | Distributed by ZGC, Inc.

Use 35mm film lenses on your mini-DV camera (Canon XL1, XL1s, or Sony PD150) to achieve virtually the same depth of field, focus, and angle of view as with a 35mm film camera. The Mini35 Digital Adapter is ideal for: film crews who want to get a true 35mm image while shooting preproduction trial footage and to e-mail filmlike quality trial footage from the field; and for professional videographers who want to reproduce the three-dimensional quality of 35mm film on video for better TV spots, Internet applications, and presentations. It's also great for film schools teaching 35mm framing, lighting, and depth-of-field control.

DREAM GEAR | LORENZE | 212

P+S TECHNIK PRO35 DIGITAL IMAGE CONVERTER | Distributed by ZGC, Inc.

The device allows broadcast videographers and digital filmmakers to attach any Arri PL mounted prime 35mm film lens to their High-Definition (HD) or Standard-Definition (SD) 2/3-inch video camera to obtain the three-dimensional quality of a 35mm film camera on videotape. By offering the three-dimensional quality of film, the Pro35 Digital Image Converter dramatically expands the look, definition, and potential of both HD and SD 2/3-inch-format video.

ZGC, Inc.
264 Morris Ave.
Mountain Lakes, NJ 07046
(973) 335-4460
www.zgc.com

LENS
CONTROLLERS

27

Arri:	WRC-1 Wireless Remote Control
Manfrotto:	522 Lanc Remote Control
16x9 Inc./Band Pro:	ZOE DV-Lanc for Mini-DV Cameras
	ZOE DVX Zoom Control for Panasonic's AG-DVX100
	ZOE II Zoom Control for Broadcast and Industrial Cameras
VariZoom:	StealthLX
	StealthZoom and StealthDVX

WRC-1 WIRELESS REMOTE CONTROL | By Arri

The WRC-1 is the new powerful remote control for all new Arri cameras (535, 535B, 435, 16SR3). With the new WRC-1 (Wireless Remote Control) Arri completes its wireless lens-control system, offering complete control of all camera parameters without cumbersome cable connections between the hand-control units and the camera. The WRC-1 allows control of camera speed, shutter angle, and lens iris. Its special strength is the many possibilities of combining and compensating parameters to keep exposure constant. Preprogrammed iris scales and an instant iris open function (Zap-button) for the quick check of the finder image add to the functionality of the system.

Arri Inc.
617 Route 303
Blauvelt, NY 10913
(845) 353-1400
www.arri.com

522 LANC REMOTE CONTROL | By Manfrotto and distributed by Bogen Photo

This versatile command center puts the essential controls for most mini-DV cameras, such as focus, record, zoom, backlight, and fader, right at your fingertips. Now, the videographer can operate both camera movement and recording controls with the same hand — finally freeing the operator to take care of creative decisions rather than having to worry about how to reach the camera buttons, follow the subject, and keep movements smooth all at the same time.

Bogen Photo Corp.
565 East Crescent Ave.
P.O. Box 506
Ramsey, NJ 07446-0506
(201) 818-9500
www.bogenphoto.com
www.manfrotto.com

ZOE DV-LANC FOR MINI-DV CAMERAS | Distributed by 16x9 Inc./Band Pro

Now mini-DV shooters can finally enjoy professional zoom moves and more — with their camcorder's existing lens — via the new ZOE DV-Lanc. Available from 16x9 Inc. and manufactured by Bebob Engineering in Germany, the easy-to-use ZOE DV-Lanc puts true variable-speed stepless zoom control at the operator's fingertips. Plus, the tiny unit also provides focus adjustment, record start/stop, and camera on/off functions. The ZOE DV-Lanc weighs just four ounces and features glitch-free proprietary software.

16x9 Inc.
3605 West Pacific Ave., Suite B
Burbank, CA 91505
(866) 800-1699
www.16x9inc.com

Band Pro Film/Video, Inc.
3403 West Pacific Ave.
Burbank, CA 91505
(818) 841-9655
www.bandpro.com

ZOE DVX ZOOM LENS CONTROL FOR THE PANASONIC AG-DVX100 | Distributed by 16x9 Inc./Band Pro

16x9 Inc. presents a professional smooth zoom lens control for the Panasonic AG-DVX100 camcorder. Manufactured by Bebob Engineering in Germany, the easy-to-use ZOE DVX puts true variable-speed stepless zoom control at the operator's fingertips. Plus, the tiny unit also provides record start/stop. The ZOE DVX weighs just four ounces and features glitch-free proprietary software specially designed to work with Panasonic's protocols.

ZOE II ZOOM CONTROL FOR BROADCAST AND INDUSTRIAL CAMERAS | Distributed by 16x9 Inc./Band Pro

Professional camera operators can now enjoy smooth zooms, without bulky and imprecise remote, with the new ZOE II. Available from 16x9 Inc. and manufactured by Bebob Engineering in Germany, compact ZOE II puts true variable-speed stepless zoom control at the operator's fingertips. In addition, the pocket-size unit provides reversible zoom direction, return function, and a record start/stop button. The ZOE II weighs just 5.29 ounces and can be used with more than one camera system and different lenses simply by exchanging the adapter cable (sold as spares).

Band Pro Film/Video, Inc.
3403 West Pacific Ave.
Burbank, CA 91505
(818) 841-9655
www.bandpro.com

16x9 Inc.
3605 West Pacific Ave.
Suite B
Burbank, CA 91505
(866) 800-1699
www.16x9inc.com

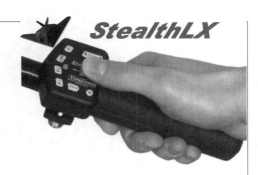

StealthLX

STEALTHLX FOR CANON AND SONY MINI-V AND HI-8 CAMCORDERS | By VariZoom

VariZoom's new StealthLX is small in size but big in performance! Its stylish and lightweight body is built with VariZoom's proprietary TAL technology and the highest degree of craftsmanship. This high-quality yet economical alternative to VariZoom's Pro-L and PG-L professional line of controls is the "must have control" for all videographers when low price and/or small size is a factor. This unique miniature control will fit on nearly any tripod, camera support, or stabilizer. Features of the StealthLX include a super-smooth pressure-sensitive zoom thumb control and an LED light to indicate record, battery low, tape out, and other indicators.

VariZoom
P.O. Box 201990
Austin, TX 78720
(888) 826-3399
www.varizoom.com

STEALTHZOOM FOR SONY AND CANON MINI-DV AND HI8 STEALTHDVX FOR PANASONIC'S AG-DVX100

By VariZoom

VariZoom's new Stealth is small in size but big in performance! This high-quality yet economical alternative to VariZoom's Pro-L and PG-L professional line of controls is the must-have control for all videographers when low price and/or small size is a factor. This unique miniature control will fit on nearly any tripod, camera support, or stabilizer. Unique features include our variable-speed zoom thumb control, which allows the user to maintain the slowest crawl or gradually ramp up speed and then decrease speed gradually all in one smooth motion!

VariZoom
P.O. Box 201990
Austin, TX 78720
(888) 826-3399
www.varizoom.com

LIGHTING 28

Arri:
Arri Daylight (Fresnel Daylight Lamphead)
Arri Daylight Compact 6000 (Fresnel Daylight Lamphead)
Arri Studio 5000 (Fresnel Tungsten Lamphead)
ArriSun 40/25 Par (Par Daylight Lamphead)
Arrilite 2000 (Open-face Tungsten Lamphead)

Chimera:
Daylite Bank
Daylite Senior and Daylite Senior Plus
MICRO Lightbank
Pancake Lantern
Plus One Lightbanks
Quartz and Quartz Plus Banks

Cool-Lux:
SL 3000 On-Camera Softlight
U-3 Broadcast Lighting

Frezzi:
MFSB-2 Soft Box
Mini-Fill Quartz Tungsten Lighting
Mini-Sun Gun HMI Lighting
SSG-200 HMI Super-Sun Gun

Innovision Optics:
Fiber Optic Lighting

Kino Flo:
Kamio System
Parabeam

Lowel:
Caselite 2/Caselite 4
Rifa-lite 44 Collapsible Softlight

LTM:
Prolight 6/12KW

PAG:
Paglight

Photoflex:
CineDome
MovieDome
WhiteDome nxt

Satellight-X:
Satellight-X HMI Softlight

ARRI DAYLIGHT
(FRESNEL DAYLIGHT LAMPHEAD)
By
Arri Inc.

The Daylight range using double-ended daylight lamps has been the mainstay of the film industry for many years. Arri AD spotlights have the largest lenses in their class and the finest light distribution so far. The smaller daylight wattages have been superseded by the smaller Compact range, while the AD18/12kW remains unrivalled.

ARRI DAYLIGHT COMPACT 6000
(FRESNEL DAYLIGHT LAMPHEAD)
By
Arri Inc.

The Arri Compact Daylight Fresnels are the preferred choice when Fresnel spotlights with daylight characteristics, compact size, high efficiency, and light weight are required. Arri's elegant modular construction, using corrosion-free aluminum extrusions and lightweight die castings, offers great structural strength and weather resistance. Together with Arri flicker-free Electronic Ballast, the rugged Compact range is the ideal choice for all locations.

Arri Inc.
617 Route 303
Blauvelt, NY 10913
(845) 353-1400
www.arri.com

ARRI STUDIO 5000 (FRESNEL TUNGSTEN LAMPHEAD) | By Arri Inc.

The Arri Studio Fresnel series is the ideal choice for TV and film studios where tungsten lampheads are required. The large short focal length lens sizes provide optimum even light output. Arri Studio Fresnels are available in both manual and pole-operated versions.

ARRISUN 40/25 (PAR DAYLIGHT LAMPHEAD) | By Arri Inc.

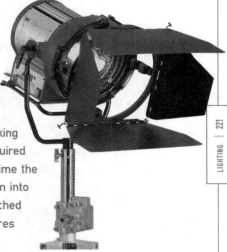

Together with the Compact range, the ArriSun is the "working horse" on location. Whenever punch or bounce light is required on a set, an ArriSun is the ultimate answer. For the first time the interaction of lamp, reflector, and converter lens was taken into consideration and computer simulated, resulting in unmatched light performance. A wide range of converter lenses ensures maximum beam control in all situations.

ARRILITE 2000 (OPEN-FACE TUNGSTEN LAMPHEAD) | By Arri Inc.

The Arrilite series is an open-face, focusing tungsten floodlight ideal for ENG (Electronic News Gathering), field production, and fast-turnaround location use. The specially designed reflector gives a balance between controllability and efficiency and provides an exceptionally even field of illumination.

DAYLITE BANK | By Chimera Lighting

Daylite Banks are designed to handle large-scale lighting jobs such as commercials and motion pictures. Their increased depth allows the full-flood beam of a large Fresnel fixture to fill the front diffusion screen of the Lightbank and deliver a beautiful, translucent quality of light. Daylite Banks have large rear openings and heat-resistant materials that enable them to be used with Fresnels up to 10,000 watts. Circular Speed Ring sizes range from 9 to 21 inches (23 to 53cm) in diameter. Daylite Banks are available in small to large.

DAYLITE SENIOR AND DAYLITE SENIOR PLUS | By Chimera Lighting

The Daylite Senior was designed for the really big jobs. Its 24- to 29-inch (61 to 74cm) Circular Speed Ring diameters work with Big Eye Teners, 12,000-, 18,000-, 20,000-watt Silver Bullets, and other similarly sized giant Fresnels. The Daylite Senior is available in one size (large), and it delivers large quantities of directional, controlled, soft light. The two-person setup/teardown method works best with the Daylite Senior.

MICRO LIGHTBANK | By Chimera Lighting

Chimera's MICRO Bank System allows the videographer the option of creating a far broader diffused light source when using a single or dual model of onboard camera light. The MICRO Bank's screen size is 5 x 7 inches (13 x 18cm) for single lights and 5 x 8 inches (13 x 20cm) for dual lights. Now with a standard density and 1/4 grid front screen. The MICRO kit includes the Lightbank, poles, and dedicated mounting bracket for your light.

PANCAKE LANTERN | By Chimera Lighting

The Pancake Lantern (our latest creation) is already making waves in Hollywood. This "flat" Lantern, with its innovative, removable, zipper-panel skirt, offers great possibilities for fine-tuning light falloff. The Lantern can be set up on any Speed Ring from the Strobe or Video Pro Bank category, but for maximum, omnidirectional effectiveness use it on a "bare bulb"-type lighting instrument. Hook and loop-attached skirts can be used to selectively block light. Available in five different sizes.

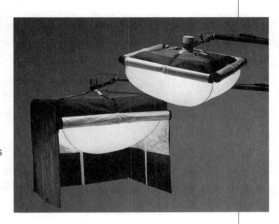

PLUS ONE LIGHTBANKS | By Chimera Lighting

Chimera has upgraded their standard line of film and video Lightbanks by making the front screens removable. Called Plus One, the new series of Lightbanks retain all the features of the Pro series, and add the flexibility of removable screens.

QUARTZ AND QUARTZ PLUS BANKS | By Chimera Lighting

Ultra heat-resistant materials and versatility make Quartz Banks the choice for jobs large and small. These standard-depth banks can accommodate Par and other open-face lights both in tungsten and HMI from 1,200 watts up to 10,000 watts. Quartz Banks fit Circular Speed Ring sizes 9 through 21 inches (23 to 53cm), plus you can combine up to four Lowel DPs or three Totas. You can even use Video Pro Rings and our Quartz to Video Pro adapter poles #4099.

Chimera Lighting
1812 Valtec Lane
Boulder, CO 80301
(888) 444-1812
www.chimeralighting.com

SL 3000 ON-CAMERA SOFTLIGHT | By Cool-Lux

Never has so much effort and technology been applied to engineering the world's finest on-camera digital video light. The remarkable SL 3000, measuring only 4" x 4" x 2" (as a softlight), delivers a higher quality of illuminating power than all other on-camera lights using a direct light beam. While enormous effort was applied to achieve the technology of the SL 3000, it takes just a push of a button to turn it on. After you push that magical button, a heavenly glow will hug your subject, giving you the best picture the world has ever seen from an on-camera light! Or, by removing the hood you can convert your on-camera softlight into a 4" x 2" on-camera broad light creating a cinema look for everyone to admire. Furthermore, the beauty of the SL 3000 design and its innovative engineering provide an on-camera light that fits in the palm of your hand!

U-3 BROADCAST LIGHTING | By Cool-Lux

This rock-solid fixture is backed by a three-year warranty and is actually six fixtures in one. You will never have to compromise artistic control with the limitations of a single light source again. A selection of three lamps allows a choice of a 20- or 35-watt flood or spot. Add or subtract light from a scene without changing its color temperature. Zoom from a single-flood close-up to long-distance action simply by shifting the light from flood to spot. You can have as much as 10 lux at 100 feet or switch back to a close-up without blinding your subjects. With the U-3, you will always have light, even if a lamp burns out, plus save battery energy when you're using only one lamp.

Cool-Lux
412 Calle San Pablo #200
Camarillo, CA 93012
(805) 482-4820
www.cool-lux.com

MFSB-2 SOFT BOX FOR FREZZI MINI-FILLS AND FREZZI HMI MINI-SUN GUNS | By Frezzi Energy Systems

The MFSB-2 is a lightweight, collapsible diffusion box that easily mounts to any Frezzi Mini-Fill or HMI Mini-Sun Gun. Designed like a professional studio light box, the MFSB-2 provides a soft, even distribution of light while eliminating hard shadows. It easily folds up to fit into a pocket and weighs only four ounces. The unique, clear front pouch on the MFSB-2 allows you to slide in the diffusion and/or color-correction filters of your choice.

MINI-FILL QUARTZ TUNGSTEN LIGHTING | By Frezzi Energy Systems

Frezzi's award-winning lighthead, the Mini-Fill was originally designed by Frezzolini for the first Mount Everest climb. It has continuously been updated and improved for the needs of the broadcasting community. The Mini-Fill's reliability, performance, and portability have established its international reputation and inspired an entire line of lighting products available today. Previously known only to the broadcasting community, this exceptional lighthead has become the light of choice for the professional videographer.

Frezzi Energy Systems
5 Valley Street
Hawthorne, NJ 07506
(800) 345-1030
www.frezzi.com

MINI-SUN GUN HMI LIGHTING

By Frezzi Energy Systems

In 1996 Frezzi revolutionized the lighting industry with the world's first camera-mountable HMI light. The tremendous popularity of the 24-watt Mini-Sun Gun inspired the expansion of Frezzi's growing line of HMIs. The Frezzi family of Mini-HMIs includes 18W, 24W, and 50W models. Now available in a sleek new ultra-lightweight rugged one-piece design, these expertly crafted HMIs operate on 12 to 14.4 volts, are 400% more power efficient than quartz-tungsten lighting, and therefore provide the advantage of long run times with high output at 5600K.

"Being CNN's reporter for nature and wildlife stories means 'assignments' are usually extended trips for more than a month to developing countries. Because my wife and I work alone, it is very important for us to minimize the number and weight of our equipment cases. When I saw the Frezzi MA-50 Sun Gun, I knew we could really use it in our work."

— Gary Stiecker, Global Environmental Reporter for CNN

Quote obtained from Frezzi's Web site

SSG-200 200-WATT HMI SUPER-SUN GUN

By Frezzi Energy Systems

Frezzi's 200-watt HMI, engineered for news gathering, produces a wide flat optical field, providing a light output unmatched in its size/weight category. At a distance of 10 feet the Frezzi Super-Sun Gun 200 produces up to two times the output of a 400W Par HMI fixture with a wide-angle lens. This incredible output is the direct result of Frezzi's computer-optimized five-inch open-face parabolic reflector. This new 200-watt fixture, constructed with a strong aluminum housing, is lightweight and compact, weighing in at only 3.5 pounds. The new dimmable Frezzi AC and DC 200W electronic ballasts are the smallest available in today's market, and may be used worldwide.

Frezzi Energy Systems
5 Valley Street
Hawthorne, NJ 07506
(800) 345-1030
www.frezzi.com

FIBER
OPTIC
LIGHTING | Distributed by Innovision Optics

Innovision's flexible ultra-bright Fiber Optic Cable and Light Source is ideal for studio, stage, underwater, and architectural lighting. The system provides end-point and linear illumination. Filters within the light source offer a range of colorful gradients and effects. Available in an array of different diameters and configurations. Fiber Optic Lighting is ideal for stage lighting, product highlighting, special effect, set design, signage, and display backlighting. It's also an ideal substitute for neon.

Innovision Optics, Inc.
1719 21st Street
Santa Monica, CA 90404
(310) 453-4866
www.innovision-optics.com

KAMIO
SYSTEM | By Kino Flo Inc.

Oh the places you'll go with this new, lightweight Kamio ring light from Kino Flo. Its unique halo of soft illumination is an ideal beauty light. The flicker-free Kamio System comes complete with a Kamio fixture and dimming ballast, and includes a reflector, detachable head extension, and matte box assembly with lens-mount clamp and filter-tray holders.

Kino Flo Incorporated
10848 Cantara Street
Sun Valley, CA 91352
(818) 767-6528
www.kinoflo.com

PARABEAM | By Kino Flo Inc.

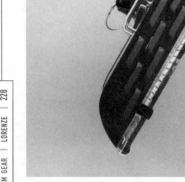

The sleek Parabeam boasts optics that compress the focal range of the light wave to produce a broad, soft source along the horizontal axis and a narrow beam on the vertical axis. The 24" x 24" Parabeam, for example, can light a four-person news desk from approximately 15 feet away. It sweeps back the darkness in the foreground without washing out the background on the set. With a simple rotation of the fixture, it can focus on just one of the four subjects.

Kino Flo Incorporated
10848 Cantara Street
Sun Valley, CA 91352
(818) 767-6528
www.kinoflo.com

CASELITE 2/
CASELITE 4

| By Lowel–Light
Manufacturing, Inc.

The current popularity of fluorescent lights in film and video production is well deserved. They offer cool, soft, and efficient light at several times the output of incandescent halogen sources. Unfortunately, they can also be too cumbersome and fragile to use on location. The Caselite 2 and Caselite 4 solve that problem by being compact, lightweight, rugged, and completely self-contained without sacrificing output or light quality. The all-in-one Caselite is both light and case combined.

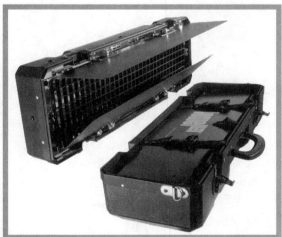

Lowel-Light Manufacturing, Inc.
140 58th Street
Brooklyn, NY 11220
(800) 334-3426
www.lowel.com

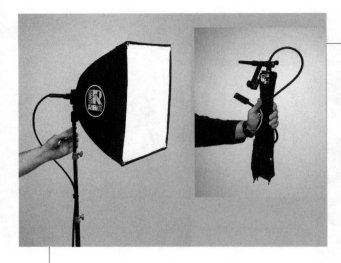

RIFA-LITE 44
(250W COLLAPSIBLE SOFTLIGHT) | By Lowel-Light Manufacturing, Inc.

Lowel-Light Manufacturing, Inc.
140 58th Street
Brooklyn, NY 11220
(800) 334-3426
www.lowel.com

Introducing the Lowel Rifa-lite 44, the "Baby Rifa" — an impressively compact, self-contained, 250-watt AC/DC, collapsible softlight that sets up in a minute or less. Bathe almost anything, from talking heads to tabletop stills, in luxurious, soft light. It's the perfect complement to today's compact, light-sensitive digital cameras and film stocks.

PROLIGHT 6/12KW | By LTM

The Prolight 6/12KW combines the advantages of single-ended lamp technology and short focal Fresnel lens to optimize light performance while considerably reducing weight and size. The light gives an extremely powerful beam in spot and smooth, wide spread in flood position. The Prolight 6/12KW is compatible with both magnetic and the new LTM 6/12KW electronic ballast.

LTM
7755 Haskell Avenue
Van Nuys, CA 91406
(800) 762-4291
www.ltmlighting.com

PAG**LIGHT** | By PAG and distributed by Ste-Man, Inc. in Hollywood

PAG's unique, patented design makes Paglight the coolest-running and most versatile camera light in the business. The Paglight is elegantly styled, and its proportions blend perfectly with the very latest professional broadcast cameras. In addition to the aesthetic and ergonomic qualities of this product, there has been a depth of scientific development embodied that sets this camera light apart from any of its competitors.

PAG USA
10663 Burbank Boulevard
N. Hollywood, CA 91601
(818) 760-8265
www.pagusa.com

Ste-Man, Inc.
10663 Burbank Boulevard
N. Hollywood, CA 91601
(818) 760-8240
www.ste-man.com

CINEDOME | By Photoflex

Our newest softbox has a narrower, deeper profile designed to maximize the light projection of your Fresnel lights. Our revolutionary Brimstone fabric is extremely heat-resistant and can easily handle up to 2,000 watts. The highly reflective silver interior ensures maximum light output from any light source. The removable face and baffle allow you to go from sharp contrast to buttery-soft lighting in seconds. Our unique, internal baffle eliminates extreme highlights and hot spots, creating even, natural lighting.

Photoflex
97 Hangar Way
Watsonville, CA 95076
(800) 486-2674
www.photoflex.com

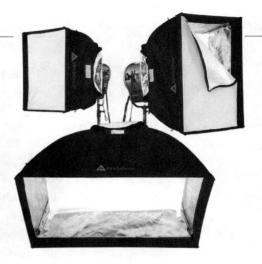

MOVIEDOME | By Photoflex

One of our newest softboxes, the MovieDome, is designed for Par, Fresnel, and open-face lights (both HMI and tungsten) to be used in movie and video production. Our revolutionary Kilnstone fabric is the most heat-resistant on the market. Coupled with our revolutionary vent flaps, it can easily handle lights in excess of 10,000 watts. Built with our Quick Release Corners, the MovieDome sets up and tears down in seconds, making it the fastest softbox on the market.

Photoflex
97 Hangar Way
Watsonville, CA 95076
(800) 486-2674
www.photoflex.com

WHITEDOME NXT | By Photoflex

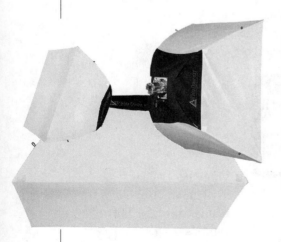

The unique, translucent design of the WhiteDome nxt produces soft, nearly shadowless lighting. With its bright, diffused light, the WhiteDome nxt is ideal for lighting your videos, films, and large sets. The WhiteDome nxt is made with our proprietary Brimstone fabric to be heat-resistant and durable. It can handle lights up to 3,000 watts including the 4-Star multihead connector (up to 1,000 watts in a small and 2,000 watts in a medium).

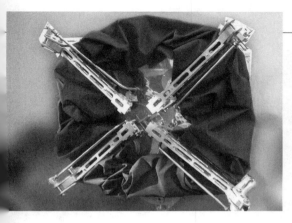

SATELLIGHT-X HMI SOFTLIGHT | By Satellight-X, Inc.

The Satellight-X is 4' x 5' x 1' and contains four 575W, individually switched HMI bulbs. Ballasts and switches are fully contained within the light. There are no header cables! To store, the Satellight-X collapses to approximately 2' x 2 1/2' x 1'. Full setup, from case to lights on, is two to three minutes for two people. Wrap time is the same. The light can be used bare or with other diffusers and gels. No other softlight device has the output, flexibility, speed, and small footprint of the Satellight-X. It can be backed into a tight corner, hung overhead, underslung, or aimed from floor level. And it's complete on one stand.

Satellight-X, Inc.
(866) 315-1400
www.satellight-x.com

If you have used this gear and want to share your own experiences, comments, and suggestions in our next edition, send an e-mail to Catherine Lorenze at *DREAMGEAR@cox.net*. We are particularly interested in innovative ways you have used the gear that will help inspire other film, video, and TV professionals.

LIGHTING KITS 29

Cool-Lux: Cool-Kit Broadcast Kit
                          Cool-Kit Location Kit

Frezzi: Standard and Dimmer Mini-Fill Kits for the Canon XL1

Lowel: ViP Kits

Mole-Richardson: DigiMole 200 AC/DC Pro Kit
                          Molequartz Tweenie/Teenie-Mole Combo Kit

Photoflex: ActionDome ENG Kits

COOL-KIT BROADCAST KIT | By Cool-Lux

The Cool-Kit Broadcast Kit was designed to anticipate the needs of the news reporter with plenty of room to expand or add your own equipment. Along with clamps, brackets, and adapters, the Cool-Kit Broadcast Kit also features a Mini-Cool Light, a 74W/12V Flood Lamp, a 22W/12V Medium Lamp, a Stand Adapter U-3 Light, and a Heavy-Duty 8 Ah NiCad Max Power Belt.

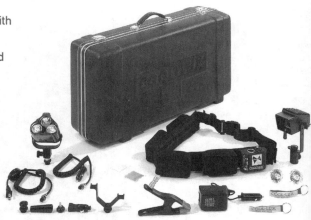

COOL-KIT LOCATION LIGHTING KIT | By Cool-Lux

The Cool-Kit Location Lighting Kit is our best start-up package for the budget-conscious individual. With room to expand, it is ideal for videotaping large groups, interviews, or weddings. Along with clamps, brackets, and adapters, the Location Lighting Kit also features two Mini-Cool Key Lights, two 150W/120V Flood Lamps, and one Micro-Lux On-Camera Light.

Cool-Lux
412 Calle San Pablo #200
Camarillo, CA 93012
(805) 482-4820
www.cool-lux.com

STANDARD AND DIMMER MINI-FILL KITS FOR THE CANON XL1 | By Frezzi Energy Systems

Each 3.5-lb. kit contains the following items: one Standard or Dimmer Mini-Fill with NP1S connector, one NPI-CB bracket to attach NP1 battery to Canon MA-100, one LS-21A 1.5" stud (shoe mount), one FNP-1S 12V 2.3 Ah battery, and one FTC-NP1 14-hour charger for FNP-1S battery.

Frezzi Energy Systems
5 Valley Street
Hawthorne, NJ 07506
(800) 345-1030
www.frezzi.com

VIP KITS | By Lowel-Light Manufacturing, Inc.

Lightweight and easy to carry, these popular kits have varying combinations of Pro and V-lights, plus lamps and accessories. With its high-intensity #2 Reflector and Prismatic Glass, the tiny and focusable Pro-light is more efficient than a mini-Fresnel of equal wattage. The V-light is powerful enough to light a small room, yet small enough to fit in a large pocket. We have updated many ViP and ViP Go Kits, adding light controls and mounting accessories to many of the kits to increase their versatility and value.

Lowel-Light Manufacturing, Inc.
140 58th Street
Brooklyn, NY 11220
(800) 334-3426
www.lowel.com

DIGIMOLE 200 AC/DC PRO KIT — TYPE 82856 | By Mole-Richardson

The DigiMole 200 is designed as a compact and lightweight fixture that will focus from flood to spot in one, easy motion. Whether you choose the Starter or Pro kit, you will be pleased with the wide range of uses this handy little fixture offers. They are great for key lighting, backlighting, and bounces, or can be used with an optional Chimera Lightbank.

Mole-Richardson Co.
937 North Sycamore Ave.
Hollywood, CA 90038
(323) 851-0111
www.mole.com

MOLEQUARTZ TWEENIE/TEENIE -MOLE COMBO KIT | By Mole-Richardson

This all-in-one kit is ideal for motion picture, video, and television as a key light, backlight, or kicker. The kit weighs a total of 61 lb. Lighting features include two 650-watt Molequartz Tweenie Solarspots and one 650-watt Molequartz Teenie-Mole.

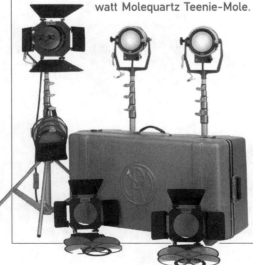

ACTIONDOME ENG KITS | By Photoflex

The ActionDome ENG Kits are designed to meet the needs of professionals who need news-gathering capabilities. Features include Diffusion to soften hard, high-contrast light, and Universal Kit Hardware that allows the softbox to be mounted to nearly any camera.

Photoflex
97 Hangar Way
Watsonville, CA 95076
(800) 486-2674
www.photoflex.com

MARINE AND UNDERWATER
PRODUCTION TOOLS

Amphibico:

Amphibicam Broadcast Video Housing
LCD High Performance Color Monitor
Optimum 110 Aspheric Wide-Angle Adapter
VHPD150 Marine Video Housing

DPA Microphones:

Hydrophone 8011 Microphone

HydroFlex:

Behind-The-Scenes (BTS) Video Cameras
HydroPar 4000W SE HMI
HydroHead Remote Pan and Tilt Head
HydroRama Lighting Fixture
IMAX IW5 Deep Water Camera Housing
SeaPar 1200W HMI
Underwater Video Monitor
35-3 RemoteAquaCam
435 RemoteAquaCam
35-3 Shallow Water Housing
35-3 Surf Housing

16x9 Inc./Bank Pro:

Betacam Splash Housing
DVCAM Splash Housing

AMPHIBICAM BROADCAST VIDEO HOUSING | By Amphibico

(Image Shows Product with Discovery Arc Lights)

For underwater feature film and broadcast production, the future is here with our Amphibicam Broadcast Video Housing. Designed for virtually all Betacams but more specifically for the Sony HDW-F900 HD Camcorder, the housing is rated to operate to a depth of 100m (330 ft.). Aspheric and Binary technology has been incorporated in our lens system, delivering wide-angle, zoom-through, zero-distortion imaging. The electronics are the most sophisticated ever developed for underwater video, providing 16 camera and lens controls at your fingertips — all designed with the diver and videographer in mind.

Amphibico
459 Deslauriers
St. Laurent, Quebec
Canada H4N 1W2
(514) 333-8666
www.amphibico.com

ACFMO350 LCD HIGH PERFORMANCE COLOR MONITOR | By Amphibico

This aluminum-constructed external monitor is for use with all Amphibico and other brand housings. It comes complete with mounting bracket, sunshade, spare o-ring kit, and underwater cable connectors for easy installation, and is designed for under or above water use. Other features include a large, 3.5-inch screen size for easy viewing at arm's length, and compatibility with NTSC or PAL at the flick of a switch.

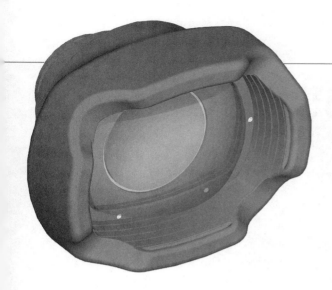

OPTIMUM 110 ASPHERIC WIDE-ANGLE UNDERWATER ADAPTER | By Amphibico

The Optimum 110 ultra-compact wide-angle underwater adapter is for all Amphibico bayonet-mounted housings. The aspheric wide-angle adapter delivers minimal distortion images while maintaining zoom capability for high-resolution close-ups. In wide-angle mode, the system focuses to the dome surface and has a field view of 100°. For macro shooting, the lens focuses to just four inches of the subject in telephoto mode.

VHPD150 MARINE VIDEO HOUSING FOR SONY'S DVCAM DSR-PD150 | By Amphibico

Designed for professional underwater use, the VHPD150 is an aluminum housing for the SONY DCR-VX2000/PD150 that allows full use of camcorder functions at depths of 330 feet. The housing features electronic push-button controls and manual controls, provides excellent underwater balance, and has a unique front camera entry design that makes camcorder installation easy. Camera weight on land is 15.5 lb. (7.04kg) fully loaded with camera battery, and in seawater 6 oz. (170g) negative buoyancy.

HYDROPHONE 8011 | By DPA Microphones

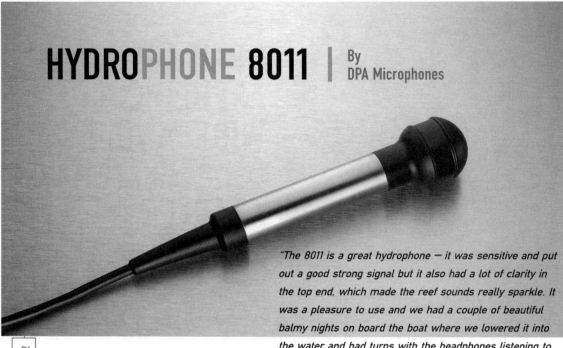

"The 8011 is a great hydrophone — it was sensitive and put out a good strong signal but it also had a lot of clarity in the top end, which made the reef sounds really sparkle. It was a pleasure to use and we had a couple of beautiful balmy nights on board the boat where we lowered it into the water and had turns with the headphones listening to the nighttime reef. On one occasion, on a glassed-out moonlit evening, working with the hydrophone from a Zodiac, I was able to capture a call from a baleen whale passing in the distance. Even though the whale was a long way off, this was a pretty special moment."

— Ashton Ward, Sound Recordist and Owner of Wild Blue Music in Australia, commenting on his use of the 8011 Hydrophone for a documentary about Raine Island for the National Geographic Channel

Quote obtained from DPA's Web site

The Type 8011 is the only 48V phantom-powered waterproof microphone specially designed to handle the high sound-pressure levels and the high static ambient pressure in water and other fluids. The hydrophone uses a piezoelectric sensing element, which is frequency-compensated to match the special acoustic conditions under water. A 10m high-quality audio cable is vulcanized to the body of the hydrophone and fitted with a standard three-pin XLR. The output is electronically balanced and offers more than 100dB dynamic range. Use it for water sports, film shoots, or broadcast shoots for effects with great results.

DPA Microphones
Gydevang 42-44
DK-3450 Alleroed
Denmark
+45 (0)4 814-2828
www.dpamicrophones.com

BEHIND-THE-SCENES (BTS) VIDEO CAMERAS | Distributed by HydroFlex

Topside crews can get information about the overall situation below the water with the Behind-The-Scenes (BTS) Video Camera. It comes with a wide-angle, fixed-focus lens that covers from four inches to infinity. The small color or black-and-white camera easily mounts to C-stands, etc. The rental kit includes a 5/8-inch spud mount, a 12V block battery, and 100 ft. of cable that terminates to a standard BNC connector. Depth rated to 1,000 ft. and manufactured by DeepSea Power & Light, San Diego.

HydroFlex, Inc.
5335 McConnell Ave.
Los Angeles, CA 90066
(310) 301-8187
www.hydroflex.com

HYDROPAR 4000W SE HMI | Distributed by HydroFlex

HydroPar lighting systems are state-of-the-art underwater lights specifically designed for feature and commercial film production. The HyroPar 4000W SE is for underwater use only. It is available with interchangeable reflectors for spot, medium, and flood configurations. Because the globe is enclosed in a tight-fitting U/V-coated quartz envelope, the beam pattern is adjusted by using interchangeable reflectors to collimate the light. We use reflectors, not Par diffuser lenses, to adjust the beam. When a Par diffuser lens is placed underwater so that both surfaces (especially the inner shaped surface) are wet, the ability of the diffuser to spread light is significantly reduced. Underwater, the glass diffuser has an effective index of refraction of 1.108 and hence not a lot of bending power. Depth rated to 100 ft., it weighs 32 lb. on the surface and 11 lb. underwater. 220V power is required.

HYDROHEAD REMOTE PAN AND TILT HEAD | Distributed by HydroFlex

The HydroHead from HydroFlex is a waterproof remote pan-and-tilt head. It is the perfect complement to our 435 and 35-3 RemoteAquaCams. The HydroHead's light weight and low profile, combined with the tubular hydrodynamics of the RemoteAquaCams, allow this system to glide through the water with less resistance than anything currently available. A large selection of camera combinations and HydroFlex custom splash bags can be fitted for above-water shooting in wet situations.

HYDRORAMA LIGHTING FIXTURE | Distributed by HydroFlex

Illuminating large areas underwater is quick and easy with the HydroRama. This powerful fixture is especially effective in creating dappled lighting effects. Depending upon your requirements, the unit can be configured with either dual 4000W SE HMIs or dual 5000W SE incandescent lamps. Designed for submersible use only, the unit is depth rated to 100 ft.

HydroFlex, Inc.
5335 McConnell Ave.
Los Angeles, CA 90066
(310) 301-8187
www.hydroflex.com

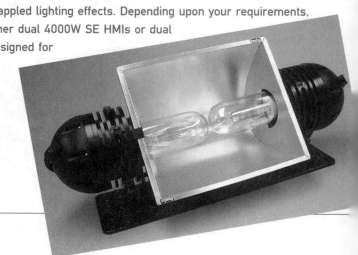

IMAX IW5 DEEP WATER CAMERA HOUSING | Distributed by HydroFlex

The IMAX housing is a unique, truly state-of-the-art camera system built for the IW5 camera with 1,000-foot magazines. This design will accommodate either the IMAX or OMNIMAX formats. The 30mm and 40mm lenses employed with this system each have their own dedicated dome ports. A specially configured low-profile camera body door with a video tap has been installed to allow for viewing on an underwater video viewfinder. The rear shell was cast from a special aluminum alloy, enabling this housing to withstand depths to 2,000 ft.

HydroFlex, Inc.
5335 McConnell Ave.
Los Angeles, CA 90066
(310) 301-8187
www.hydroflex.com

SEAPAR 1200W HMI | Distributed by HydroFlex

The original underwater HMIs designed by Richard Mula and Pete Romano for the movie *The Abyss*, the SeaPar 1200W HMI has been extensively used in the motion picture and commercial industries on countless projects worldwide. This light made such a profound impact on the industry that in 1991 the lamp received a Technical Achievement Award from The Academy of Motion Picture Arts and Sciences for "Safety and Portability On Wet or Dry Sets." To date, the SeaPar lighting system is the only underwater lighting to be allowed in NASA's Neutral Buoyancy Lab (NBL) in Houston. On the surface the SeaPar 1200W weighs 28 lb., and underwater just 4.5 lb. Depth rated to 120 ft.

HydroFlex, Inc.
5335 McConnell Ave.
Los Angeles, CA 90066
(310) 301-8187
www.hydroflex.com

UNDER**WATER** VIDEO MONITOR | Distributed by HydroFlex

This HydroFlex underwater video monitor incorporates a flat 5.6-inch color screen in an aluminum housing with a built-in hood. It offers excellent off-axis viewing and the ability to mount the unit on a ball-joint arm, a swivel-type yoke, or handheld. It works great as a director's video assist monitor mounted on a foam float when shooting in flooded sets.

HydroFlex, Inc.
5335 McConnell Ave.
Los Angeles, CA 90066
(310) 301-8187
www.hydroflex.com

35-3 REMOTE**AQUA**CAM | Distributed by HydroFlex

Designed primarily for use with remote heads for on the water or wet filming, the HydroFlex 35-3 RemoteAquaCam represents a new approach to waterproof motion picture camera systems. Incorporating an Arriflex 35-3 body (standard 12 volt or Pan Arri 24 volt), custom SL Cine 400-foot magazines, and Preston remote focus and iris controls, this low-profile camera system fits inside an 11-inch-diameter tube and weighs in at only 62 lb. fully loaded. Zeiss, Cooke, or Panavision spherical and

anamorphic lenses can easily be fitted. In the handheld mode, a HydroFlex 5.6-inch monitor allows the operator to set the frame while the camera assistant rolls camera and pulls focus and iris from as far as 100 ft. away. The complete system is depth rated to 100 ft.

435 REMOTE**AQUA**CAM

Distributed by
HydroFlex

The 435 RAC (RemoteAquaCam) was engineered primarily for use with remote three-axis heads on cranes for at sea or wet stage work. Field testing has also proven the 435 RAC to be as useful for handheld filming under the water or floating on the surface. Designed around a standard Arriflex 435, custom SL Cine 400-foot magazines, and Preston remote focus and iris controls, this low-profile camera system can be easily fitted with Cooke, Zeiss, or Panavision spherical and anamorphic lenses. Fully loaded, the system weighs 62 lb. and is depth rated to 100 ft.

35-3 SHALLOW WATER HOUSING

Distributed by
HydroFlex

Designed primarily for use above water in wet environments, the HydroFlex 35-3 Shallow Water Housing is constructed of fiberglass with a new aluminum front. The housing fits a standard Arriflex 35-3 camera with 400-foot magazines, a Cinematography Electronics motor control base, and Zeiss, Cooke, or Panavision lenses. When fitted with its custom lead pack for underwater use, the HydroFlex Shallow Water Housing is well balanced, neutrally buoyant, and easy to maneuver, making it the perfect swimming pool housing, as it can also be used underwater to a depth of 12 ft.

HydroFlex, Inc.
5335 McConnell Ave.
Los Angeles, CA 90066
(310) 301-8187
www.hydroflex.com

35-3 SURF HOUSING | Distributed by HydroFlex

Action water photography demands lightweight, portable equipment. The HydroFlex 35-3 Surf Housing, designed around a stock Arri 35-3, is ideal for shooting in the surf and wet, action-oriented situations. For above-water filming in rain or wet sets, an optional lens port spray deflector system shoots air across the lens area, keeping drops of water from registering on the film. The 35-3 Surf Housing accepts Zeiss PL T1.3 and 2.1 series of lenses and Panavision spherical and anamorphic lenses. The complete system weighs only 36 lb. and is depth rated to only 2 ft.

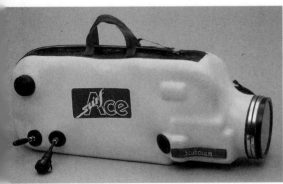

16x9 Inc.
3605 West Pacific Ave., Suite B
Burbank, CA 91505
(866) 800-1699
www.16x9inc.com

Band Pro Film/Video, Inc.
3403 West Pacific Ave.
Burbank, CA 91505
(818) 841-9655
www.bandpro.com

BETACAM SPLASH HOUSING | Distributed by 16x9 Inc./Band Pro

The Betacam Splash Housing is made from 2.5mm-thick natural latex and is sealed using a heavy-duty watertight zip. The housing is designed to fit various models of Betacams manufactured by Sony and Ikegami. The zoom servo can be felt and operated through the flexible material, and an integral glove on the left-hand side of the housing accesses the iris and focus controls on the lens. Behind the front port is a collar into which the lens fits. To prevent the port falling over the front of the lens, three step-down rings with internal diameters of 86mm, 95mm, and 100mm are supplied. When the zip is fully closed, the unit can be submerged to a maximum depth of 4 meters.

DV**CAM** SPLASH HOUSING

This housing is made from 2.5mm-thick natural latex and sealed using a heavy-duty watertight zip. The camera is mounted on an internal adjustable quick-release plate, allowing the lens to be positioned as close to the front port as possible, thus reducing refraction and eliminating corner cutting. The basic model has the option to be upgraded with a dump valve, 5-meter underwater audio cable, or 10-meter underwater video cable. The DVCAM/ DVCPRO splash bag is designed to fit all cameras manufactured by Phillips, Sony, Ikegami, and Panasonic. When the zip is fully closed, the unit can be submerged to a maximum depth of 7 meters.

Band Pro Film/Video, Inc.
3403 West Pacific Ave.
Burbank, CA 91505
(818) 841-9655
www.bandpro.com

16x9 Inc.
3605 West Pacific Ave., Suite B
Burbank, CA 91505
(866) 800-1699
www.16x9inc.com

MICROPHONES 31
HANDHELD AND
STUDIO CONDENSER

AKG:	C 12 VR Tube Condenser Microphone
	C 4500 B-BC Studio Condenser Microphone
Audio-Technica:	AT815b Line Gradient Condenser Microphone
	AT822 One Point X/Y Stereo DAT Microphone
Audix:	SCX-one Studio Condenser Microphone
	VX-10 Studio Condenser Microphone
Shure:	VP88 Stereo Condenser Microphone
Sony:	C800GPAC Studio Tube Condenser Microphone

C 12 VR TUBE CONDENSER HANDHELD MICROPHONE | By AKG Acoustics

The AKG C 12 VR (Vintage Reissue) is the modern equivalent to the classic C 12 produced beginning in 1953. The C 12 VR continues to set the standard for quality, providing its famed warmth and presence, which are direct results of its unique tube, diaphragm, and transformer design. The available pickup patterns include omnidirectional, cardioid, and figure eight with six intermediate patterns.

AKG Acoustics USA
914 Airpark Center Drive
Nashville, TN 37217
(615) 620-3800
www.akgusa.com

C 4500 B-BC STUDIO CONDENSER MICROPHONE | By AKG Acoustics

The C 4500 B-BC was developed to meet the demands associated with digital broadcasting. A front-address, large-diaphragm condenser microphone, the C 4500 B-BC is immune to electrostatic and magnetic fields and provides an extremely wide dynamic range and low self-noise. Features include a switchable 20dB pad and a switchable low-frequency roll-off (6dB/octave below 120Hz). Internal shock mounting is provided. The C 4500 B-BC operates on all phantom-power voltages. H 100 spider suspension and W 4000 windscreen are included.

AT815B LINE GRADIENT CONDENSER MICROPHONE

| By
Audio-Technica U.S., Inc.

The AT815b Line Gradient Condenser Microphone was designed for professional recording, broadcasting, and film/TV/video production. It provides the narrow acceptance angle desirable for long-distance sound pickup, has excellent sound rejection from the sides and rear of the mic, has switchable, low-frequency roll-off, and operates on battery or phantom power.

AT822 ONE POINT X/Y STEREO DAT MICROPHONE

| By
Audio-Technica U.S., Inc.

The AT822 is ideal for DAT recording as well as television, FM, and field applications. Its compact, lightweight design is perfect for camera-mount use, and closely matched elements provide the spatial impact and realism of a live sound field. The AT822 operates on battery power only.

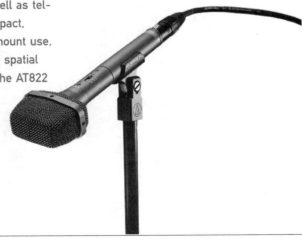

Audio-Technica U.S., Inc.
1221 Commerce Drive
Stow, OH 44224
(330) 686-2600
www.audio-technica.com

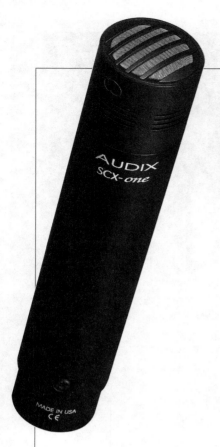

SCX-ONE STUDIO CONDENSER MICROPHONE | By Audix Corporation

This microphone provides exceptionally flat response, making it perfect for any ultra-critical recording or live sound application. The mic is extremely quiet, making it ideal for critical digital or analog recording. It operates on standard phantom power of 48-52 volts DC. The SCX-one is a high-quality, U.S.-made condenser comparable to the very finest European condenser microphones. It incorporates Surface Mount Technology (SMT), making it compact and durable enough for years of reliable performance both in the recording studio and for sound reinforcement and broadcast use. Matched pairs may be special ordered for stereo use.

VX-10 STUDIO CONDENSER MICROPHONE | By Audix Corporation

The VX-10 is a true condenser microphone designed to set new performance standards in the areas of live sound and broadcast applications. With a smooth, uniform response over a frequency range of 40 to 20kHz, the VX-10 is highly sensitive to transient response and will reproduce vocals and speech with exceptional detail and realism. Some of the many applications include speech, live broadcasts, and on-air announce microphone.

Audix Corporation
P.O. Box 4010
Wilsonville, OR 97070
(800) 966-8261
www.audixusa.com

VP88 STEREO CONDENSER MICROPHONE | By Shure Incorporated

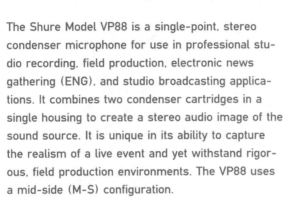

The Shure Model VP88 is a single-point, stereo condenser microphone for use in professional studio recording, field production, electronic news gathering (ENG), and studio broadcasting applications. It combines two condenser cartridges in a single housing to create a stereo audio image of the sound source. It is unique in its ability to capture the realism of a live event and yet withstand rigorous, field production environments. The VP88 uses a mid-side (M-S) configuration.

Shure Incorporated
5800 W. Touhy Ave.
Niles, IL 60714
(800) 25-SHURE
www.shure.com

C800GPAC STUDIO TUBE CONDENSER MICROPHONE | By Sony Electronics

Excellent for vocal recording in studios and film postproduction houses, Sony's C800G Studio Tube Condenser Microphone is designed for the highest possible sound reproduction quality. The C800G features a high-quality dual large diaphragm for true reproduction of vocal qualities, vacuum-tube warm sound quality through a 6AU6 vacuum tube, a unique Peltier-based cooling system to achieve optimum tube operating temperature, and an electronically selectable pickup pattern (Omni/Uni) for various recording applications. The package includes a power supply (AC-MC800G) and all the necessary accessories.

Sony Electronics
One Sony Drive
Park Ridge, NJ 07656
(800) 686-7669
www.sony.com/professional

If you have used this gear and want to share your own experiences, comments, and suggestions in our next edition, send an e-mail to Catherine Lorenze at *DREAMGEAR@cox.net*. We are particularly interested in innovative ways you have used the gear that will help inspire other film, video, and TV professionals.

MICROPHONES 32
HANDHELD AND
STUDIO DYNAMIC

AKG: D 230 Dynamic Handheld ENG Microphone

Shure: SM7B Studio Dynamic Microphone
                              SM63 Handheld Dynamic Microphone
                              VP64A and VP64AL Handheld Dynamic Microphones

D 230 DYNAMIC ENG MICROPHONE | By AKG Acoustics

This rugged, dynamic ENG microphone delivers exceptional sensitivity and clarity in the demanding news-gathering field. The extended shaft allows for easy placement of a TV/radio station flag without typical handling problems. The body is made of extremely rugged, die-cast metal with a nonreflective surface for low-profile, on-camera operation.

AKG Acoustics USA
914 Airpark Center Drive
Nashville, TN 37217
(615) 620-3800
www.akgusa.com

SM7B STUDIO DYNAMIC MICROPHONE | By Shure Incorporated

The Model SM7B dynamic microphone has a smooth, flat, wide-range frequency response appropriate for music and speech in all professional audio applications. It features excellent shielding against electromagnetic hum generated by computer monitors, neon lights, and other electrical devices. The SM7B has been updated from earlier models with an improved bracket design that offers greater stability. In addition to its standard windscreen, it also includes the A7WS windscreen for close-talk applications.

Shure Incorporated
5800 W. Touhy Ave.
Niles, IL 60714
(800) 25-SHURE
www.shure.com

SM63 HANDHELD
DYNAMIC MICROPHONE | By Shure Incorporated

Elegant yet rugged, the high-output SM63 series dynamic, omni-directional microphones are designed for professional applications where performance and appearance are critical. Their smooth, wide frequency response is tailored for optimum speech intelligibility, and includes a controlled low-frequency roll-off for reduced pickup of stand and wind noise. A built-in hum-bucking coil makes the microphones virtually immune to strong hum fields, such as those produced by studio lighting. The three models differ only in length and color. The champagne-finished SM63 is designed for handheld use onstage and in broadcast, recording, and television studios. The champagne-finished SM63L and the black-finished SM63LB are ideal for remote interviews, sports broadcasts, and other situations where longer microphones are desirable.

VP64A AND VP64AL HANDHELD
DYNAMIC MICROPHONES | By Shure Incorporated

The VP64A and VP64AL are high-output, omnidirectional, handheld dynamic microphones designed for professional audio and video production. They combine exceptional per-formance and comfortable feel with a handsome on-camera appearance. The VP64A and VP64AL are identical except for handle length. The 200mm (7 7/8 inch) VP64A is ideal for close-up use and can be used outside as well as indoors. The VP64AL is well suited to location interviews, sports broad-casting, and other situations where the 244mm (9 5/8 inch) length is an advantage. The VP64A series also features a tailored frequency response with an upper midrange presence rise that adds crispness and clarity to speech. A water-resistant mesh grille allows the microphone to be used during the most challenging weather conditions.

If you have used this gear and want to share your own experiences, comments, and suggestions in our next edition, send an e-mail to Catherine Lorenze at *DREAMGEAR@cox.net*. We are particularly interested in innovative ways you have used the gear that will help inspire other film, video, and TV professionals.

MICROPHONES
LAVALIER
33

Professional Sound Corp.:	**MilliMic Lavalier Microphone**
Shure:	**MC50B and MC51B Lavalier Microphones**
	SM93 Micro-Lavalier Microphone

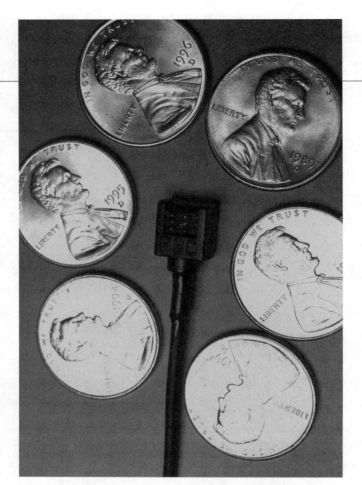

MILLIMIC PRODUCTION
LAVALIER MICROPHONE | By Professional So
Corporation

Incorporating the latest in capsule design, the MilliMic boasts miniature size, very high output, a low inherent noise floor, and exceptional shielding against electromagnetic interference. The soft, flexible and nonreflective finish of the MilliMic cable will also better isolate handling noise and keep the MilliMic unobtrusive on camera. Included in the MilliMic's attractive storage case are a wide variety of MilliMic mounting accessories including a tie bar, tape-down mount, cable mount, vampire clip, windscreen clip, and the exclusive Professional Sound Corporation Guard Mount, useful in applications where concealment is mandatory and clothing noise must be negated.

Professional Sound Corporation
28085 Smyth Drive
Valencia, CA 91355
(661) 295-9395
www.professionalsound.com

MC50B AND MC51B SUBMINIATURE LAVALIER MICROPHONES | By Shure Incorporated

Shure models WL50/MC50 (omni) and WL51/MC51 (unidirectional) are subminiature, electret-condenser lavalier microphones. They provide uncompromised sound quality and high reliability with minimal visibility in sound-reinforcement applications such as television broadcasting and stage performances. Despite its small size, the microphone's condenser element provides full, clear, and natural reproduction of speech. Each microphone is supplied with two foam windscreens to minimize wind noise. The supplied mounting accessories consist of a lapel clip, a tie clip, a pin mount, and a magnet mount, giving the user a wide variety of options for placement.

SM93 MICRO-LAVALIER MICROPHONE | By Shure Incorporated

The SM93 is an economical, omnidirectional, subminiature lavalier condenser microphone designed for use in speech applications. Despite its small size, the 93 microphone element provides full, clear sound comparable to that of much larger microphones. Its frequency response is tailored to body-worn applications, with low-end roll-off and presence rise. The SM93 is supplied with a sew-on mounting bracket, a mounting block with attached tie bar, and an acoustic windscreen to minimize wind noise in outdoor applications. The SM93 is also supplied with a dual mounting block with attached tie bar.

Shure Incorporated
5800 W. Touhy Ave.
Niles, IL 60714
(800) 25-SHURE
www.shure.com

If you have used this gear and want to share your own experiences, comments, and suggestions in our next edition, send an e-mail to Catherine Lorenze at *DREAMGEAR@cox.net*. We are particularly interested in innovative ways you have used the gear that will help inspire other film, video, and TV professionals.

MICROPHONES
SHOTGUN
34

Audio-Technica:	**AT835ST Stereo Shotgun Microphone**
Shure:	**SM89 Condenser Shotgun Microphone**
Sony:	**ECM670 Short Shotgun Microphone**

AT835ST STEREO SHOTGUN MIC | By Audio-Technica U.S., Inc.

Audio-Technica U.S., Inc.
1221 Commerce Drive
Stow, OH 44224
(330) 686-2600
www.audio-technica.com

Audio-Technica's AT835ST Stereo Shotgun Mic was designed for broadcasters, videographers, and sound recordists. Its compact, lightweight design is perfect for camera-mount use. Features include: independent line-cardioid and figure eight condenser elements; switchable low-frequency roll-off; switch selection of non-matrixed M-S mode; and two internally matrixed left/right stereo modes.

SM89 CONDENSER SHOTGUN MICROPHONE | By Shure Incorporated

The Model SM89 is a highly directional condenser shotgun microphone with distant pickup characteristics suitable for on-location film and television production. The SM89 can also be used for theater sound reinforcement, spot news coverage, or wildlife recording. The SM89 discriminates at a distance in favor of desired dialogue or effects and against ambient noise — even in noisy surroundings. The on-axis frequency response of the SM89 is very smooth and extended. For clarity and speech intelligibility, a slight presence rise optimizes the high-frequency response to compensate for high-frequency losses. A low-frequency roll-off minimizes pickup of wind, mechanical vibration, ambient noise, and rumble without affecting voice frequencies.

Shure Incorporated
5800 W. Touhy Ave.
Niles, IL 60714
(800) 25-SHURE
www.shure.com

ECM670 SHORT SHOTGUN MICROPHONE | By Sony Electronics

The ECM670 is a short shotgun microphone for use on cameras. No battery operation — 48V phantom power only. The compact and lightweight design offers a high-performance, electret-condenser microphone with super-cardioid characteristics. Low-cut switch provides a low-frequency roll-off for optimum voice pickup, reducing pop and wind noises.

Sony Electronics
One Sony Drive
Park Ridge, NJ 07656
(800) 686-7669
www.sony.com/professional

If you have used this gear and want to share your own experiences, comments, and suggestions in our next edition, send an e-mail to Catherine Lorenze at *DREAMGEAR@cox.net*. We are particularly interested in innovative ways you have used the gear that will help inspire other film, video, and TV professionals.

MISCELLANEOUS 35

Cinetransformer: Mobile 95-Seat Digital Theater

Mole-Richardson: Cob Web Maker
                          Fog Machine
                          Wind Machine

MOBILE
STATE-OF-THE-
ART DIGITAL
THEATER | By Cinetransformer

Cinetransformer is a transportable, totally self-contained, state-of-the-art, 95-seat digital theater. Designed to bring a true cinema experience to the world's communities with no access to movie theaters, Cinetransformer also brings high-tech promotional events and educational programs wherever there is a road and an audience. Whether it be via movies, satellite television, or two-way high-speed Internet, Cinetransformer is the mobile communications solution.

Cinetransformer International Corporation
9601 Wilshire Boulevard, Penthouse
Beverly Hills, CA 90210
(310) 274-8300
www.cinetransformer.com

COB WEB MAKER | By Mole-Richardson

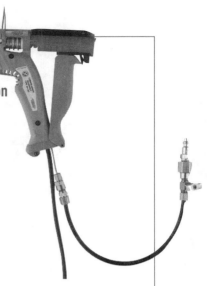

When used in conjunction with an air compressor, the Cob Web Maker creates cobweb and aging effects using harmless and removable hot glue sticks.

FOG MACHINE | By Mole-Richardson

Create the effects of fog, smoke, haze, and mist with Fog Juice. Once the internal heating element reaches optimum temperature, the unit can be operated cordless.

WIND MACHINE | By Mole-Richardson

The Wind Machine is designed to create maximum airflow with minimum noise. A rheostat control varies the speed of the fan to produce wind effects from a light zephyr to a stiff breeze.

Mole-Richardson Co.
937 North Sycamore Ave.
Hollywood, CA 90038
(323) 851-0111
www.mole.com

If you have used this gear and want to share your own experiences, comments, and suggestions in our next edition, send an e-mail to Catherine Lorenze at *DREAMGEAR@cox.net*. We are particularly interested in innovative ways you have used the gear that will help inspire other film, video, and TV professionals.

MOBILE
PRODUCTION VEHICLES

36

Core Digital:	HD601 Hybrid Mobile Unit
E–N–G Mobile Systems:	OmniLink Family of SNG/ENG Vehicles

HD601 HYBRID MOBILE UNIT | By Core Digital Technologies

Core Digital introduces the world's first and only mobile unit capable of simultaneous production of both HD and Standard 601 signals. Although the unit is designed to broadcast both formats simultaneously, it can be used for all HD or straight 601 broadcasts. The most immediately striking feature is its giant, continuous, flat-screen monitor wall. The truck is outfitted with 12-bit Ikegami 790 HD cameras for the highest-quality picture output available today. Another piece of cutting-edge equipment on the truck is the Ikegami Mongoose. This is a one-of-a-kind conversion system that allows HD cameras to be run with either SMPTE fiber or triax cable. Onboard Avid DS/HD edit bays are available, and the truck houses the TV industry's premier multitrack audio-production system.

Core Digital Technologies
303 S. River Ave.
Tempe, AZ 85281
(480) 707-1000
www.coredigital.com

OMNILINK FAMILY OF SNG/ENG VEHICLES

By
E-N-G Mobile Systems

E-N-G's line of OmniLink SNG and SNG/ENG news vehicles offers the widest possible range of choices and configurations for state-of-the-art news gathering. The models are available for both digital and analog transmission and may be equipped for SNG only or SNG and ENG capabilities.

E-N-G Mobile Systems, Inc.
2245 Via de Mercados
Concord, CA 94520
(800) 662-4522
www.e-n-g.com

If you have used this gear and want to share your own experiences, comments, and suggestions in our next edition, send an e-mail to Catherine Lorenze at *DREAMGEAR@cox.net*. We are particularly interested in innovative ways you have used the gear that will help inspire other film, video, and TV professionals.

MONITORS
SIGNAL AND DISPLAY

37

PERSONAL MONITOR | By AccuScene Corporation

For professional moviemakers — get your dailies today! The amazing new AccuScene personal monitor is a new way to instantly view your shots. Using a live feed from your camera, the personal monitor allows you to see what your camera sees — what your audience will eventually see — live and in full color. Features include: a robust and compact size, accurate colorimetry, high resolution (1280 x 1024 pixels), focus and contrast adjustment, and digital micro display technology. Power requirements: 12V DC, 10W.

AccuScene Corporation
1 St. David's Drive
St. David's Business Park
Dunfermline, Fife KY119PF
Scotland
+44 (0)1 383-828-880
www.accuscene.com

WM-3001 PORTABLE WAVEFORM MONITOR | By Astro Systems, Inc.

The WM-3001 is a portable HD/SD waveform monitor that supports 17 HD formats currently in use in the HD world. This compact monitor can provide all necessary functions such as picture, waveform, vector scope, and status display for an overall solution. For outdoor use, an Anton Bauer or Sony lithium battery can be mounted on its back for greater power flexibility. Input signals can be either HD SDI (SMPTE-292) or Analog YPbPr including SD-SDI/601 digital NTSC.

Astro Systems, Inc.
425 S. Victory Blvd., #A
Burbank, CA 91502
(877) 882-7876
www.astro-systems.com

SUNLIGHT VIEWABLE LCD MONITORS | By IMP Electronics

No sun hood is required for this portable, rugged, battery-operated 15-inch monitor. From boats to helicopters, this monitor is for all high-ambient-light applications including video assist outdoors on location; next to big, glass windows in modern, bright buildings; or in well-lit atriums with multimedia centers. The radical optical construction controls reflective glare with wipe-clean optical-coated glass. Some additional features include: PAL and NTSC standards, 16:9 letterbox, and built-in speakers with a headphone outlet.

IMP Electronics
The Rocol Building
3 Glebe Road, Huntingdon
Cambridgeshire PE29 7DL, UK
+44 (0)1 480-411-822
www.imp-electronics.com

4.5-INCH LCCS COLOR MONITOR | By JVC

This unique, portable monitor uses a 4-inch liquid crystal color shutter in front of a high-resolution monochrome picture tube to create unbelievably high-resolution images — even in bright environments (daytime, direct sunlight). Some features include: more than 400 lines of resolution, weight of only 7.2 lb., NTSC/PAL, and 16:9.

JVC Headquarters
1700 Valley Road
Wayne, NJ 07470
(973) 317-5000
www.jvc.com/pro

DVCAM VIDEO WALKMAN WITH I.LINK | By Sony

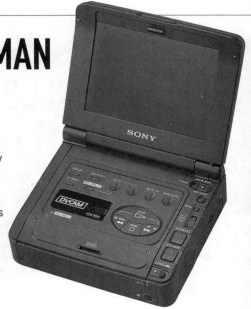

Designed for professional-quality video and audio, the DSRV10 has a built-in 5.5-inch LCD monitor and battery operation capability. With the optional DSRM-E1 Editing Adapter and a DVCXAM camcorder, the DSRV10 can form a simple field-editing system. Or it can be used as a lightweight field monitor, a back-up VTR, or a handy desktop viewer.

Sony Electronics
One Sony Drive
Park Ridge, NJ 07656
(800) 686-7669
www.sony.com/professional

HD ULTRABRITE COLOR VIDEO MONITOR FOR STEADICAM | A Steadicam product by Tiffen

The HD UltraBrite is built for today's demanding needs for versatility and flexibility. Tiffen has created an LCD monitor that attaches to the Steadicam unit and can easily be viewed in daylight. Some features include: selectable color temperature, portrait/landscape image rotation, vertical and horizontal flip capabilities, adjustable image scaling, image zoom and freeze-frame features, and automatic video format switching.

The Tiffen Company, LLC
90 Oser Avenue
Hauppauge, NY 11788-3886
(631) 273-2500
www.tiffen.com
www.steadicam.com

VTM-150 MULTI-FORMAT ON-SCREEN MONITOR

By Videotek, Inc.

The VTM-150 Multi-Format On-Screen Monitor combines a cost-effective display output at 800 x 600 resolution to monitor and measure 601 digital, CAV, and composite analog (NTSC or PAL) video and analog audio signals. The output display includes a waveform and vector overlay, alarms, and analog stereo audio levels mixed or keyed over internally generated color background or picture. Inputs include two composite analog NTSC/PAL with one shared CAV and two 601 SDI digital inputs. Standard output is compatible for display on any 800 x 600 resolution computer monitor.

Videotek, Inc.
243 Shoemaker Road
Pottstown, PA 19464-6433
(800) 800-5719
www.videotek.com

PRODUCTION
PREP AND
MANAGEMENT TOOLS

38

Apogee: Session Tools Software

The Badham Company: ShotMaster Software

Easy Budget: Easy Budget for Commercials Software
                               Easy Budget for Feature Films Software

Entertainment Partners: Entertainment Partners Budgeting Software
                               Movie Magic Scheduling Software
                               Virtual Production Office Software

Final Draft: Final Draft AV Prof. Audio-visual Script Processor
                               Final Draft Scriptwriting Software

Kinetic Impulse: PECS Manager
                               Shot (List) Generator Wizard Software

PowerProduction Software: AutoActuals Bidding Software
                               StoryBoard Artist Software
                               StoryBoard Quick Software

StuffBak: StuffBak Loss Protection Service

Thomson/Grass Valley: ProSet — Production Setup Application

Wide Screen Software: SunPATH Sun Tracking Software

"With the number of projects I work on every year, I need my sessions to be completely organized. That's why we developed Session Tools."

— Bob Clearmountain, award-winning engineer and developer of Session Tools Software

Quote obtained from Apogee Digital's Web site

SESSION TOOLS
SOFTWARE | Distributed by Apogee Electronics Corporation

Session Tools is a stand-alone, networkable studio management database application available for both Macintosh and Windows computers. It offers a series of layouts with comprehensive features for every aspect of the operation of a modern recording or mixing facility, including: a full client database, booking forms, and work orders; asks all the questions that need to be answered when taking a booking; handles studio operations with or without an assistant engineer; materials and hours logging, including customizable multiple rates and lockout provisions; tape-library management, including source location, storage, format, and shipping information; and much, much more.

Apogee Electronics Corporation
3145 Donald Douglas Loop South
Santa Monica, CA 90405-3210
(310) 915-1000
www.apogeedigital.com

SHOTMASTER SOFTWARE | By The Badham Company

ShotMaster Software makes a working director's job easier by organizing thoughts, ideas, sequences, and storyboards. Designed for the director who cannot draw at all, the software has two main features. First, it helps you create a shot list with drag-and-drop storyboards using hundreds of pre-drawn figures, simple self-drawn diagrams, or scans of professionally drawn storyboards. Second, it provides a good place to keep your thoughts and notes relative to each scene. The shot lists can then be printed in an easy-to-read form, complete with thumbnail versions of the storyboards and shot diagrams for disbursement to the crew. Crews love these illustrated shot lists because they get a clear idea of the day's work ahead. If there are changes, the shot-list plan is easily and quickly updated. ShotMaster Software was created by John Badham, award-winning director of *Saturday Night Fever*, *War Games*, *Blue Thunder*, and many other feature films.

The Badham Company
www.shotmaster.com

EASY BUDGET FOR COMMERCIALS
SOFTWARE | By Easy Budget

Finally, commercial production bidding can be easy to do! This specially designed program will produce bid estimates that conform with the industry-standard format. It will actualize a budget anytime during or after production. It's also an excellent tool for budgeting television programs, documentaries, and corporate videos. The industry-standard format means your bid will be accepted by everyone, and our online labor database supplies all the important labor information you'll need. The software is even powerful enough to do your payroll too! Detailed totals and subtotals are provided for every cast or crew member.

EASY BUDGET FOR FEATURE FILMS SOFTWARE | By Easy Budget

"Easy Budget has been my program of choice for the past three years. It's user-friendly and fast and there is great technical support."

— David Landau, Emmy award-winning commercial producer
Quote obtained from Easy Budget's Web site

This is the budget software to use for estimating the cost of a feature film and presenting those figures to the people who will be financing or insuring the production. Fine-tuned and perfected from 20 years of production experience, it's a comprehensive checklist of all typical expenses and a versatile tool for testing and adjusting a film budget. Easy Budget has been used to estimate budgets from next-to-nothing to more than 140 million dollars! Easy Budget knows when a particular labor contract provision benefits you and automatically makes the most cost-efficient selection. And the software lets you easily compare changes — without having to create another budget to test for a "what if?" situation.

The Easy Budget Company
17724 Lemarsh Street
Northridge, CA 91325
(800) 356-7461
www.easy-budget.com

ENTERTAINMENT PARTNERS
BUDGETING SOFTWARE | By Entertainment Partners

Introducing budgeting for the 21st Century! Create and edit budgets of all sizes for all types of productions. Entertainment Partners' clients have long requested a budgeting application that would address the expanded range of needs facing cost estimators today, including: greater flexibility with a wide range of options for comparing budgets and examining individual components; capacity for an additional level of detail; more timesaving features; a facility for making notations; and interaction with Movie Magic Budgeting files. In response, we proudly introduce EP Budgeting. Isn't it time for a change?

Setup Globals for Love.mmb				
Add	Remove	Print		Default status
D	Name	Description		E
☐	S	Shoot Weeks Total		LocWks+[
☐	LocWks	5-Day Weeks		0
☐	DistWks	6 - Day Weeks		0
☐	PostProd	Post- Production Weeks		0
☐	LH	Local Weekly Pay-hrs		70
☐	DH	Distant Weekly pay-hrs		96

MOVIE MAGIC
SCHEDULING | By Entertainment Partners

Automating the time-tested scheduling strip-board process, Movie Magic Scheduling has improved the production scheduling process. Producers, production managers, and assistant directors want script breakdown and scheduling software that is intuitive, easy to use, and timesaving — so they rely on this invaluable tool as a necessity. Movie Magic Scheduling handles changes in the production schedule with ease, and convenient import into Movie Magic Budgeting allows decision-makers to view multiple production scenarios with ease. Keeping everyone informed and on time, Movie Magic Scheduling is the industry's highest-rated and most widely used scheduling software.

Entertainment Partners
2835 North Naomi Street
Burbank, CA 91504
(818) 955-6000
www.ep-services.com

Shoot Schedule #1

IT'S A WONDERFUL LIFI
Shooting Schedule

Day Out Of Days

Abbreviations
Start: SW   Finish: WF
Work: W   S-W-F: SWF
Hold: H   Holiday: /
Drop: WD   Travel: T
Pickup: PW   Co Travel: M

Column
Width: 0
Starting C
IDs: 0
Names: 0
Table: 2

VIRTUAL PRODUCTION OFFICE | By Entertainment Partners

Managing the massive amounts of documentation generated throughout the production process can be challenging and frustrating. Entertainment Partners' Virtual Production Office offers a highly secure online solution. Archive, deliver, and update key production documents (reports, memos, budgets, script drafts, and much more) anytime, from anywhere. Carefully controlled access ensures that users view only the information they are authorized to see. EP Payroll clients enjoy the added benefit of performing payroll edits directly via VPO.

Entertainment Partners
2835 North Naomi Street
Burbank, CA 91504
(818) 955-6000
www.ep-services.com

FINAL DRAFT AV
PROFESSIONAL AUDIO-VISUAL
SCRIPT PROCESSOR | By
Final Draft, Inc.

VIDEO	AUDIO
A WOMAN HOLDING A BOX OF "WAVE" LAUNDRY DETERGENT STANDING IN A TYPICAL AMERICAN KITCHEN. A SIX YEAR OLD BOY ENTERS THE KITCHEN HOLDING UP A SHIRT LOOKING UPSET.	WOMAN: WAVE DETERGENT GETS MY CLOTHES AS CLEAN AS THE OCEAN, AND HAS 1/3 LESS CARCINOGENS THAN THE LEADING LAUNDRY DETERGENT. BOY: (frantic) MOM! YOU RUINED MY NEW SWEATSHIRT. IT'S FULL OF HOLES! I'M TOO EMBARRASSED TO GO TO SCHOOL.
WOMAN TAKES THE SHIRT AND STARTS EXAMINING IT.	WOMAN: DON'T WORRY SON. THAT'S JUST THE SUPER CLEAN SCRUBBING POWER OF THE WAVE DETERGENT. NO OTHER DETERGENT IS STRONGER THAN WAVE. WAVE CONTAINS THE CLEANING POWER OF THE OCEAN.
BOY LOOKS PUZZLED AND IS SMILING TO HIDE HIS CONFUSION.	BOY: WOW, THAT'S GREAT, MOM. SMELLS REALLY CLEAN TOO. ANNCR (VO): SIZE OF HOLES MAY VARY DEPENDING ON TYPE OF WATER USED AND MATERIAL OF CLOTHING. DO NOT USE ON ANIMALS, DO NOT BREATHE IN FUMES, USE IN WELL-VENTILATED AREAS.

Final Draft AV is a full-featured script processor specifically designed for audiovisual scriptwriting. It combines powerful word processing with a variety of industry-standard formats, all in one self-contained, easy-to-use system. Final Draft AV lines up multiple audio/video columns automatically and keeps them aligned when text is added, edited, or deleted. There are no complicated commands to learn, no frustrating tables to deal with. In addition, scripts created in Final Draft (for screenplays) can be interchanged with Final Draft AV and vice versa. Whether you are creating a 60-second commercial, a 15-second radio spot, a half-hour speech, or a four-hour training film, Final Draft AV's ease of use allows you to focus on writing.

Final Draft, Inc.
16000 Ventura Blvd., Suite 800
Encino, CA 91436
(888) 320-7555
www.finaldraft.com

FINAL DRAFT PROFESSIONAL SCRIPTWRITING SOFTWARE | By Final Draft, Inc.

"The new Final Draft 6 is fast, fluid, intuitive and as always, state-of-the-art. Final Draft 6 makes me look good and feel old all at the same time."

— Christopher McQuarrie, Academy Award Winner and Writer/Producer of *The Usual Suspects*

Final Draft is the number-one choice among Hollywood's professional writers. Specifically designed for writing movie scripts, TV episodes, and stage plays, it combines powerful word processing with professional script formatting in one self-contained, easy-to-use package. There is no need to learn about script formatting rules — Final Draft automatically paginates and formats your script to industry standards as you write. Use your creative energy to focus on the content; let Final Draft take care of the style.

Final Draft, Inc.
16000 Ventura Blvd.
Suite 800
Encino, CA 91436
(888) 320-7555
www.finaldraft.com

```
7        INT. HOUSE IN SAYERVILLE - DAY                          7
         Bob and Bryan move to the kitchen.

                         BOB
                  Any trouble finding the place?

                         BRYAN
                  No...no problem at all.  Your
                  wife's directions were perfect.
                  Gorgeous home you have here Mr.
                  Williams.
                       (MORE)

                                            (CONTINUED)
```

```
                                          My Story   4.
7        CONTINUED:                                             7
                         BRYAN (CONT'D)
                  Did you decorate yourself?...Silly
                  question, I'm sure you did...
                  wonderful taste.
```

PECS
MANAGER | By Kinetic Impulse

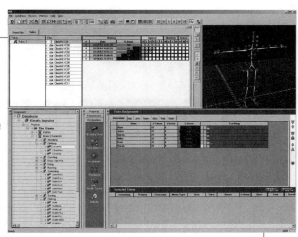

PECS Manager is the ultimate Motion Capture Production/Pipeline Software. Database driven and utilizing secure file storage and retrieval, PECS Manager helps you keep your productions on time and on budget. Handling the complete pipeline from shot-list generation (including imports for "Shot Generator Wizard" files), to preproduction, on-set data capture, data cleaning, and delivery, PECS Manager ensures that you and your team work efficiently and accurately on multiple projects simultaneously. Available in stand-alone and network modes, PECS Manager can also handle remote team members in different offices or locations around the world.

Kinetic Impulse
87 Hadlow Road
Tonbridge, Kent
TN9 1QD UK
+44 (0)7 788-710-481
www.kinetic-impulse.com

SHOT (LIST)
GENERATOR WIZARD | By Kinetic Impulse

Shot Generator Wizard is the leading Motion Capture preparation tool to reduce lead times, improve productivity, and increase team understanding of your project. Enabling you to break down your preproduction into logical structures including Props, Stunt Equipment, and Human/Animal Performances, Shot Generator Wizard manages your project directly in conjunction with any facility running PECS Manager, or exports to a human-readable text file for use in spreadsheet applications. Including information such as methods of delivery, data file formats, video and audio reference media, as well as character descriptions and directorial notes, this package helps you stay in control of MoCap specifications as well as the performances.

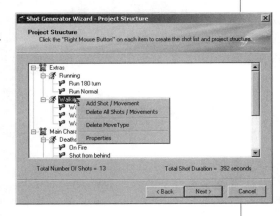

AUTOACTUALS BUDGETING/BIDDING SOFTWARE | By PowerProduction Software

AutoActuals is an easy-to-use bidding and actualizing template for AICP producers and coordinators who use Microsoft Excel. Enter POs into the log and then select AutoActualize from the menu. Each AICP line item is totaled and placed in the bidding template. Includes a time-sheet module to compute and actualize crew payroll. AutoActuals is used around the world for instant actualizing of commercial productions and is also available for commercial editorial houses. For special production company needs, customization is available.

STORYBOARD ARTIST | By PowerProduction Software

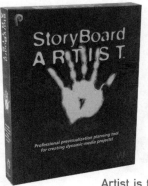

"StoryBoard Artist is changing the way storyboarding is done and there's nothing like it on the market that's as fast and easy to use. It's opened the doorway to getting storyboards closer to film. Anyone can use it with just 30 minutes' worth of training, especially artists."

— Ken Harsha, Storyboard Artist, DreamWorks

Quote obtained from PowerProduction's Web site

Successful media projects need a blueprint to follow. StoryBoard Artist is the all-in-one industry standard for digital storyboarding of both feature films and games. Created for graphically savvy media producers, StoryBoard Artist has all the features of StoryBoard Quick and adds a time line for run-time playback with sounds and nonlinear linking for multipath stories.

PowerProduction Software
15732 Los Gatos Blvd. #300
Los Gatos, CA 95032
(800) 457-0383
www.powerproduction.com

STORYBOARD QUICK | By PowerProduction Software

Creative minds don't always come with the ability to draw, but all creative minds know that a successful visual project needs visual planning. That's why StoryBoard Quick has become the industry's best-selling storyboarding tool. Even better than pencil and paper! It's the previsualization software tool that gets the job done. It's the no-nonsense tool for creating shooting boards. Whether you are an expert or just getting started, StoryBoard Quick helps you create the visuals you need in order to bring your ideas to reality and get your ideas on the screen.

STUFF**BAK** LOSS PROTECTION SERVICE | By StuffBak

StuffBak is a loss protection service that helps you get back your missing possessions.

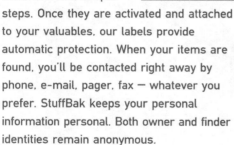

Just place our unique ID labels and tags on all of your important gear. If something "disappears," the label tells the finder how to return it easily, and get a reward too. You can purchase StuffBak labels and activate them in a few, simple

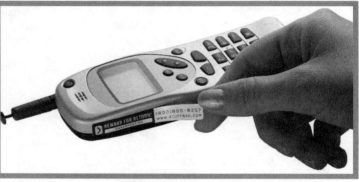

steps. Once they are activated and attached to your valuables, our labels provide automatic protection. When your items are found, you'll be contacted right away by phone, e-mail, pager, fax — whatever you prefer. StuffBak keeps your personal information personal. Both owner and finder identities remain anonymous.

StuffBak
7960 Niwot Road, Bldg. B12
Niwot, CO 80503
(800) 800-8257
www.stuffbak.com

PROSET – PRODUCTION SETUP
APPLICATION | A Grass Valley product by
Thomson Broadcast & Media Solutions

Our ProSet software provides production setup capabilities for OB vans and production facilities with a single click. A graphical user interface (GUI) provides access to stored configurations and other system information (e.g., router status), then forwards this data to controlled subsystems. ProSet software provides bitmap representations of production setups in an attractive and clear hierarchical display view. Some features include: significantly reduced production setup time, and three-layer, hierarchical access rights security mechanism.

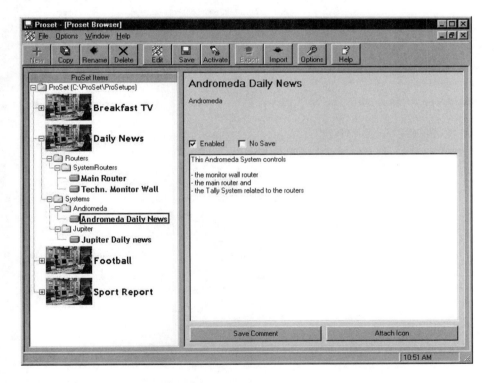

Thomson Broadcast & Media Solutions
400 Providence Mine Road
Nevada City, CA 95959
(530) 478-3000
www.thomsongrassvalley.com

SUNPATH SUN TRACKING SOFTWARE

By
Wide Screen Software

"The last producer I worked with called me Merlin because I was so accurately predicting where the sun would be and when."

— Rob Draper, Director of Photography, ASC

Quote obtained from Wide Screen Software's Web site

"I keep blowing my clients away with the printout from your program and I believe it's starting to be a regular enclosure in our production books down here in Florida."

— Ed McNamara, Florida Producer

Quote obtained from Wide Screen Software's Web site

Wide Screen Software
7838 Saint Clair Ave.
North Hollywood, CA 91605
(818) 764-3639
www.wide-screen.com

The sunPATH software tracks the position of the sun for any day, anywhere on earth. The program includes a comprehensive database of more than 39,000 locations worldwide. The database includes latitude, longitude, time zone, daylight savings time, and magnetic declination information for each location. Users select a location without the need to enter any information other than the date range. Expensive GPS equipment is not required. With sunPATH, directors of photography, directors, producers, assistant directors, photographers, and location managers will accurately predict the sun's position worldwide. This can be a tremendous aid in production scheduling and set construction, allowing efficient management of the limited and expensive production time.

TELECINE 39

Sony: FVST1000 Multi-Resolution Telecine

Thomson/Grass Valley: Scream System for Grain Reduction
                           Shadow Telecine System
                           Spirit DataCine System

FVST1000 MULTI-RESOLUTION TELECINE BASE UNIT | By Sony Electronics

The FVST1000 includes digital light valve primary color correction, selectable ND filters, 35mm and 16mm film gates and zoom lenses. Operates at all standard frame rates (23.98, 24, 24.975, 25, 29.97, 30fps) plus variable frame rates from 5fps to 30fps. Single-step forward and reverse, true still frame mode, 5X shuttle speed in forward and reverse.

Sony Electronics
One Sony Drive
Park Ridge, NJ 07656
(800) 686-7669
www.sony.com/professional

DREAM GEAR | LORENZE | 298

SCREAM GRAIN REDUCER | A Grass Valley product by Thomson Broadcast & Media Solutions

As an internal processing option for the Spirit, Specter, and Shadow telecine systems, our Scream system is the only real-time, 2K, resolution-independent grain-reduction tool available. Designed by our Emmy award-winning film-imaging team, it features three independent channels (one for each dye layer), custom film-stock profiles, and real-time de-flicker. Features include split-screen mode for comparison before/after processing.

Thomson Broadcast &
Media Solutions
400 Providence Mine Road
Nevada City, CA 95959
(530) 478-3000
www.thomsongrassvalley.com

SHADOW TELECINE
SYSTEM | A Grass Valley product
by Thomson Broadcast & Media Solutions

Our Shadow Telecine system is a low-cost telecine designed specifically for television production in standard and High-Definition resolutions. Leveraging key technologies and proven concepts from our Spirit DataCine system, it features advanced CCD scanning technology and an all-digital design to ensure the lowest possible operational and maintenance costs and high system availability. Designed specifically for SD and HD television production, other features include diffuse illumination that reduces the visibility of scratches and dirt.

SPIRIT DATACINE
SYSTEM | A Grass Valley product
by Thomson Broadcast & Media Solutions

With more than 200 units installed worldwide, our Spirit DataCine system is the industry standard for high-resolution film transfers. Whether it's commercial postproduction, feature-film mastering, or electronic cinema, it delivers outstanding results. With 2K data-scanning functionality, it expertly addresses the growing demand for digital intermediate feature productions — supporting SDTV, HDTV, or 2K data from 35mm, 16mm, or Super 8mm film. Features include built-in creative tools, 2K six-sector color processor, Scream Grain Reducer, and Steadiscan 35mm image-stabilization system.

**Thomson Broadcast &
Media Solutions**
400 Providence Mine Road
Nevada City, CA 95959
(530) 478-3000
www.thomsongrassvalley.com

If you have used this gear and want to share your own experiences, comments, and suggestions in our next edition, send an e-mail to Catherine Lorenze at *DREAMGEAR@cox.net*. We are particularly interested in innovative ways you have used the gear that will help inspire other film, video, and TV professionals.

TELEPROMPTERS 40

Barber Tech Video Products: EZ Prompter

Mirror Image: FP-120 Field Prompter
LC-70 Prompter for Steadicams, Jib Arms
LC-160 and LC-160HB Field Prompters
SF-200-LCD 20-Inch Prompter
SF-1550-LCD Studio Prompter

EZ PROMPTER | By Barber Tech Video Products

2002 NAB Pick of Show

2002 Prime Time Emmy Awards Engineering Award for Outstanding Achievement in Engineering Development

With EZ Prompter, your talent will look more confident, authoritative, and professional. EZ Prompter easily fits all 85mm (82mm filter thread) lenses, and can be easily fitted for most broadcast and industrial lenses that are smaller than 85mm O.D. Lens adapters are available for cameras ranging from the Canon XL1 to the JVC GY-DV500U to Sony's VX-1000 and many others. Weighing around 2 lb., the EZ Prompter is great for jibs, handheld cameras, Glidecams, and Steadicams. It works great outdoors and requires only 10 seconds to set up. No power and no operator required.

Barber Tech Video Products
P.O. Box 248
Sun Valley, CA 91353
(818) 982-7775
www.barbertvp.com

FP-120 FIELD PROMPTER | By Mirror Image Teleprompters Inc.

The FP (field prompter) series consists of fold-down capable mirrors and housing for easy shipping. Quick setup times are also a plus. Removable side panels are included. All use our top-quality beam-splitter mirror. Weight listed includes counterweight. Depending on camera used, a counterweight may not be required. The FP-120, our popular multi-camera field prompter, features a 12-inch composite fold-down monochrome camera prompter. Universal 110/220 volts AC power-ready and will accept NTSC or PAL video signals via BNC connectors. Weighs 40 lb. Mirror size: 15.5" x 12.75".

Mirror Image Teleprompters Inc.
2189 Abraham Lane
Oshkosh, WI 54904
(920) 232-0220
www.teleprompters.com

LC-70 PROMPTER FOR STEADICAMS AND JIB ARMS | By Mirror Image Teleprompters Inc.

This series is extremely lightweight and requires no counterweight. All LC models feature a fold-down mirror and hood design for ease of shipping. Includes removable side panels for hood. The LC-70 is the prompting answer for Steadicams and jib arms. This 7-inch LCD system weighs just 7 lb. The LC-70 accepts composite NTSC signals and runs on 120 volts AC or 12 volts DC. Includes two universal camera mounts that accept almost any camera. Fold-down hood and easy breakdown design.

LC-160 AND LC-160HB FIELD PROMPTERS | By Mirror Image Teleprompters Inc.

The LC-160 is our first-class 15-inch LCD field prompter. It works anywhere in the world and is great for prompting text, Webcasting, or teleconferencing. Accepts SVGA computer inputs, which are extremely sharp, as well as PAL or NTSC composite video signals. Powered by 110/220 volts AC or 12 volts DC. Weighs 18 lb. Mirror size: 15.5" x 12.75".

The LC-160HB is our top-of-the-line field/studio prompter. With up to 1600 NTS, this is the brightest 15-inch prompter on the market. Recommended for outside shoots and six times brighter than a conventional CRT screen, the LC-160HB is great for prompting text, Webcasting, or teleconferencing. Accepts SVGA computer inputs, which are extremely sharp, as well as PAL or NTSC composite video signals. Powered by 110/220V AC or 12V DC. Weighs 18 lb. Mirror size: 15.5" x 12.75".

Mirror Image Teleprompters Inc.
2189 Abraham Lane
Oshkosh, WI 54904
(920) 232-0220
www.teleprompters.com

SF-200-LCD STUDIO CAMERA PROMPTER | By Mirror Image Teleprompters Inc.

The SF-200-LCD is the largest studio camera prompter on the market. This system features the ultimate 20-inch color LCD panel. It accepts SVGA high-quality video signals directly from your computer via a 15-pin cable or composite video signal including NTSC/PAL/Secam. Universal power 110/220 volts AC or 12 volts DC. Weighing just 28 lb., the SF-200-LCD has a large, 20-inch trapezoidal hood. No counterweight required. Camera mount for most of today's ENG/EFP cameras.

SF-1550-LCD STUDIO PROMPTER | By Mirror Image Teleprompters Inc.

The SF-1550-LCD is our top-selling studio prompter. Use it anywhere in the world. This 24-lb. system features a 15-inch color panel that accepts NTSC/PAL or Secam inputs and runs on 110/220 volts AC or 12 volts DC.

Mirror Image Teleprompters Inc.
2189 Abraham Lane
Oshkosh, WI 54904
(920) 232-0220
www.teleprompters.com

TRIPODS
AND MONOPODS

41

Cartoni:	Maxi Tripod
	Studio Tripod
Cinekinetic:	Jib Stix
Manfrotto:	542 A.R.T. Road Runner
	754 MDeVe Carbon Fiber Video Tripod
Sachtler:	Cine 2000
	ENG 75/2 D
	Hot Pod CF
	Monopod 2 CF
	OB 2000
	Speed Lock CF HD
16x9 Inc./Band Pro:	DuoPod Pro
Telemetrics:	TELEVATOR
Vinten:	Fibertec Tripod

MAXI TRIPOD

The Maxi Tripod is provided with 25mm-diameter tubes and a two rotary clamping mechanism on each leg. Entirely manufactured in die-cast alloy, this tripod features a Mitchell Flat Base or a 150mm bowl and interfaces with a heavy-duty spreader or dolly. Ideal for Lambda and Omega fluid heads, the Maxi Tripod provides for a 200kg (440 lb.) payload.

By Cartoni and distributed by Ste-Man, Inc. in Hollywood

STUDIO TRIPOD

The Studio Tripod is entirely manufactured in die-cast alloy and fitted with a two rotary clamping mechanism on each leg. The single-stage version, featuring 22mm-diameter tubes, performs with unsurpassed torsional rigidity and structural integrity, while the locking knobs, which include overtightening protection, ensure maximum clamping efficiency maintained over the tripod lifetime. On the two-stage version, higher rigidity is obtained with a combination of 22 and 25mm-diameter tubes. Ideal for C40 S, this tripod can be supplied with an interchangeable 150mm bowl base or flat Mitchell base.

By Cartoni and distributed by Ste-Man, Inc. in Hollywood

Cartoni S.p.A
Via Giuseppe Mirri, 13
01159 Rome, Italy
+39 (0)6 438-2002
www.cartoni.com

Ste-Man, Inc.
10663 Burbank Blvd.
N. Hollywood, CA 91601
(818) 760-8240
www.ste-man.com

JIB STIX | By Cinekinetic

Cinekinetic U.S.A.
1405 Vegas Valley Drive,
#177
P.O. Box 73063
Las Vegas, NV 89170
(702) 731-4700
www.cinekinetic.com

Cinekinetic's Jib Stix holds up to a 250-lb. payload. This makes it one of the most robust tripods on the market. Designed primarily to support a jib arm, the monotubular legs provide the utmost stability. Jib Stix is loaded with extra features not found on other tripods. Its legs are etched with colored markings. This makes leveling easy and convenient. Our rubber feet are inexpensive to replace if lost. And Jib Stix comes supplied with a 100mm bowl. A 150mm bowl, Mitchell mount, and a range of non-standard bowls are available as options. With the supplied spreader attached, Jib Stix weighs 21 lb. with a collapsed length of 33 inches.

542 A.R.T ROAD RUNNER | By Manfrotto and distributed by Bogen Photo Corp.

The 542 uses our patented A.R.T. (Advanced Release Technology) mechanism for the fastest opening, positioning, and closing of any video tripod — ideal for news crews filming under pressure. Complete with all of the features and practical innovations that have made the Manfrotto 540 A.R.T. tripod among the most popular video tripods in the world, the new carbon fiber 542 A.R.T. offers the added benefit of a unique "squid" spreader that delivers even more flexibility for shooting in tight spaces. Unlike most other spreaders, the squid allows the user to fine-tune the spreader brace angle to suit virtually any working position.

Bogen Photo Corp.
565 East Crescent Ave.
P.O. Box 506
Ramsey, NJ 07446-0506
(201) 818-9500
www.bogenphoto.com
www.manfrotto.com

754 MDEVE CARBON FIBER
VIDEO TRIPOD | By Manfrotto and distributed by Bogen Photo Corp.

The 754 is the top of the range of the MDeVe tripod series due to a combination of extremely low weight (carbon fiber) and high load capacity. This two-stage video tripod allows the video camera to be positioned at a height just under 5 ft. and can support up to 13 lb. of equipment! Its unique center column construction in carbon fiber and precision-machined red anodized aluminum includes a built-in 50mm leveling-ball system locked by a detachable rotating grip built at the bottom of the center column. This allows the camera operator to level the camera and even adjust its height without needing to make micro adjustments to each individual tripod leg.

Bogen Photo Corp.
565 East Crescent Ave.
P.O. Box 506
Ramsey, NJ 07446-0506
(201) 818-9500
www.bogenphoto.com
www.manfrotto.com

CINE 2000 | By Sachtler Corporation

With its all-metal construction and 35mm (1.4-inch) tube diameter, the Cine 2000 is an extremely stable tripod. The optional spreader and rubber feet are attached to the bottom of the tripod spike by an eccentric clamp. This ensures incredibly smooth operation, even when using the strongest damping drags. And you can adjust the friction between the tripod bowl and the legs.

Sachtler Corporation of America
55 North Main Street
Freeport, NY 11520
(516) 867-4900
www.sachtler.com

ENG 75/2 D | By Sachtler Corporation

Sachtler's new tripod, the ENG 75/2 D, does justice to the wide range of lightweight DV camcorders and convertible cameras on the market. With their compact dimensions, these tripods are indispensable companions. The proven Touch & Go system enables fast changeover, so camera operators can go from using the tripod to shooting from the shoulder within a matter of seconds. In combination with fluid heads DV 4 II and DV 2 II, this tripod system is ideal for mini-DV camcorders starting from around 1kg (2.2 lb.).

HOT POD CF | By Sachtler Corporation

The fastest tripod in the world is the perfect companion for the DV 8/100, DV 12, DV 15, and Video 18 Plus/Sensor. All that's needed to change the fluid head is a touch of the button — no tools are required! With its centering function, the Hot Pod's locking system simultaneously releases and locks all three legs. The pneumatic center column easily lifts loads up to 25kg (55.1 lb.) to lens heights of more than 2m (6.6 ft.) and has a factory-set elevation force that is maintenance-free. And if you need to move quickly, the Hot Pod CF has both a handle and a strap for easy carrying.

Sachtler Corporation of America
55 North Main Street
Freeport, NY 11520
(516) 867-4900
www.sachtler.com

MONOPOD 2 CF | By Sachtler Corporation

Sachtler's support for shoulder cameras is outstanding. Our lightweight carbon fiber technology is very fast and easy to handle. Users can choose double extension Monopods fitted with either the proven Sandwich Touch & Go system or a Betacam quick-release system. The Monopod 2 CF greatly reduces weight by avoiding the use of tripod adapter plates from camera manufacturers.

OB 2000 ALUMINUM TRIPODS | By Sachtler Corporation

The OB 2000 is the tripod for heavy cameras. The single-stage, heavy-duty, flat-base tripod has a built-in stabilizer that can hold a hand-crank column and lock it into place. Rotating rubber feet are built into the tripod legs. The built-in bubble and tripod leg scaling provide simple and precise leveling. The OB 2000 supports all common flat-base heads, including Mitchell video fittings, which do not require an adapter.

Sachtler Corporation of America
55 North Main Street
Freeport, NY 11520
(516) 867-4900
www.sachtler.com

SPEED LOCK CF HD 100MM DOUBLE EXTENSION CARBON FIBER TRIPODS | By Sachtler Corporation

The Speed Lock CF is the fastest two-stage tripod in the world! Simply release the three easy-to-reach clamps and the Speed Lock CF is ready for action. This extremely sturdy and twist-resistant carbon fiber tripod ensures that you're already shooting while the others are still setting up. The Speed Lock CF weighs less than 3kg (6.6 lb.), only a couple of hundred grams more than the ENG 2 CF, highly favored by camera crews all over the world. And if you need strength, the HD model has an amazing clamping force of 95kg (209 lb.).

DUOPOD PRO | Distributed by 16x9 Inc./Band Pro

DuoPod supports you in more ways than one — by combining the advantages of a tripod with those of a monopod, a simple but ingenious design that allows the impracticalities associated with using a monopod to be overcome. The DuoPod forms a brace between the user and monopod, providing the stability of a tripod whilst retaining the flexibility of a monopod. The units are waterproof up to the first joint as the bottom outer leg slides up over a thinner inner leg that does not allow water, sand, or silt to be sucked up into the unit. Each DuoPod is supplied with a rubber slipper that snaps onto the spiked foot of the DuoPod for use indoors on polished surfaces.

16x9 Inc.
3605 West Pacific Ave., Suite B
Burbank, CA 91505
(866) 800-1699
www.16x9inc.com

Band Pro Film/Video Inc.
3403 West Pacific Ave.
Burbank, CA 91505
(818) 841-9655
www.bandpro.com

TELEVATOR | By Telemetrics Inc.

The Telemetrics EP-PT Elevator Pedestal (TELEVATOR) is a remotely controlled, motorized telescoping tripod. It is designed to add pedestal height control to the Telemetrics Robotic Pan/Tilt product line. Additionally, the system can be used as a stand-alone teleprompter elevation system for studio applications. Optional Pan/Tilt mounting extensions available (6", 12", and 18").

Telemetrics Inc.
6 Leighton Place
Mahwah, NJ 07430
(201) 848-9818
www.telemetricsinc.com

FIBERTEC TRIPOD | By Vinten

Fibertec is up to three times more rigid than its nearest competitor, an ideal characteristic when using high levels of drag and long lenses, particularly in windy outdoor conditions. The unique design of the Fibertec's lever-operated clamping system is a significant contributory factor in the overall performance of the tripod. With long-term reliability, ease of operation, and minimal maintenance in mind, our designers have introduced a system that utilizes the entire length of the leg overlap. So the more the legs are nested, the bigger the clamping area, almost doubling the maximum carrying capacity of a traditional Vinten 100mm tripod to an impressive 45kg.

Vinten
709 Executive Boulevard
Valley Cottage, NY 10989
(845) 268-0100
www.vinten.com

VIDEO
CHARACTER
GENERATION SOFTWARE

42

Chyron:

Duet LEX
SOLO Laptop-Based CG System

Pinnacle Systems:

FXDeko II
PostDeko

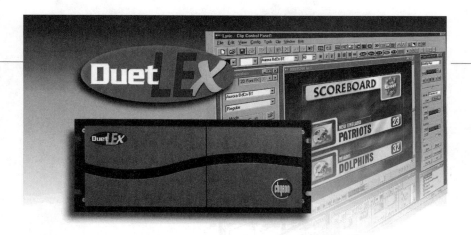

DUET LEX | By Chyron

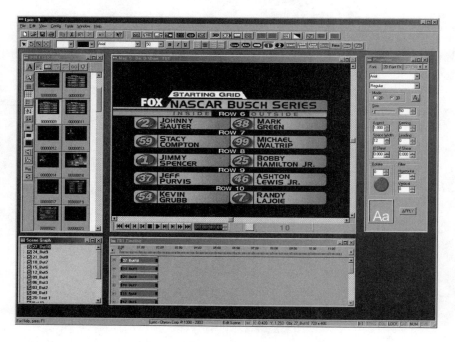

Duet LEX brings outstanding graphics with real-time animation to applications that require the highest quality yet need an economical price. It capitalizes on the compact cost-effectiveness of Duet LE while incorporating some of the sophisticated features of Duet SD, such as real-time animations and Chyron's CAL application. With multiple expansion slots, you have total flexibility to configure a system to fit your exact needs.

SOLO LAPTOP-BASED CG SYSTEM | By Chyron

With SOLO, a producer can create broadcast-quality content and then play it out all from a remote location. Harnessing the power of the Duet LEX in a 3-lb. chassis, SOLO is a one-channel, portable workhorse. SOLO brings outstanding graphics with real-time animation to applications that require the highest-quality DVEs and squeezeback in a portable solution. Sophisticated features of the Duet LEX such as Chyron's CAL application are run on state-of-the-art laptop hardware featuring a digital downstream keyer with bypass. SOLO SB features dual-channel squeeze-back containing the power of the Chyron PCI Squeezeback. With its superior blend of features, performance, and price, SOLO is the perfect solution for your demanding mobile application.

Chyron USA
5 Hub Drive
Melville, NY 11747
(631) 845-2000
www.chyron.com

FXDEKO II ON-AIR
CHARACTER GENERATOR | By
Pinnacle Systems, Inc.

"Before, we were often transcribing handwritten information from a piece of paper or a phone call. With Deko we have the ability to remove human errors, which is a great step up. When you're talking 400-500 graphics a day, it helps a lot."

— Patrick Twomey, Manager of Graphics Operation for CNBC, explaining how the FXDeko II can copy text directly from a reporter's e-mail into the Deko software to create a graphic
Quote obtained from Pinnacle Systems' Web site

DREAM GEAR | LORENZE | 316

Pinnacle Systems' flagship character generator, FXDeko II, delivers stunning multichannel-effects capability in a fully featured on-air graphics creation and play-out workstation. FXDeko II enables you to independently move text, graphics, and textures through 3-D space in real time. Additionally, with our content-independent effects, you can change text or elements and still maintain your look without adjustment. Individual objects can have actions independent of any other element or effect on the screen such as video squeezeback or continuous crawls.

Pinnacle Systems, Inc.
280 North Bernardo Ave.
Mountain View, CA 94043
(650) 526-1600
www.pinnaclesys.com

POSTDEKO
SOFTWARE-BASED
CHARACTER
GENERATOR | By
Pinnacle Systems, In

PostDeko provides a complete software-based character-generation solution for video production. As a stand-alone solution, PostDeko delivers a complete range of tools for creating anything from simple lower thirds to an entire look. PostDeko can also be networked with any turnkey Deko to provide a cost-effective second-user station for creating motion graphics that are ready for use on air. Automation capability and database integration enable PostDeko to play a vital role within any broadcast environment.

VIDEO
CONVERSION TOOLS

43

ADS Tech: Pyro A/V Link

Canopus: ADVC-100 DV Converter
                             ProCoder Format Converter

Datavideo: DAC-100 Composite Video Converter

JVC: BC-D2300U HDTV Upconverter

PYRO A/V LINK

By
ADS Technologies

The ultimate tool for capturing and converting video into professional-quality DV format and just as valuable for exporting edited DV content to analog videotape recorders. With PYRO A/V Link you can capture from any video source, including DV camcorders. Mix and match your video content to create a truly unique video production. Edit the video with Video Studio 6 SE DVD and add video filters, transition effects, video overlays, narration, background music, and more. When your video production is a wrap, export to any VCR or VTR, save as MPEG-2, and burn a DVD or publish to the Internet.

ADS Technologies
12627 Hidden Creek Way
Cerritos, CA 90703
(800) 888-5244
www.adstech.com

ADVC-100 DV CONVERTER

By
Canopus Corporation

Convert your S-VHS, Hi8, and 8mm analog tapes to DV in one simple step using the ADVC-100. The converted DV streams are transferred to your PC or Mac via IEEE1394 (i.Link, FireWire) and stored on your hard drive, where they can be manipulated using your favorite photo or video editing applications. This device is ideal for all OHCI and DV-only capture cards for Macintosh or PC.

Canopus Corporation
711 Charcot Ave.
San Jose, CA 95131
(888) 899-EDIT
www.canopus.com

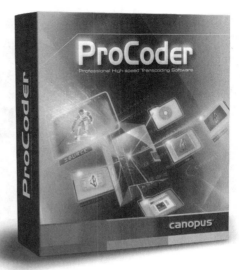

PROCODER FORMAT CONVERTER | By Canopus Corporation

Whether you're encoding MPEG for DVD production or a Windows Media for streaming, ProCoder makes conversion from one video format to another quick and easy. Featuring Canopus' highly optimized DV and MPEG CODECs, ProCoder provides high-quality output without the long wait and guesswork of similar tools. Stitching allows you to link multiple sources of various formats together to create a single seamless result, preventing you from having to combine the sources in an editor.

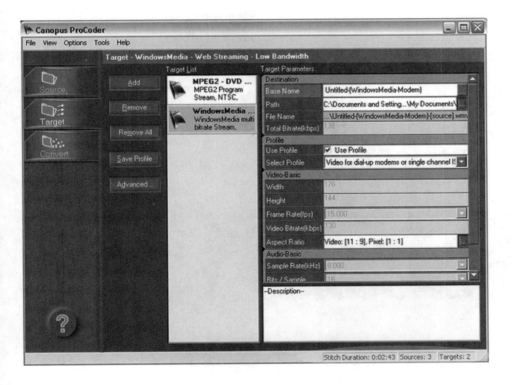

Canopus Corporation
711 Charcot Avenue
San Jose, CA 95131
(888) 899-EDIT
www.canopus.com

DAC-100 COMPOSITE VIDEO CONVERTER | By Datavideo Corporation

PC, PowerMac, and iMac platform video editors now have a simple, competent solution for transferring video and audio back and forth between analog tape and DV. Some key features include: selectable video standard — NTSC (525 lines/60Hz), PAL (625 lines/50Hz); inputs — DV, Y/C, Composite; outputs — DV, Y/C, Composite; formats — DV (i.Link), Digital 8, Video 8, Hi8, VHS, S-VHS, VHS-C, S-VHS-C, U-Matic, etc.

Datavideo Corporation
12300-U East Washington Blvd.
Whittier, CA 90606
(562) 696-2324
www.datavideo-tek.com

BC-D2300U HDTV UPCONVERTER | By JVC

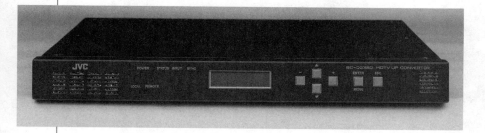

JVC's BC-D2300U HDTV Upconverter is a powerful new solution for broadcasters and post houses that smoothly converts 480i/4:2:2 component digital to high-quality 720P or 1080i. Some features include JVC's original "Advanced Bi-directional Motion Adaptive Architecture," SDI input with embedded audio, built-in audio resynchronization, aspect convert 4:3, and letterbox and squeeze.

JVC Headquarters
1700 Valley Road
Wayne, NJ 07470
(973) 317-5000
www.jvc.com/pro

VIDEO
DISK RECORDERS

44

Datavideo: DV Bank Video Disk Recorder/Playback

FOCUS Enhancements: FireStore DTE Solutions

IMP Electronics: HDVR Combo Video Disk Recorder/Video Assist

Sony: DSR-DU1 DVCAM Video Disk Unit

DV BANK VIDEO DISK RECORDER | By
Datavideo Corporation

The DV Bank is an instant-on, easy-to-use, reliable disk-based FireWire video recorder/player. Every DV Bank is specially formatted and has a self-contained processor optimized for storing video streams. A 60-Gigabyte hard drive (4.5 hours) or 120 GH HDD (9 hours) is available. VTR-style controls with large, illuminated buttons and a two-line backlit LCD display let the user select play, record, rewind, fast forward, fast reverse, pause, frame advance, file selection, file delete, and loop play. Its FireWire (IEEE1394) interface allows direct capture from digital camcorders, other digital VTRs, analog VTRs with a converter, or DV mixers. Other features include seamless repeat loop play (for trade shows), variable-speed forward or reverse play and play one frame at a time forward or reverse. DV Bank's accessories add utility to the obvious advantages of a disk recorder.

Datavideo Corporation
12300-U East Washington Blvd.
Whittier, CA 90606
(562) 696-2324
www.datavideo-tek.com

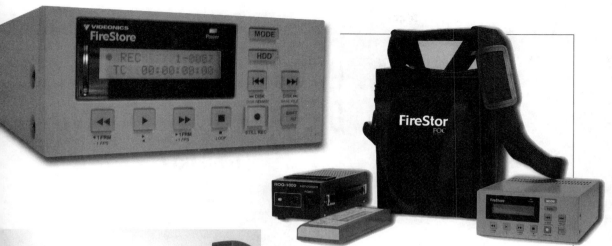

FIRESTORE DTE SOLUTIONS

By FOCUS Enhancements

FireStore series products convert any IEEE1394 (FireWire, i.Link) drive into high-performance digital disk recorder/players. Record directly to disk from your digital camcorder, VTR, or mixer. When you are ready to edit, your clips are immediately available to your NLE system — there is no need to capture, transfer files, or render! Mount FS-3 or DR-DV5000 directly to full-size DV camcorders and record directly to disk while you shoot! These FireStore models are ideal for ENG, field production, videography, and other applications that require DTE technology in the field. DR-DV5000 features unique capabilities for JVC camcorders. If you edit with applications from Adobe, Apple, Avid, Canopus, Matrox, Pinnacle, Sonic Foundry, Ulead, and many others, FireStore's DTE technology is the only solution that can save you up to 25 hours a month by recording clips to disk in your NLE's native file format!

FOCUS Enhancements
1370 Dell Avenue
Campbell, CA 95008
(408) 866-8300
www.focusinfo.com

IMP Electronics
Rocol Building
3, Glebe Road, Huntington
Cambridgeshire, PE29 7DL, UK
+44 (0)1 480-411-822
www.imp-electronics.co.uk

DSR-DU1 DVCAM VIDEO DISK UNIT | By Sony Electronics

Sony Electronics
One Sony Drive
Park Ridge, NJ 07656
(800) 686-7669
www.sony.com/professional

HDVR COMBO VIDEO DISK RECORDER AND VIDEO ASSIST | By IMP Electronics

The HDVR Combo Video Disk Recorder is a critically acclaimed instant-replay machine that works alongside the Panavision and Arri film cameras in a video assist role. Its immediate video playback allows film directors to make decisions that previously had to wait for the next day's developed film. The HDVR Combo features film-friendly controls, variable speeds, mixes live camera with stored shots for comparison, and has an input/output panel uniquely suited to studio and location film work. Movie credits include *Tomb Raider*, *Harry Potter*, and *Star Wars II*.

By connecting the unit to compatible DVCAM shoulder-type camcorders with the new CA-DU1 camera adapter or handheld-type DVCAM camcorders, both via the i.LINK DV I/O connection, the DSR-DU1 can record video and audio signals in the internal hard disk drive in parallel with the tape in the camcorder, enabling the DSR-DU1 to serve as a complementary recording device. The DSR-DU1 can also serve as an extension to the recording time being provided by the tape. Allowing acquisition in both media of hard disk and tape, the DSR-DU1 offers workflow innovation by providing production efficiency and flexibility as well as enhancing confidence of shooting within a DVCAM system. After shooting, content in the DSR-DU1 can be instantly reviewed through the camera viewfinder. Indexing is also available, enabling edit preparation even in the field. The DSR-DU1 can then be connected to a computer and provide 2X transfer of the recorded material via SBP2 connection, helping to avoid downtime and streamlining the editing process.

VIDEO
EFFECTS SOFTWARE
AND SYSTEMS

45

Adobe:	After Effects Visual Effects Software
Apple:	Shake Compositing and Effects Software
Aurora Video Systems:	Igniter RT311 Studio Bundle
Boris FX:	RED Effects and Rendering Software
Digital Anarchy:	Aurora Sky Plug-In Geomancy Plug-In Psunami Plug-In
Discreet:	Flame Visual Effects System Inferno Visual Effects System
Pinnacle Systems:	DVEXtremePlus
Quantel:	QEdit Pro QColor
Silicon Graphics:	Octane2
StageTools:	MovingPicture Plug-In
Thomson/Grass Valley:	Shout Restoration Software

AFTER EFFECTS MOTION GRAPHICS AND VISUAL EFFECTS SOFTWARE | By Adobe

Adobe After Effects 6.0 software sets new standards for motion graphics and visual effects. It delivers the speed, precision, and powerful tools you need to produce visually innovative motion graphics and effects for film, video, DVD, and the Web. After Effects 6.0 is available in two editions: After Effects 6.0 Standard provides core 2-D and 3-D compositing, animation, and visual effects tools. After Effects 6.0 Professional adds motion tracking and stabilization, advanced keying and warping tools, more than 30 additional visual effects, a particle system, render automation and network rendering, 16-bit-per-channel color, 3-D channel effects, and additional audio effects.

Adobe Systems Incorporated
345 Park Ave.
San Jose, CA 95110
(408) 536-6000
www.adobe.com

"Because Shake's 2-D motion blur is so fast, and in certain situations is indiscernible from 3-D motion blur, we were able to meet the critical render deadline and get the trailer out to the theaters on time."

— Andrew Beddini, Compositing Lead & Lightings TD at Blue Sky Studios, commenting on production of the all-CGI film *Ice Age*

Quote obtained from Apple's Web site

SHAKE COMPOSITING AND VISUAL EFFECTS SOFTWARE | By Apple

Shake is the industry's most advanced compositing software designed for large-format productions by major motion picture studios and leading visual effects houses. Shake features the fastest resolution-independent software rendering engine on the market, a production-proven visual effects toolset, and a compositing architecture that supports multiple bit depths within a single project. Shake has been used in the production of more than a hundred motion pictures, including all three films in the Academy Award-winning *Lord of the Rings* trilogy.

Apple
1 Infinite Loop
Cupertino, CA 95014
(800) MY-APPLE
www.apple.com

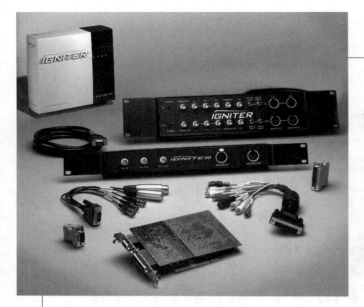

IGNITER
RT311
STUDIO
BUNDLE

By
Aurora Video Systems

"Here at the Simpsons' TV show, we use the Aurora Igniter with (Adobe's) Premiere to shoot pencil test animations at 24 frames per second, so the writers and directors can see their shows and make changes. I've tested dozens of high-end capture cards, and the Aurora Igniter was the only one that worked for us. The image quality is hands-down the best. The quality is so good, I recommended the Igniter to several other animation shows we do here at Film Roman."

— Reid Kramer, Animator with Film Roman *(The Simpsons* and *King of the Hill)*

Quote provided by Aurora Video Systems

Designed exclusively for the Mac, Aurora's family of innovative Igniter video capture and editing cards have helped thousands of postproduction professionals in more than 30 countries revolutionize their facilities and creative processes. Widely recognized as an industry pioneer, Aurora introduced the world's first Mac-only, Betacam-compatible card that works without converters and provides real-time, 24fps editing for Final Cut Pro and true offline editing for Mac OSX. Among the world-class professionals and facilities that rely on Aurora to deliver superior results on time and within budget are Walter Murch (*Godfather II, Apocalypse Now, The English Patient*), Film Roman (*The Simpsons, King of the Hill*), Magic Film and Video Works (*ER, NYPD Blue, West Wing*), and the Oxygen Network.

Aurora Video Systems
7633 Nineteen-Mile Road
Sterling Heights, MI 48314
(586) 726-5320
www.auroravideosys.com

RED EFFECTS AND RENDERING SOFTWARE | By Boris FX

"The titles I do with RED don't look like anybody else's, which is a big part of creating a visual identity for our station. The most important thing that titles need to do is reinforce the message of the words being spoken. We recently did a story about the water on some airlines being unsafe, so I started with a title, quickly nested a QuickTime movie in the font, then added a ripple filter to make the whole thing move like water. I also added a ripple on the background and masked in some color effects."

— Kristi Joiner-Simpson, Senior Promotion Producer for CBS 5 — KPHO in Phoenix

Quote obtained from the Boris FX Web site

Boris RED 2.5 offers an unprecedented range of options for integrated 3-D compositing, titling, and effects creation and adds stand-alone rendering capabilities. Some highlights include motion tracking and stabilization, vector paint and rotoscoping, and can import, extrude, and animate EPS/Illustrator files.

Boris FX
381 Congress Street
Boston, MA 02210
(888) 772-6747
www.borisfx.com

AURORA SKY
PLUG-IN | By Digital Anarchy

Aurora Sky allows you to create realistic three-dimensional skies in After Effects and Final Cut Pro. This plug-in gives you a wide variety of special effects that are substantially more powerful and flexible than simple fractal clouds. Create suns, stars, haze, volumetric light — anything you can imagine. Aurora takes advantage of the new 3-D capabilities of After Effects. You can use texture and cloud shaping maps to create wildly custom sky-scapes. And Aurora gives you the option of truly volumetric 3-D clouds (with a bit of a render hit) that let you create clouds like smoke and fog.

GEOMANCY
PLUG-IN | By Digital Anarchy

Geomancy is a three plug-in set that creates and animates lines and shapes. While these common design elements are easy to create, they can be quite tedious to animate. We make this easy for you. A particle system generates the shapes, and "randomness" options abound. Parameters include thickness, length, location, path of motion, growth rate, and growth constraint. From rapid wormlike lines to flowing electricity or water, to basic squares, stars, and Xs, Geomancy is flexible and dynamic for creating patterns and texture, shapes and lines.

PSUNAMI
PLUG-IN | By
Digital Anarchy

Psunami 1.0 generates precise 3-D geometry of an ocean surface, then produces ultra-realistic ray-traced output that is practically indistinguishable from the real thing. With Psunami, artists can design, animate, and render 3-D oceanographic effects completely within After Effects 4.x/5.x. Psunami utilizes the RenderWorld ray-tracing render engine from Arete Image Software, for render quality previously unavailable except in high-end 3-D systems. It's been used on a number of feature films, television productions, and commercials.

Digital Anarchy
120 Pierce Street, Suite 10
San Francisco, CA 94117
(415) 621-0991
www.digitalanarchy.com

FLAME VISUAL EFFECTS SYSTEM | By Discreet

Flame is a high-performance visual effects system, designed to empower the world's leading digital artists to work interactively on projects ranging from intensely complex visual effects of feature film to the fast-paced sessions of online commercial spots. Flame offers artists one of the most comprehensive toolsets for visual effects design available today — everything from state-of-the-art keying, tracking, and color-correction tools to one of the most sophisticated 3-D compositing environments ever designed.

Discreet Corporate Headquarters
10 rue Duke
Montreal, Quebec
H3C 2L7 Canada
(800) 869-3504
www.discreet.com

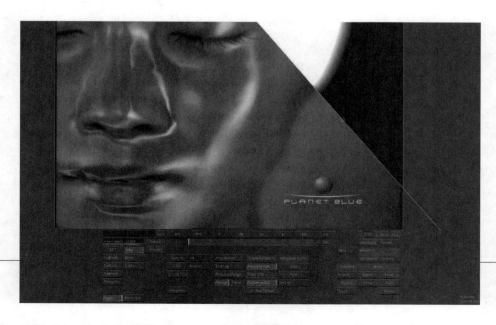

INFERNO VISUAL EFFECTS SYSTEM | By Discreet

The ultimate visual effects system, Inferno is Discreet's Academy Award-winning solution for fast, interactive creative design. Used by the world's leading artists, the Inferno system delivers incredible performance combined with one of the most sophisticated visual effects toolsets on the market today. Designed for fast project turnaround under the tightest production schedules, Inferno provides an interactive 3-D design environment with real-time capabilities for standard-definition video, HDTV, DTV, and 2K digital cinema. The Inferno Visual Effects System is used extensively on projects ranging from feature film effects work, opening title sequences, and trailers to commercial spots, music videos, broadcast IDs, and promos.

Discreet Corporate Headquarters
10 rue Duke
Montreal, Quebec
H3C 2L7 Canada
(800) 869-3504
www.discreet.com

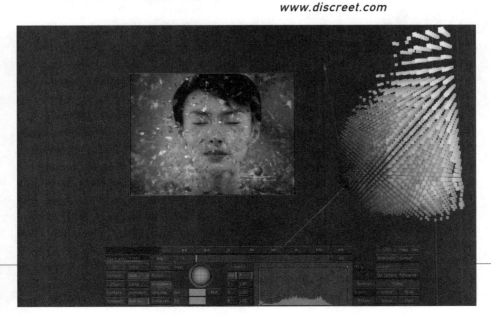

DVEXTREME PLUS | By Pinnacle Systems

DVEXtremePlus is the culmination of Pinnacle Systems' decade of experience, five Emmy awards and more than 18,000 real-time production DVE systems around the world. DVEXtremePlus adds features that will greatly enhance your productions. Global 3-D Highlights allow you to add two types of light sources that interact in 3-D space. The 3-D Flood Light has adjustments for position, intensity, ambient, diffuse, specular, and attenuation. The 3-D Spot Light adds adjustments for beam rotation and cone angle. Wipe patterns with borders are now available on each channel.

Pinnacle Systems, Inc.
280 North Bernardo Ave.
Mountain View, CA 94043
(650) 526-1600
www.pinnaclesys.com

QEDIT PRO | By Quantel

QEdit Pro is the price performance leader in PC-based NLEs. Quantel performance and quality hit the mainstream with this all-new editing and effects system designed from the ground up for today's multi-format world. QEdit Pro is an uncompressed, 10-bit AAF-compliant SD/HD, PC-based NLE with unrivalled finishing performance. Combining Quantel hardware, PC openness, a new source/record editing model effects and compositing based on the legendary Henry and Paintbox systems, QEdit Pro sets a new benchmark for price, performance, and quality in PC-based NLEs.

Quantel
Headquartered in Newbury, UK, Quantel has offices in the USA, Europe, Asia, Japan, Korea, and Australia
www.quantel.com

QCOLOR | By Quantel

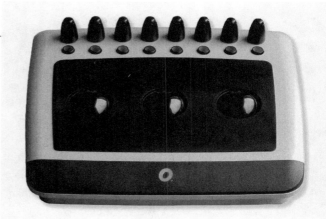

QColor is an integrated hardware and software option for eQ offering an additional set of color-correction tools and an entirely new approach to grading. QColor's flexible toolset and ergonomics make it ideal for a wide range of HD and SD grading projects. Advanced compositing tools such as tracker-linked masked correction and the ability to keyframe every part of the QColor interface allow for the creation of complex effects easily and quickly.

OCTANE2 VISUAL WORKSTATION | By Silicon Graphics, Inc.

Silicon Graphics, Inc.
1500 Crittenden Lane
Mountain View, CA 94043
(650) 960-1980
www.sgi.com

"Sulley (the monster voiced by John Goodman in Monsters, Inc.*') is covered with shaggy fur consisting of millions of individual hairs. All that hair was positioned and styled interactively on the Octane2 workstations, and the motion of the hair was computed using our proprietary algorithms for dynamics simulation."*

— Darwyn Peachey, Vice President of Technology, Pixar Animation Studios

Quote Obtained from Silicon Graphics' Web site

Octane2 delivers a suite of industry-leading options including the award-winning, DMediaPro DM2 video option for the most powerful High-Definition solution on the desktop. Complementing DM2 is the new DMediaPro DM5 for high-quality uncompressed HD and SD graphics-to-video output from 3-D graphics, 2-D imagery, and video data. Other innovative options include the Dual Head and Dual Channel Display options, which maximize your visualization resources, and the new, cost-effective PowerDuo configuration, which allows two users to share the same high-performance system.

"See the SGI ad featuring the new Silicon Graphics® Tezro™ visual workstation at the back of this book in the RESOURCES section."

MOVINGPICTURE PLUG-IN | By StageTools LLC

MovingPicture allows documentary and industrial filmmakers to pan and zoom on high-resolution images (up to 8000 x 8000 pixels). Rather than use an expensive and bulky motion-control rig or animation stand, often requiring expensive photographic prints, MovingPicture takes high-resolution scanned images and allows for perfectly repeatable pans and zoom moves on a desktop computer.

StageTools LLC
34313 Welbourne Road
Middleburg, VA 20117
(540) 592-7001
www.stagetools.com

SHOUT RESTORATION TOOL | A Grass Valley product by Thomson Broadcast & Media Solutions

Designed primarily for film applications, our software-based Shout Restoration Tool is working-resolution independent and can remove typical film-related artifacts such as dirt, scratches, and other common frame defects. Using powerful motion-estimation algorithms for every frame, it can identify and mark defects automatically, letting an operator accept or reject a proposed repair. Shout is available as a stand-alone software application for standard SGI platforms or as a preconfigured workstation package.

Thomson Broadcast & Media Solutions
400 Providence Mine Road
Nevada City, CA 95959
(530) 478-3000
www.thomsongrassvalley.com

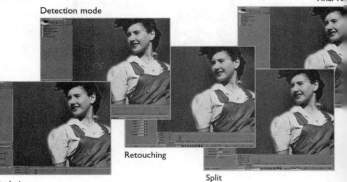

Detection mode

Retouching

Original picture

Split

Final re

VIDEO
NONLINEAR
EDITING SOLUTIONS

46

Adobe:	**Premiere**
Apple:	**Final Cut Pro**
Avid:	**Avid Media Browse** **Avid Media Composer Adrenaline**
Edirol:	**DV-7 Digital Video Workstation**
Leitch:	**dpsVelocity** **dpsVelocityQ**
Panasonic:	**newsBYTE50**
Pinnacle Systems:	**CineWave** **Liquid Blue** **Liquid Purple** **TARGA 3000**
Quantel:	**eQ** **iQ**

PREMIERE | By Adobe

Delivering unmatched hardware support, Adobe Premiere 6.5 software is the most adaptable DV-editing tool on the market. Now you can work more productively with Real-Time Preview. And you can take advantage of the sophisticated new Adobe Title Designer, MPEG-2 export, DVD authoring, powerful audio tools, and more to create extraordinary video productions. Whether you want to edit digital video on your laptop or work with multiple layers of analog footage on a professional, hardware-based, real-time system, Adobe Premiere is the hands-down choice for desktop video editing.

Adobe Systems Incorporated
345 Park Ave.
San Jose, CA 95110
(408) 536-6000
www.adobe.com

FINAL CUT PRO | By Apple

Final Cut Pro 4 is the creative, professional, and extensible tool for editing and finishing in SD and HD formats. From the innovative OfflineRT and DV to uncompressed 10-bit 601 or HD, Final Cut Pro 4 is perfect for editing and finishing a wide variety of programs at virtually any resolution or frame rate. Video pros will appreciate the rich, new editing tools and new customization features. RT Extreme, a sophisticated, multi-stream, real-time architecture, supports an increased number of video streams and effects. Final Cut Pro gives digital artists the freedom to explore their creativity. And with support from DVCPRO50 built in, it has the power to deliver professional, broadcast-quality 4:2:2 images from the field.

Apple
1 Infinite Loop
Cupertino, CA 95014
(800) MY-APPLE
www.apple.com

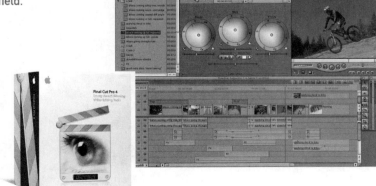

AVID MEDIA BROWSE | By Avid

Journalists aren't always trained editors. But sometimes they need to work like they are. Maybe they need precise shot lists so that the editor can focus on crafting a professional package instead of wasting time looking for footage. Or the schedule is so tight that they need a frame-accurate, cuts-only story to send directly to play out. Only Avid Media Browse workstations put these powerful tools on the journalist's desktop. Avid Media Browse systems take the journalist from writing to script to telling a story.

AVID MEDIA COMPOSER ADRENALINE | By Avid

Avid Technology, Inc.
Avid Technology Park
One Park West
Tewksbury, MA 01876
(978) 640-6789
www.avid.com

"To me, the Media Composer is designed for spot work. It's a really good packaging of rather sophisticated tools that allows you to create what looks like a darned-near finished spot. I remember the old days of workprints and grease pencil marks and splicing tape — the editor was really the only one who could tell what the thing was going to look like when it was finished. Nowadays, there tends to be a lot less difference between the rough cut and the finished piece. I've even had people ask me if those time code numbers are going to be there in the finished ad."

— Editor Dan Swietlik, Owner of Swietlik, whose company edited the *Terry Tate* and *Streaker* Super Bowl ads for Reebok

Quote obtained from Avid's Web site

Designed for high-pressure, time-sensitive production environments, the new Media Composer Adrenaline system is a revolutionary new architecture combining the power of next generation Media Composer software with state-of-the-art Avid Adrenaline Digital Nonlinear Accelerator (DNA) hardware — purpose built for 10-bit video, 24-bit 96kHz audio, HD expansion, and flash upgradability. Up to seven real-time uncompressed SD video streams with room to grow. Backward compatible with AVR and Meridien projects and media. Support for even more media formats — mixable right in the timeline. New high-quality, real-time Open GL 2D and 3D DVE. Patent-pending AutoCorrect technology that color corrects entire sequences automatically. Facility-class connectivity and compatibility. Everything you expect from the Media Composer system and much more.

DV-7 DIGITAL VIDEO WORKSTATION | By Edirol Corporation

The DV-7 provides all of the tools for loading video and audio, creating titles, editing, processing, and output of the finished job in one integrated package. Pursuing zero loss in source image quality, the DV-7 Digital Video Workstation uses the same native DV format used by digital video cameras. This means you can connect a digital video camera to the DV port and transfer audio and video without any loss in picture quality. The DV-7 also records analog audio and video in DV format, and after editing there is little discernible difference in quality.

Edirol Corporation North America
425 Sequoia Drive, Suite 114
Bellingham, WA 98226
(360) 594-4273
www.edirol.com

DPSVELOCITY | By Leitch Technology International Inc.

The acclaimed dpsVelocity nonlinear editing system is the ultimate "no compromise" dual-stream real-time solution for digital video and content creation professionals. dpsVelocity combines dual-stream real-time hardware with powerful NLE software to produce exceptional integrated editing solutions with guaranteed real-time performance and an unparalleled level of efficiency, reliability, and ease of use. dpsVelocity is also ideal for live Webcasting, because live video from a camera or deck can be combined in real time with titles, transitions, and previously captured clips and then streamed live to the Internet.

Leitch Technology International Inc.
150 Ferrand Drive, Suite 700
Toronto, Ontario
M3C 3E5 Canada
(416) 445-9640
www.leitch.com

DPSVELOCITYQ | By Leitch Technology International Inc.

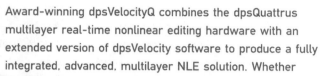

Award-winning dpsVelocityQ combines the dpsQuattrus multilayer real-time nonlinear editing hardware with an extended version of dpsVelocity software to produce a fully integrated, advanced, multilayer NLE solution. Whether producing content for video, broadcast, CD-ROM, DVD, or the Web, dpsVelocityQ provides the features and workflow that professionals have come to depend on. With real-time features including full-quality simultaneous playback of four video streams, up to six graphics streams, and four channels of real-time 3-D DVE, dspVelocityQ raises the bar for real-time performance.

NEWSBYTE50 | By Panasonic

The newsBYTE50 is the world's first and only DVCPRO50/DVCPRO native nonlinear editing system with a dual built-in 50Mbps, 4:2:2 DVCPRO50/DVCPRO VTR. The newsBYTE50 includes the high-end features you expect in a leading news-editing system yet is as simple to learn as many cuts-only editors. The newsBYTE50 allows you to streamline the production process, boost operational efficiency, and dramatically improve time to air. Panasonic's Emmy award-winning DVCPRO format is used daily at more than 750 U.S. television stations — making DVCPRO the most rapidly adopted digital broadcast format in history.

Panasonic Broadcast & Television Systems Co.
1 Panasonic Way
Secaucus, NJ 07094
(800) 528-8601
www.panasonic.com/broadcast

CINEWAVE | By Pinnacle Systems

"In many cases, we might record a rehearsal for a complicated stunt on the computer and play it back at four or five different speeds. Once the director has decided on a speed, he can shoot the 'take' on film at his desired speed without risking the stunt man's health. With CineWave HD as part of our video assist solution, the producer no longer has to mentally visualize a shot but can see it in High-Definition or in uncompressed SD in real time with added effects, multiple speeds, and compositing." (During the filming of Matrix Reloaded, *Ocean Wave recorded a car chase sequence and used CineWave to show multiple speed previews. The directors wanted to film the chase sequence with a high-speed camera at 120 frames per second. With traditional video assist technology, it's impossible to show slow- or fast-motion playback at various speeds. With the CineWave system, Ocean Video was able to play the scene at 20% of real time.)*

— Jeb Johenning, Co-Owner of Ocean Video, on their use of CineWave for *Matrix Reloaded*

Quote and background information obtained from Pinnacle's Web site

CineWave is software and hardware working together to seamlessly deliver unprecedented quality and flexibility on the Mac G4. Work with your favorite applications without sacrificing image quality or interoperability. With infinite layering, awesome effects, advanced nonlinear editing, the fastest and most accurate motion tracker, and paint and compositing tools, CineWave allows you the freedom to create and the power to produce.

Pinnacle Systems, Inc.
280 North Bernardo Ave.
Mountain View, CA 94043
(650) 526-1600
www.pinnaclesys.com

LIQUID BLUE | By Pinnacle Systems

Pinnacle Liquid Blue delivers complete native support for every video format — that means no more transcoding and no more degradation by recompression. You get the best-possible image quality for every project and the tools you need to create finished masterpieces. Designed for seamless integration within existing broadcast and post-production facilities, Pinnacle Liquid Blue supports a variety of network solutions and topologies from simple transfer networks to large storage area networks.

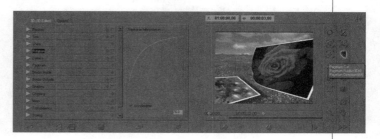

"In 30 days' time, we changed the entire look of the station (logos, station promos, etc.). We couldn't have done that on another system. The advantages of what Pinnacle Liquid had, how efficient it is, how fast it is — we could never have gotten the station off the ground so fast with any other product. We would have been in rendering hell."

— Brian Cisek and Joe Mustacchi,
Editors at AZTV Cable Station in Arizona
Quote obtained from Pinnacle's Web site

LIQUID PURPLE | By Pinnacle Systems

Pinnacle Liquid Purple is the ideal desktop solution for broadcast, independent film, education, corporate, and any video professional who needs a cost-effective solution for creating dazzling video content. Pinnacle Liquid Purple begins with Pinnacle Liquid, the same intelligent application found on the Pinnacle Liquid Blue, Liquid Chrome, and Liquid Silver solutions. This common interface means that your skills and your footage move seamlessly between all our editing systems as your needs change.

Pinnacle Systems, Inc.
280 North Bernardo Ave.
Mountain View, CA 94043
(650) 526-1600
www.pinnaclesys.com

TARGA 3000 | By Pinnacle Systems

"We routinely create trade show and internal videos for Intel and Microsoft, and have created high-end videos for car companies like Nissan, Toyota, and Hyundai. TARGA 3000's real-time rendering option helps create projects faster and easier because we can now tweak things on the timeline and render much faster."

— Judah and Ben Jehoshua, Owners of Image Line Media
Quote obtained from Pinnacle's Web site

The TARGA 3000 desktop editing and compositing solution provides impeccable quality including true, uncompressed video as well as MPEG-2 and DV video processing. TARGA 3000 includes tools for 3-D animators and Web producers with native support for video and key as well as the Animation Recorder and OneStep capture plug-ins. TARGA 3000 includes such real-time FX as interpolated slow-motion, curve-fitting color correction, and sub-pixel DVEs with masks.

Pinnacle Systems, Inc.
280 North Bernardo Ave.
Mountain View, CA 94043
(650) 526-1600
www.pinnaclesys.com

EQ | By Quantel

eQ is a completely new nonlinear postproduction environment. Designed for full-resolution, mixed-format, online SD and HD effects and finishing, eQ eliminates the barriers of today's multi-format post environments by using Resolution Coexistence, the exclusive Quantel technology that allows real-time mixing and output of any SD or HD format — no format conversion time is required, nor is drive space wasted storing multiple formats. Format conversion and aspect-ratio conversion happens instantly via the powerful Quantel hardware — no rendering is required in editing or output.

Quantel
Headquartered in Newbury, UK, Quantel has offices in the USA, Europe, Asia, Japan, Korea, and Australia
www.quantel.com

IQ | By Quantel

"[iQ] really is an extremely versatile beast. Color correction on iQ is fantastic, rendering time is megafast, and its multi-resolution capabilities put it in a class of its own. Audience expectations are much higher these days and it was important to the producers that the added depth which HD brings to the images on screen was maintained. We knew this was going to be a tricky project and we didn't have the time to mess around or get it wrong."

— Vicki Braden, Editor at Henninger 1150 Post in Washington, DC, and editor of Bob Ballard's National Geographic documentary *The Quest for Noah's Flood*

Quote obtained from Quantel's Web site

iQ is Quantel's Digital Intermediate system that brings new levels of immediacy and creative feedback to the production pipeline and helps filmmakers realize their vision more completely than ever before. For the biggest Hollywood blockbuster right through to the low-budget, local-interest feature, Quantel DI puts the director totally in control. iQ is a visionary technology that lets postproduction facilities radically rethink the way they work to compete in today's multi-resolution world.

Quantel
Headquartered in Newbury, UK, Quantel has offices in the USA, Europe, Asia, Japan, Korea, and Australia
www.quantel.com

If you have used this gear and want to share your own experiences, comments, and suggestions in our next edition, send an e-mail to Catherine Lorenze at *DREAMGEAR@cox.net*. We are particularly interested in innovative ways you have used the gear that will help inspire other film, video, and TV professionals.

VIDEO
PORTABLE
EDITING TOOLS

47

Avid:	Avid NewsCutter XP
1 Beyond:	DV Pro 3000 Laptop ND Video Pro Mobile Editor
Sony:	DNWA25WS Betacam Portable Editing Recorder
Thomson/Grass Valley:	NewsEdit LT Laptop

AVID NEWSCUTTER XP | By Avid

Avid NewsCutter XP systems provide an affordable, full-featured nonlinear editing suite in a powerful software package for organizations that are beginning their newsroom upgrade, and for craft editors and journalist-editors who want to record to timeline in an intuitive, high-speed environment. This solution includes all the editing and creative features of the Adrenaline FX model with single-stream DV25, DV50, and 50Mb IMX editing — all on the same timeline. Add the Avid Mojo DNA hardware, and you'll gain comprehensive I/O with composite and S-video inputs — right over FireWire — and with QuickRecord, you'll be able to edit complete packages right from the VTR.

Avid Technology, Inc.
Avid Technology Park
One Park West
Tewksbury, MA 01876
(978) 640-6789
www.avid.com

DV PRO 3000 LAPTOP | By 1 Beyond, Inc.

1 Beyond is the first company to develop a laptop specifically for the video professional because its design alleviates the five constraints found in consumer laptops: power — the latest desktop Dual P4 with Hyper/Threading takes advantage of software optimized for dual processors; speed — desktop processors now allow the execution speed to be increased to 3.06GHz; data flow — the desktop bus is 533MHz; disk speed — the single disk of consumer laptops is replaced by dual to quadruple raided drives yielding 70MBs; and space — the raided hard drives of the DV Pro 3000 can provide up to 240GBs internally.

1 Beyond, Inc.
61 Medford Street
Somerville, MA 02143
(877) 663-2396
www.1beyond.com

ND VIDEO PRO MOBILE EDITOR AND ON-SITE BROADCASTER | By 1 Beyond, Inc.

The ND Video Pro Mobile Editor and On-Site Broadcaster offers the same high performance as our desktop systems but in a portable case. It's a unique combination of power, portability, lossless native DV video editing, live Webcasting, and Web video streaming. The configuration includes the power to create high-quality native DV video with Adobe Premiere 6.0 and related tools including hardware-accelerated special effects and real-time DV editing; broadcast live to the Web; and prepare edited video for on-demand Web streaming.

DNWA25WS BETACAM SX WIDE-SCREEN CAPABLE PORTABLE EDITING RECORDER | By Sony Electronics

Sony's DNWA25WS is small, lightweight, and rugged, and includes a built-in LCD video monitor. Ideal for ENG field editing, this unit is small enough to be carried by hand and versatile enough to be used internationally. It features frame-accurate insert editing functions, as well as Betacam and Betacam SP tape playback, making it a very flexible product for broadcast stations bridging the analog and digital worlds. The DNWA25WS can be docked with a second DNWA25WS to form a complete portable editing package and can also be used as a feeder or as a third VTR for A/B roll with the DNWA225.

Sony Electronics
One Sony Drive
Park Ridge, NJ 07656
(800) 686-7669
www.sony.com/professional

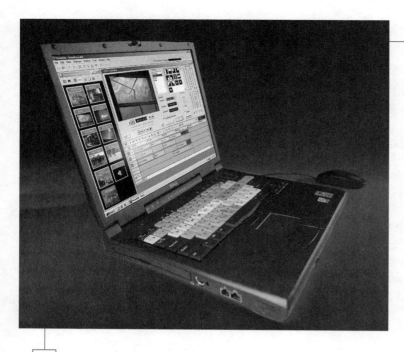

Up twice as fast as traditional nonlinear editing applications, our NewsEdit LT system is the fastest available for field journalists. You can see edits as they're being made, eliminating the edit review process — and start editing before a feed ingest is complete, speeding things further. With its cuts-only edit-bay capabilities, traditional A/B roll suite functions, and a highly networked design, this turnkey system offers an unmatched toolset for journalists who need instant mobility.

NEWSEDIT LT LAPTOP

A Grass Valley product by
Thomson Broadcast & Media Solutions

Thomson Broadcast &
Media Solutions
400 Providence Mine Road
Nevada City, CA 95959
(530) 478-3000
www.thomsongrassvalley.com

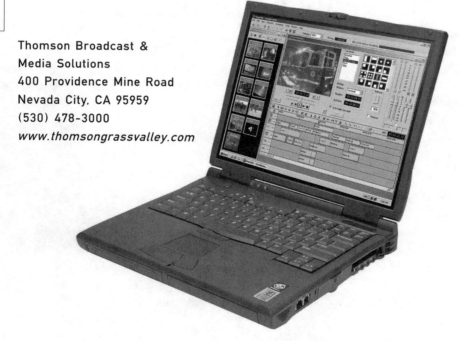

VIDEO
RECORDERS AND
PLAYBACK TOOLS
48

JVC: SR-VDA300US Recorder
                        SR-VD400US D-VHS Player

Sony: DVW250 Digital Betacam Portable Recorder
                        HDW250 HDCAM Field Recorder

Y-Vamp: DigiClam Digital Video Recorder/Video Assist

SR-VDA300US PRO-HD MASTERING RECORDER | By JVC

Now you can master Pro-HD recordings using JVC's "pro-scramble" content protection with this advanced 25Mbps bitstream recorder. The SR-VDA300US is ideal for digital dailies and economical distribution of High-Definition recordings. Features include: high-quality picture (25Mbps), JVC's Original Scramble technology, password protection for individual copies, and an ASI interface to pro-MPEG-2 HD encoder.

SR-VD400US D-VHS RECORDER/PLAYER, PRO-HD PLAYER | By JVC

Distribution of true, High-Definition programming has never been simpler and more economical. JVC's SR-VD400US plays all variations of D-VHS including password- and non-password-protected Pro-HD (pro-scramble) recordings, standard D-VHS, and D-Theater. In addition to outstanding High-Definition recording and playback, the SR-VD400US has a built-in MPEG-2 encoder (SD) and can be used to record digital standard definition in both scrambled and unscrambled modes, with or without password protection.

JVC Headquarters
1700 Valley Road
Wayne, NJ 07470
(973) 317-5000
www.jvc.com/pro

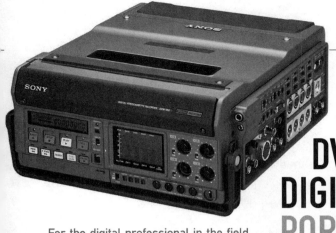

DVW250
DIGITAL BETACAM
PORTABLE
RECORDER | By Sony Electronics

For the digital professional in the field, Sony's DVW250 Digital Betacam Portable Recorder/Player records 4:2:2 10-bit component digital video and four channels of digital audio. The unit will operate for two hours on Sony's optional lithium-ion battery (BPL-60A). Both BNC and 26-pin SDI inputs are provided along with analog component/composite. The four channels of analog audio interface via standard XLR connectors or are embedded with video on SDI.

HDW250 HDCAM
FIELD RECORDER | By Sony Electronics

For capturing those important images in the field, a top-of-the-line field recorder is key. Sony's HDW250 portable HDCAM VTR can be used with a variety of Sony High-Definition cameras, including the HDC-750A multipurpose camera, DXC-H10 compact camera, HDW-700A camcorders, and HDW750. It is compatible with both 1035 and 1080 line signals. The HDW250 inherits all of the advantages of the DVW250 Digital Betacam portable VTR, especially the familiarity of its operation. There are multiple inputs including a 26-pin camera input and HD-SDI. There are multiple outputs including HD-SDI, analog HD component, and composite down-converted NTSC.

Sony Electronics
One Sony Drive
Park Ridge, NJ 07656
(800) 686-7669
www.sony.com/professional

DIGI**CLAM** | By Y-Vamp Corporation

The DigiClam is a digital video recorder that plays back at variable speeds. It is compact, with a durable design, and is highly mobile. Its features are simple and easy to operate. DigiClam is intended to replace aging 8mm combos. Its large, internal hard drive stores up to 150 hours of video and makes it the perfect recorder for video assist and security systems. Some main features include: rugged mini-size — 7.5" x 10" x 3.5" (19 x 25.4 x 9cm); broadcast-quality MPEG-2 recording and playback; programmable compression ratio for optimum quality; anamorphic 2.35:1, 16:9, 4:3 selectable aspect ratio; instant replay on normal/slow/fast/freeze playback; and playback of any fps ±1fps to ±1200fps.

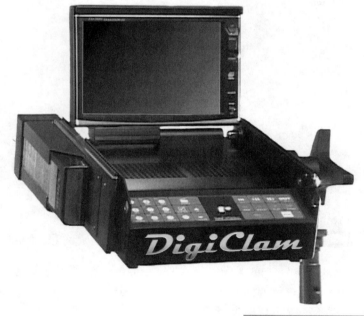

Y-Vamp Corporation
100 The East Mall, Unit 8
Toronto, ON
M8Z 5X2 Canada
(416) 255-5558
www.y-vamp.com

INDEX

U

V

MANUFACTURERS AND VENDORS CONTACT INFORMATION

Aaton	www.aaton.com	+33 (0)4 76-42-95-50
Abel Cine Tech	www.abelcine.com	(888) 223-1599
AccuScene Corporation	www.accuscene.com	+44 (0)1 383-828-880
Adobe	www.adobe.com	(408) 536-6000
ADS Technologies	www.adstech.com	(800) 888-5244
AKG Acoustics	www.akgusa.com	(615) 620-3800
Alan Gordon Enterprises	www.alangordon.com	(323) 466-3561
Amphibico	www.amphibico.com	(514) 333-8666
AMS Neve	www.ams-neve.com	+44 (0)1 282-457-011
Angenieux	www.angenieux.com	+33 (0)4 77-90-78-00
Apogee Digital	www.apogeedigital.com	(310) 915-1000
Apple	www.apple.com	(800) MY-APPLE
Arri Inc.	www.arri.com	(845) 353-1400
Astro Systems, Inc.	www.astro-systems.com	(877) 882-7876
Audio-Technica U.S., Inc.	www.audio-technica.com	(330) 686-2600
Audix Corporation	www.audixusa.com	(800) 966-8261
Aurora Video Systems	www.auroravideosys.com	(586) 726-5320
Avid Technology, Inc.	www.avid.com	(978) 640-6789
The Badham Company	www.shotmaster.com	not available
Band Pro Film/Video, Inc.	www.bandpro.com	(818) 841-9655
Barber Tech Video Products	www.barbertvp.com	(818) 982-7775
BeachTek	www.beachtek.com	(416) 690-9457
B. E. Meyers & Co. Inc.	www.bemeyers.com	(800) 327-5648
Bogen Photo	www.bogenphoto.com/www.manfrotto.com	(201) 818-9500
Boom Audio and Video	www.boom-audio.com	+33 (0)2 99-05-35-83
Boris FX	www.borisfx.com	(888) 772-6747
CamMate Systems	www.cammate.com	(480) 813-9500
Canada Camera Car	www.canadacameracar.com	(905) 602.6996
Canon	www.canondv.com	(800) OK-CANON

Canopus Corporation	www.canopus.com	(888) 899-EDIT
Cartoni	www.cartoni.com	+39 (0)6 438-2002
Century Optics	www.centuryoptics.com	(800) 228-1254
Chapman/Leonard	www.chapman-leonard.com	(888) 88-DOLLY
Chimera Lighting	www.chimeralighting.com	(888) 444-1812
Chyron	www.chyron.com	(631) 845-2000
Cinekinetic	www.cinekinetic.com	(702) 731-4700
Cinetransformer	www.cinetransformer.com	(310) 274-8300
Cool-Lux	www.cool-lux.com	(805) 482-4820
Coptervision	www.coptervision.com	(818) 781-3003
Core Digital Technologies	www.coredigital.com	(480) 707-1000
Crystal Partners	www.parabs.com	(800) 244-3277
Datavideo Corporation	www.datavideo-tek.com	(562) 696-2324
Davis & Sanford	www.tiffen.com	(631) 273-2500
Digidesign	www.digidesign.com	(800) 333-2137
Digital Anarchy	www.digitalanarchy.com	(415) 621-0991
Discreet	www.discreet.com	(800) 869-3504
Doggicam Systems	www.doggicam.com	(818) 845-8470
DPA Microphones	www.dpamicrophones.com	+45 (0)4 814-2828
The Easy Budget Company	www.easy-budget.com	(800) 356-7461
Edirol Corporation	www.edirol.com	(360) 594-4273
Electrophysics	www.electrophysics.com	(973) 882-0211
E-N-G Mobile Systems	www.e-n-g.com	(800) 662-4522
Entertainment Partners	www.ep-services.com	(818) 955-6000
Euphonix, Inc.	www.euphonix.com	(650) 855-0400
EZ FX	www.ezfx.com	(800) 541-5706
Filmair International	www.filmairinternational.com	(416) 207-2051
Final Draft, Inc.	www.finaldraft.com	(888) 320.7555
FLIR Systems	www.flir.com	(800) 322-3731
Flying-Cam, Inc.	www.flying-cam.com	(310) 581-9276
Focus Enhancements	www.focusinfo.com	(408) 866-8300
Fostex	www.fostex.com/www.fostexdvd.net	(562) 921-1112
Frezzi	www.frezzi.com	(800) 345-1030
Fujinon	www.fujinon.com	(973) 633-5600
Gillard Industries, Inc.	www.gillardindustries.com	(604) 328-2052
Glidecam	www.glidecam.com	(800) 600-2011
GPI	www.pro-gpi.com	(818) 982-3991
Ground Support Equipment	www.biomorphdesk.com	(888) 302-DESK
Herman Miller, Inc.	www.hermanmiller.com	(888) 443-4357
HHB Communications	www.hhbusa.com	(805) 579-6490

Hitachi	www.hdal.com	(516) 682-4429
Hollywood General Machining, Inc.	www.porta-jib.com	(323) 462-2855
Hollywood Lite	www.hollywoodlite.com	(310) 871-7386
HydroFlex, Inc.	www.hydroflex.com	(310) 301-8187
Ikegami Electronics	www.ikegami.com	(800) 368-9171
IMP Electronics	www.imp-electronics.com	+44 (0)1 480-411-822
Innovision Optics	www.innovision-optics.com	(310) 453-4866
J. L. Fisher, Inc.	www.jlfisher.com	(818) 846-8366
JVC	www.jvc.com/pro	(973) 317-5000
Kata	www.kata-bags.com	+972-25-38-88-45
K&H Products, Ltd.	www.portabrace.com	(800) 442-8171
Kinetic Impulse	www.kinetic-impulse.com	+44 (0)7 788-710-481
Kino-Flo	www.kinoflo.com	(818) 767-6528
Leitch Technology International	www.leitch.com	(905) 780-2600
Losmandy	www.porta-jib.com	(323) 462-2855
Lowel-Light Manufacturing, Inc.	www.lowel.com	(800) 334-3426
Lowepro	www.lowepro.com	(707) 575-4363
LTM	www.ltmlighting.com	(800) 762-4291
Manfrotto	www.bogenphoto.com/www.manfrotto.com	(201) 818-9500
Marketec	www.marketec.com	(800) 557-8861
Microdolly Hollywood	www.microdolly.com	(818) 845-8383
Mirror Image	www.teleprompters.com	(920) 232-0220
Mole-Richardson	www.mole.com	(323) 851-0111
Nagra	www.nagrausa.com	(800) 813-1663
NCS Products	www.intervalometer	(888) 333-1666
1 Beyond	www.1beyond.com	(877) 663-2396
Optex	www.optexint.com	+44 (0)2 084-412-199
PAG	www.pagusa.com/www.ste-man.com	(818) 760-8265
Panasonic	www.panasonic.com/broadcast	(800) 528-8601
Panavision	www.panavision.com	(818) 316-1000
Panther	www.panther.tv	+49-89-61-39-00-01
Photoflex	www.photoflex.com	(800) 486-2674
Photo-Sonics Inc.	www.photosonics.com	(818) 842-2141
Pinnacle Systems, Inc.	www.pinnaclesys.com	(650) 526-1600
Portabrace	www.portabrace.com	(800) 442-8171
PowerProduction Software	www.powerproduction.com	(800) 457-0383
Preston Cinema Systems	www.prestoncinema.com	(310) 453-1852
Professional Sound Corporation	www.professionalsound.com	(661) 295-9395
ProMax	www.promax.com	(800) 977-6629
Quantel	www.quantel.com	not available

Russ Basssett	www.russbassett.com	(562) 945-2445
Sachtler	www.sachtler.com	(516) 867-4900
Satellight-X	www.satellight-x.com	(866) 315-1400
Shotmaker	www.shotmaker.com	(818) 623-1700
Shure Incorporated	www.shure.com	(800) 25-SHURE
Silicon Graphics	www.sgi.com	(650) 960-1980
16x9 Inc.	www.16x9inc.com	(866) 800-1699
Sony Electronics	www.sony.com/professional	(800) 686-7669
Sound Devices	www.sounddevices.com	(608) 524-0625
Spintec	www.spintec.co.il	+972-2-579-7999
SpyderCam	www.spydercam.com	(661) 775-9058
StageTools	www.stagetools.com	(540) 592-7001
Steadicam	www.tiffen.com/www.steadicam.com	(631) 273.2500
Ste-Man	www.ste-man.com	(818) 760-8240
StuffBak	www.stuffbak.com	(800) 800-8257
Tascam	www.tascam.com	(323) 726-0303
Telemetrics, Inc.	www.telemetricsinc.com	(201) 848-9819
Television Equipment Associates	www.swatheadsets.com	(310) 457-7401
Thomson/Grass Valley	www.thomsongrassvalley.com	(530) 478-3000
Tiffen	www.tiffen.com	(631) 273-2500
Trew Audio	www.trewaudio.com	(800) 241-8994
Tyler Camera Systems	www.tylermount.com	(800) 390-6070
VariZoom	www.varizoom.com	(888) 826-3399
Videotek	www.videotek.com	(800) 800-5719
Vinten	www.vinten.com	(845) 268-0100
Wescam	www.wescam.com	(818) 785-9282
Wide Screen Software	www.wide-screen.com	(818) 764-3639
Winsted Corporation	www.winsted.com	(800) 447-2257
Wohler	www.wohler.com	(888) 5-WOHLER
Y-Vamp	www.y-vamp.com	(416) 255-5558
Zaxcom, Inc.	www.zaxcom.com	(201) 652-7878
ZGC, Inc.	www.zgc.com	(973) 335-4460

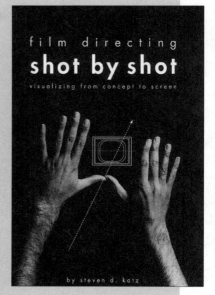

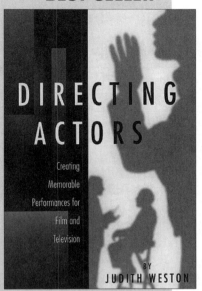

DIGITAL MOVIEMAKING
2nd Edition

All the Skills, Techniques, and Moxie You'll Need to Turn Your Passion into a Career

Scott Billups

This book is geared to professional-minded people who have hopefully had prior experience in some aspect of production and who understand the fundamental difference between a hobby and a career. It's about how to be successful at making movies by taking an opportunity to experiment and demonstrating your abilities.

Scott Billups' goal is to kick your professionalism, your toolset, and your image quality up a notch so that you can compete in the real world of cinema. There are no simple solutions, secret tricks, instant remedies, or gizmos that will turn you into a moviemaker. In fact, the odds are against you. But Billups promises that by the time you've finished this book, your odds of success will have improved.

"If you are in or entering the new world of digital filmmaking and you want to know everything about everything... read this book by Scott Billups. You'll be sorry if you don't."

— David Lynch, Director

"An individualist in a town where conformity can be a Zen-like state of grace, Billups is not afraid to lock horns with mainstream studios as he seeks to invent 'the new Hollywood.'"

— Paula Parisi, *Wired Magazine*

Scott Billups is an award-winning director/producer who has produced, directed and written countless feature films, television programs, and commercials.

$26.95 | 300 Pages | Order # 107RLS | ISBN: 0-941188-80-9

DIGITAL FILMMAKING 101

DIGITAL FILMMAKING 101
An Essential Guide
to Producing
Low-Budget Movies

Dale Newton and John Gaspard

The Butch Cassidy and the Sundance Kid of do-it-yourself filmmaking are back! Filmmakers Dale Newton and John Gaspard, co-authors of the classic how-to independent filmmaking manual *Persistence of Vision*, have written a new handbook for the digital age. *Digital Filmmaking 101* is your all-bases-covered guide to producing and shooting your own digital video films. It covers both technical and creative advice, from keys to writing a good script, to casting and location-securing, to lighting and low-budget visual effects. Also includes detailed information about how to shoot with digital cameras and how to use this new technology to your full advantage.

As indie veterans who have produced and directed successful independent films, Gaspard and Newton are masters at achieving high-quality results for amazingly low production costs. They'll show you how to turn financial constraints into your creative advantage — and how to get the maximum mileage out of your production budget. You'll be amazed at the ways you can save money —and even get some things for free — without sacrificing any of your final product's quality.

"These guys don't seem to have missed a thing when it comes to how to make a digital movie for peanuts. It's a helpful and funny guide for beginners and professionals alike."

> — Jonathan Demme
> Academy Award-Winning Director
> *Silence of the Lambs*

Dale Newton and John Gaspard, who hail from Minneapolis, Minnesota, have produced three ultra-low-budget, feature-length movies and have lived to tell the tales.

$24.95 | 283 pages | Order # 17RLS | ISBN: 0-941188-33-7

RESOURCES

If you would like to be included in
Dream Gear's Resources Section,
please contact *DREAMGEAR@cox.net*
or *kenlee@mwp.com*
for advertising specs and rates.

If you have used this gear and want to
share your own experiences, comments,
and suggestions in our next edition,
send an e-mail to Catherine Lorenze at
DREAMGEAR@cox.net. We are
particularly interested in innovative
ways you have used the gear that will
help inspire other film, video, and TV
professionals.

sgi®

Obliterate the envelope.
sgi.com/tezro

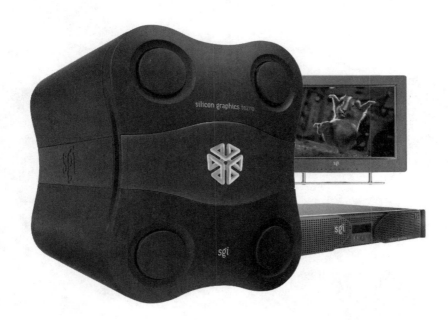

Don't just push the edge of the envelope. Power past it. Introducing the Silicon Graphics® Tezro™ visual workstation. Tezro is the world's most advanced desktop system with its quad-processor capability, industry-leading I/O, and balanced system throughput. By delivering the ultimate in performance, visualization, and reliability, Tezro helps you knock down workflow barriers. Power is knowledge. Silicon Graphics Tezro. It's time to leave the rules behind.

SILICON GRAPHICS | The Source of Innovation and Discovery™